Nasser Tolba

Student Culture in a Changing World

KINDHEIT – FAMILIE – PÄDAGOGIK

Herausgegeben von
Steffen Großkopf,
Ulf Sauerbrey,
Michael Winkler

Band 4

ERGON VERLAG

Nasser Tolba

Student Culture in a Changing World

The Paradox of Politics, Education, and Religion

ERGON VERLAG

Umschlagabbildung:
© Nasser Tolba

Bibliografische Information der Deutschen Nationalbibliothek
Die Deutsche Nationalbibliothek verzeichnet diese Publikation in der
Deutschen Nationalbibliografie; detaillierte bibliografische Daten sind im
Internet über http://dnb.d-nb.de abrufbar.

www.ergon-verlag.de

ISBN 978-3-95650-588-1 (Print)
ISBN 978-3-95650-589-8 (ePDF)
ISSN 2509-8659

To the Martyrs
of the January 25th Revolution of 2011,
I Hereby Dedicate this Work

Acknowledgment

I would like to express my appreciation to my advisor (Doktorvater), Professor Dr. Michael Winkler; my academic and professional developments are products of his unreserved guidance. You gave me trust, encouragement, and confidence that were crucial to complete this work. You never hesitated to give me advice, time, independence, and rich discussions despite your overload of academic responsibilities. A couple of lines are not sufficient to express my heartfelt gratitude for you Professor Winkler. I would also like to acknowledge Professor Dr. Bettina Hünersdorf for her assistance, guidance, and remarkable insights which were curical when it came to confronting data analysis difficulties.

I would like to thank the participants for their time given to participate in this study. I know that it was difficult and sensitive to conduct these interviews at that time, but their willingness and interest made the research easy for me. I also want to acknowledge Professor Dr. Susan E. Keefe (Department of Anthropology, Appalachian State University, USA) for her assistance when this study was just a simple idea. The author acknowledges the Egyptian Ministry of Higher Education (Cultural Affairs and Missions Sector) for the financial support during this work. I also want to recognize the staff of the Graduate Academy of the Friedrich Schiller University of Jena for their assistance and support that facilitated my stay and study here in Jena.

Finally, I would like to express my sincere gratitude to all my family members (my father, my Mother, my Brothers, my Wife, and my Kids Nadine and Nouran) for their support and prayers. Without their love, sympathy, and understanding that have embraced me, I would not have been able to continue this work and tackle all the challenges. I wished that all of you could be here to share with me these wonderful moments in my academic career.

Nasser Tolba, Jena 2018

Table of Contents

Table of Figures

Vorwort

1. Unter Historikern gelten Zeit- oder gar Gegenwartsgeschichte als eher heikel. Man überlässt sie gerne jenen, die als Publizisten bezeichnet werden. Diese geben dann über aktuelle Entwicklungen mehr oder weniger kluge Urteile ab, welche am nächsten Tag überholt sein können. Wartet man nicht ohnedies auf die Freigabe von Dokumenten, wird man als Historiker stets eine Art Distanzfrist einhalten, die besser nicht unter zwei Jahrzehnten liegen sollte. Alles andere bleibt entweder den Politikwissenschaftlern oder den ereignisnah agierenden Journalisten überlassen, wobei der Ruf beider Gruppen zumindest mit kratzigen Nebentönen verbunden wird; ihn rettet nur die mediale Heiligung als Experten. Und die dürfen bekanntlich immer irren.

Für sozialwissenschaftlich und erziehungswissenschaftlich interessierte Forscherinnen und Forscher erweist sich die Lage indes als noch komplizierter; zunehmend sind sie ja als Experten gefragt. In vielerlei Hinsicht können und dürfen sie sich daher nicht die Zeit nehmen, auf die Historiker zu verweisen. Ihre Befunde kämen dann zu spät, zumal wenn sie sich mit Entwicklungen auseinandersetzen, die durchaus Züge einerseits des Einmaligen und Besonderen tragen, andererseits aber wenigstens die Vermutung nahelegen, in struktureller Hinsicht oder für das sinnhafte Handeln der Akteure längerfristige Relevanz zu besitzen. Die Erziehungswissenschaft, oder besser: die wissenschaftliche Beschäftigung mit Fragestellungen der – im weitesten Sinne des Ausdrucks – Pädagogik, befindet sich in einer zusätzlich schwierigen Lage: Zwar präsentiert sie sich gerne als international ausgerichtet, doch bezieht sie sich dabei eher auf Bildungssysteme, genauer auf Schulen und deren Effekte, während die Beobachtung und Analyse von sozialen oder auch Jugendbewegungen in den Hintergrund getreten sind; Strukturen, Institutionen beschäftigen mehr, insbesondere seitdem die internationalen, meist ökonomisch motivierten Leistungsvergleiche dominieren, während jugendliche Akteure und ihre Lebenswelten nur wenig Aufmerksamkeit genießen.

Das hängt sicher mit methodischen Problemen zusammen. Einschlägige Forschungsfelder erweisen sich als unübersichtlich und komplex, zudem kommt nationalen und sogar regionalen Kulturen wie Mentalitäten ein solches Gewicht zu, dass zumindest außenstehende Beobachter kaum zu einem hinreichenden oder gar angemessen Verständnis der Sinnhaftigkeit von Handlungen kommen werden. Und man muss wohl auch zugeben: Oft, nein: meist fehlt das Wissen um die soziale, kulturelle und politische Entwicklung in anderen Ländern, übrigens nicht nur in den ferneren. Nüchtern betrachtet vollzieht sich nämlich parallel zu aller Globalisierung eher ein geradezu paradox erscheinender Verlust an Informationen und Kenntnissen selbst schon über nahe liegende Gesellschaften, erst recht über die ferner liegenden. Selbst international agierende Medien – wie etwa BBC-World – berichten doch nur punktuell und partiell, manche durchaus auch positionell, wie dies etwa Al Jazeera vorgeworfen wird.

2. Die von Nasser Tolba vorgelegte Untersuchung bewegt sich in diesem Spannungsfeld. Dabei fällt eigentlich schon die disziplinäre Zuordnung schwer – zumindest wenn man an solchen Zuordnungen noch festhalten will und nicht, international üblichen Gepflogenheiten folgend, eine gegenständliche Problematik oder Thematik als Ausgangspunkt und Fokus nimmt. Disziplinär betrachtet bewegt sich Tolba zum einen im Bereich der Zeitgeschichte, dann in dem einer an Sozialisationsprozessen interessierten Soziologie: Er greift ferner Fragestellungen und Perspektiven auf, die mit der Analyse politischer Bildung verbunden werden können, letztlich nimmt er ein geradezu klassisches, zuletzt aber eher vernachlässigtes Thema der Erziehungswissenschaft auf, nämlich die Frage nach Jugend und jugendkulturellen Aktivitäten – wobei diese nach langer Vernachlässigung erst zuletzt wieder in den Fokus der Aufmerksamkeit getreten sind, wie etwa der 15. Kinder- und Jugendbericht der deutschen Regierung belegt.

Wählt man eine inzwischen fast erklärungsbedürftige, weil traditionell wirkende Denkweise, dann kann man mit Fug und Recht sagen, dass Tolba sich in geradezu vorbildlicher Weise mit einem Untersuchungsgegenstand befasst, der als Bildung zu begreifen ist – im ernsthaften und klassischen Sinne des Ausdrucks, bevor dieser auf Schule reduziert worden ist. Es geht ihm nämlich um die Frage, wie sich junge Menschen kollektiv wie individuell ihre soziale, kulturelle und politische Welt aneignen, wie sie diese aufnehmen, um sich selbst in ihr zu entwickeln und zu verändern. Er zeichnet nach, wie sie letztlich als Personen aktiv werden, durchaus im Alltagsleben einer sich verändernden studentischen Kultur, dann aber im politischen oder gesellschaftlichen Engagement – mit aller Brisanz übrigens, die sich in einem Land zeigt, das von einer fast dramatischen Veränderungsdynamik gekennzeichnet ist, deren Richtung völlig offen ist. Zugespitzt könnte man sagen: Es geht um eine – als studentische durchaus privilegierte – Jugend, die zwischen Diktatur und Demokratie aufwächst, überschattet übrigens von zunehmender Verarmung weiter Kreise der Bevölkerung.

Dabei fokussiert er auf einen Bereich, der als empirischer Forschungsgegenstand eher vernachlässigt worden ist, nämlich auf studentische Kulturen. Diese sind zwar als Thema allgemeiner soziokultureller oder politischer Erörterung präsent, nicht zuletzt in den Medien. Studentische Kulturen werden aber nur selten methodisch empirisch untersucht, zumindest mit Blick auf soziale Zusammenhänge, welche, durch Wohn- und Alltagsleben konstituiert, eine Lebensform begründen. Der Grund dafür liegt auf der Hand: Die Wohnform von

Studierenden ist wenig durch den engen und geradezu abgezirkelten Zusammenhang eines Campus bestimmt und insofern identifizierbar, vielmehr lässt sie sich nur als eine Art Mentalitätsmuster rekonstruieren, das in einem durch überwiegend studentische Bevölkerung geprägten Stadtviertel entstehen mag; Ähnlichkeiten bestehen freilich dort, wo studentische Aktivitäten etwa politische Auseinandersetzungen und insbesondere solche mit einer Hochschulleitung bestimmen.

Ausgangspunkt der Untersuchung war dabei *einerseits* die Beschäftigung mit dem, was vereinfachend als *Arabische Revolution* bezeichnet werden kann, wie sie sich in den letzten fünfzehn Jahren in einer Vielzahl von arabischen und afrikanischen Ländern vollzogen hat und noch vollzieht, zuweilen mit erheblicher Enttäuschung in großen Teilen der Bevölkerung verbunden. Insbesondere der Mittelstand und die akademisch interessierte Jugend wirkten als Träger der Veränderungen. Sie sehen sich jetzt mit zuweilen desaströsen, zuweilen existenziell bedrohlichen Entwicklungen konfrontiert. Nicht nur restituierten sich autoritäre Strukturen, vielmehr breiteten sich Spaltungen und Armutslagen aus. Insofern lassen sich kaum Prognosen für die Zukunft formulieren, denn die weitere Entwicklung der studentischen Kulturen bleibt unklar. Als Krisenpotenzial deutet sich das schon dort an, wo die Studierenden eine bessere, zielführende Qualifikation durch die Hochschule für ihre mögliche Berufstätigkeit einfordern. Nur nebenbei: Allein die Diagnose dieser Entwicklungen gibt der Untersuchung Brisanz, weil sie zumindest andeutet, wo künftig Migrationsentwicklungen entstehen könnten.

Andererseits war Nasser Tolba an einem Vergleich zwischen der Entwicklung in Ägypten und den Veränderungen in den studentischen Kulturen, die sich während und nach der Wende in der DDR und somit in Deutschland bzw. in den osteuropäischen Ländern ergeben haben, interessiert. Parallelen zeigen sich übrigens zu dem, was sich an tschechischen Universitäten während der Revolution in der Wendezeit ergeben hat. Dieses Interesse ist gleichwohl in den Hintergrund getreten, es klingt vorrangig in der umfassenden Literaturrecherche an, die er durchgeführt hat. Allerdings lässt sich eine Interessenverschiebung schon aus methodischen Gründen nachvollziehen: In dem von ihm gewählten qualitativ-rekonstruktiven Zugang wäre ein solcher Vergleich durch einen Einzelnen kaum zu bewältigen gewesen, ganz abgesehen von der Komplexität der Ereignisse in Ägypten, die sich nun in der Tat als ein eigener Forschungsgegenstand erweisen.

3. Die Untersuchung bewegt sich auf mehreren Ebenen: Sie kann und darf zunächst als Dokument einer tiefgreifenden gesellschaftlichen und politischen Veränderung in Ägypten gelesen werden, die – unvermeidlich – mehr exemplarisch als repräsentativ an der Gruppe der Studierenden, genauer: der organisierten Studierenden untersucht wird. Zweifellos ist diese Gruppe privilegiert, weil sie Zugang zu einer Institution des höheren Bildungswesens hat. Dies prägt den

sozialen Status der Beteiligten und schlägt sich nicht zuletzt in Freiheiten der alltäglichen Lebensführung nieder, die großen Teilen der Bevölkerung verwehrt bleiben. Aber: zugleich haben sich in der Vergangenheit und im Vergleich die Studierenden immer als Promotor und Indikator für soziale, kulturelle und politische Veränderungen erwiesen.

Dabei konzentriert sich die Darstellung auf Phänomene der Veränderung im Alltagsleben der Studierenden, einerseits im Verhältnis zu der sie in ihren Aktionen bestimmenden Institution, andererseits – als Folge der Veränderungen – in ihrem Verhältnis zu den von den Studierenden wahrgenommenen Problemen in der Lebenslage von Menschen außerhalb der Institution Hochschule. Allerdings schlägt sich eine historische Dramatik im Beobachtungsfeld nieder – zuweilen fast mit Wucht: Den Zeitraum der Beobachtung zeichnen nämlich drei ganz unterschiedliche Dynamiken aus. Dem offenen revolutionären Aufbruch folgt eine Phase der inneren Differenzierung, in der die Gruppen der beteiligten Akteure sich organisieren, unterschiedliche Interessen entwickeln und zugleich Formen der Auseinandersetzung ausbilden – es entsteht also eine Struktur der mehr oder weniger demokratischen Konfliktgestaltung. All dies kommt zu einem Ende in dem, was Nasser Tolba als „coup" bezeichnet, einem Putsch, der in eine zumindest autoritäre, wenn nicht diktatorische Situation führt, die mit einer desaströsen Lage für große Teile der Bevölkerung einhergeht.

Diese Dynamik durchwirkt die gesamte Untersuchung, die aber dem klassischen Aufbau wissenschaftlicher Arbeiten gehorcht. Nasser Tolba konzentriert sich dabei zunächst auf das verfügbare Wissen über studentische Kulturen schlechthin, um dann in einem weiter angelegten Überblick die historische, politische und soziale Situation Ägyptens anhand der verfügbaren Befunde und Daten zu beschreiben und zu analysieren, ehe er nach einem Blick auf sein methodisches Verfahren für die eigenen empirischen Studien diese in zentralen Befunden vorstellt.

Weil die Arbeit in englischer Sprache vorliegt, erlaube ich mir, ihre Inhalte kurz zu referieren. Eine solche Übersicht ersetzt nicht die gründliche Lektüre, bietet aber eine Art Grundinformation und erleichtert so vielleicht den Zugang.

Das erste Kapitel führt in die Thematik ein und expliziert den Gegenstandsbereich sowie das Forschungsfeld, dann vor allem die Forschungsfragen. Das Interesse gilt zunächst einmal einem grundlegenden Verständnis von studentischer Kultur. Diese wird gleichzeitig als alltägliche Lebenspraxis und als Situation mit hoher Wandlungsdynamik gefasst. Dies lenkt die Aufmerksamkeit auf die Jänner-Revolution von 2011, die forschungsstrategisch nahezu als eine Experimentalsituation für die Erkundung einer studentischen Kultur erscheint. Nasser Tolba bewertet die Ereignisse als Befreiung von einengenden Mauern und Überwindung von Ungerechtigkeit. Dabei bewegt ihn schon, was er später fast ein wenig nebenbei bemerkt, nämlich die Schwäche des politischen Bewusstseins unter den Studierenden, die er mit den eher autoritären, wenn nicht repressiven Strukturen an den Universitäten verbindet, wie sie aus den früheren Zeiten etwa unter Staatspräsident Mubarak resultieren.

Im Übergang zum zweiten Kapitel findet sich eine Art Begriffsdefinition nicht nur für studentische Kultur, wobei doch deutlich wird, dass im Grunde alle Kernbegriffe offen und in gewisser Weise „ungenau" sein müssen – nicht zuletzt übrigens, weil die empirische Untersuchung schließlich das Selbstverständnis der Akteure zeigen soll und kann. Damit wird auch deutlich, dass und wie die Untersuchung doch hermeneutisch angelegt ist. Allzumal die Schlüsselkonzepte wie das der Revolution (etwa in Abgrenzung zur Revolte) oder vor allem das der Kultur, bleiben deutungsoffen. Dabei knüpft Nasser Tolba mit seinem Kulturbegriff als Ausdruck einer Lebensform u. a. an Raymond Williams und Paul Willis an, indem er etwa die alltäglichen Gewohnheiten und Lebens- wie Essensweisen der Studierenden thematisiert; sie spielen in den von ihm geführten Interviews dann eine herausragende Rolle.

Das zweite Kapitel präsentiert eine umfassende Literaturrecherche, die – in Rezeption vorrangig angelsächsischer Studien – zunächst allgemein und weit ausgreifend sowie in kritischer Auseinandersetzung mit Schlüsselaspekten der Debatten um Jugend- und Studentenkulturen einsetzt. Ein zweiter Abschnitt fokussiert dann auf die Auseinandersetzungen mit studentischer Kultur in Ägypten. Hier kommen auch die von Williams und Clarke eingeführten Unterscheidungen zum Tragen, etwa im Blick auf das Verhältnis von übergreifender bzw. durch Klassenzugehörigkeit geprägter Stamm-Kultur und Subkultur. Studenten in Ägypten werden durch ein intergenerationell transformiertes Erbe beeinflusst; skeptisch beurteilt Tolba die Wirkung der Massenmedien. In der Summe belegt die Forschungsliteratur, wie sehr Einstellungen und Haltungen der Studierenden sich verändert haben – durchaus in eine Richtung, die als westlich bezeichnet werden kann.

Das dritte Kapitel untersucht zeitgeschichtlich, dabei politikwissenschaftlich und soziologisch angelegt, die Revolution von 2011. Sie bildet einen Kern der Untersuchung, wobei in der Konkretisierung und Detailorientierung der Darstellung Neuland betreten werden musste. Nach einem kurzen, eher phänomenologisch ausgerichteten Überblick befasst sich Tolba mit den sozialen, politischen und ökonomischen Bedingungen, die Ägypten in einen Krisenzustand geführt haben, auf den unterschiedlichste Bewegungen reagiert haben (als Indikator hierfür erwähnt er übrigens die Zunahme der Straßenkinder in Äygpten). Zudem zeigt die Untersuchung, wie die ägyptische Wirtschaftsökonomie in einer Art staatsmonopolitischer Form organisiert ist.

Die Besonderheit der ägyptischen Revolution liegt darin, dass und wie sie sich umfassend und zugleich in weiten Bereichen des sozialen Lebens sehr spontan vollzogen hat. Sie war populär und friedlich, wurde besonders von der jungen Generation getragen, die jugendspezifische Medien genutzt hat. Politische Parteien wirkten kaum mit. Allerdings lassen sich die revolutionären Vorgänge nicht in die gängigen Schemata und Kategorien politischer Deutung und Lagerbildung einordnen. Sie sind in sich widersprüchlich geblieben. Insbesondere die Aktivisten der Muslim Brotherhood zielten dann doch wiederum auf die Übernahme der politischen Macht, ohne jedoch die ökonomischen Probleme des Landes ernsthaft lösen zu können.

Ein ausführlicher Abschnitt befasst sich mit den mehrdeutigen Effekten der Revolution vom 25. Jänner 2011. Diese führt zur Konstitution einer neuen, durch eine Verfassung geregelten Ordnung und löst das alte autoritäre Regime ab. Bis weit hinab auf die lokalen und kommunalen Ebenen setzen sich neue Formen der Beteiligung durch – so etablieren sich auch in der anschließend vorrangig untersuchten Fayoum-Universität neue Möglichkeiten demokratischer Mitwirkung. Im weiteren Verlauf des Geschehens wird der Prozess der Demokratisierung sowohl gesamtgesellschaftlich wie in der Universität wenigstens unter-, wenn nicht abgebrochen. Die revolutionären Gruppen können sich nicht einigen, streiten miteinander, so dass sie ihre Kraft verlieren.

Das bisher Skizzierte ist spannend genug, doch stellt es nur eine Rahmenhandlung für die eigentliche empirische Untersuchung dar. Wie es sich gehört, diskutiert Tolba daher – im vierten Kapitel – das methodische Design seiner Studie. Insbesondere begründet er die Wahl eines qualitativen, rekonstruktiven Verfahrens, mithin die Verbindung einer Fallstudie mit Methoden der grounded theory. Er verweist auf die Spezifika des Forschungsfeldes: Eine kleine Universität im ländlichen Raum kann als Untersuchungsgegenstand als nachteilig angesehen werden, wenn und sofern generalisierende Aussagen über Studentenkulturen getroffen werden sollen, da diese häufig städtisch geprägt sind. Sie bietet aber zugleich den Vorteil einer klar umrissenen, gewissermaßen experimentellen Situation.

Methodisch noch mehr Herausforderungen stellen sich bei der Auswahl der Interviewpartner und in der eigentlichen Erhebung. Streng genommen bewegt sich Nasser Tolba zwischen teilnehmender Beobachtung, Deskription und einer ersten Analyse, die doch noch als explorative Fallstudie bezeichnet werden muss. Dabei gelingt ihm eine *dichte Beschreibung*, wenngleich er sich ausdrücklich auf die *grounded theory* bezieht und diese seiner Auswertung zu Grunde legt. So stützt sich Tolba auf Daten, die durch teilnehmende Beobachtung in den unterschiedlichen Formierungen studentischer Kultur sowie an studentischen Aktionen gewonnen wurden.

Zum Teil war der Autor auf Zugänge angewiesen, die als hoch riskant investigativ gelten müssen. Das gilt insbesondere für die Beobachtungen und Analysen von Gruppen, die der Muslim Brotherhood angehören. Methodisch sei dabei angemerkt, dass er seine Interviews mehrfach codiert und ausgewertet hat, ohne gänzlich dem Sprachproblem zu entkommen, nämlich der Aufnahme der

Daten in arabischer Sprache und ihrer Übersetzung in englische Sprache. Insofern lässt sich über die Datenqualität und die Transparenz der Interpretationen streiten, man ist und bleibt ein wenig auf Treu und Glauben angewiesen. Aber dieser Preis muss wohl in gesellschafts- und kulturvergleichender Forschung entrichtet werden, allzumal wenn diese sich auf aktuelle soziale Prozesse bezieht.

Das fünfte Kapitel stellt nun die Befunde vor. In der Auswertung der Interviews ergeben sich dabei sechs Themen und Sinnstrukturen für die Akteure: Nasser Tolba setzt ein mit den täglichen Gewohnheiten und somit der alltäglichen Lebensform, beobachtet Kleidung und Essensweisen sowie Hobbies und Freizeit. Ein zweiter Themenbereich ergibt sich mit den Mustern der Wahrnehmung, die die Studierenden für ihre eigene Universität und ihre Strukturen entwickelt haben. Nicht zuletzt spielt hier die Frage nach der Qualität der Lehre sowie die nach der Verwertbarkeit des Wissens auf dem Arbeitsmarkt eine Rolle; sie wird als unzureichend beurteilt, wie auch das Urteil über die Dozenten eher kritisch ausfällt. Man kann prognostizieren, dass sich hieraus ein weiterer Anlass zur Empörung ergeben wird. Im dritten Themenbereich fokussiert Tolba auf die hochschulinternen Aktivitäten der Studierenden, wobei insbesondere die Wahlen auf Studentenebene, dann jedoch auf der nationalen und insofern gesamtgesellschaftlichen Ebene Aufmerksamkeit finden. Hier zeichnet sich eine Interaktion zwischen „großer" Politik und universitätsinterner, „lokaler" Demokratisierung ab, die sich dann als mittelfristig problematisch erweist. Die Gegenreaktion nach dem Ausklingen des Revolutionsprozesses schlägt sich als Repression im Universitätscampus nieder und wird insofern als besonders hart erfahren. Das gilt vor allem vor dem Hintergrund der im vierten Bereich angesprochenen Erfahrungen. Hier zeigt Tolba, wie sich zunächst neue Formen der Solidarität und Auseinandersetzung unter den Studierenden ausbilden, die aber dann zu neuen Machtkonstellationen führen. Der fünfte Themenbereich ergibt sich in dem – für Revolutionen in Studentenkulturen durchaus üblichen – Ausgriff in die unmittelbare soziale Umgebung: Freiwilliges und ehrenamtliches Engagement zeigt sich als wichtiges Handlungs- und Erfahrungsfeld. Mit dem sechsten Themenbereich wendet sich der Autor der symbolischen Kommunikation, mithin der Sprache der Studierenden und ihren eigenen Ausdrucksformen zu.

Ein kurzes, sechstes Kapitel fasst noch einmal zentrale Merkmale der Veränderung in der Studentenkultur an der Fayoum-Universität zusammen, um dann eine vorsichtige, gewissermaßen kleine Theorie der Beziehungen zwischen den einzelnen Feldern bzw. Achsen der Analyse zu entwerfen. Tolba bleibt zurückhaltend, nicht zuletzt, weil das von ihm erhobene Datenmaterial dazu Anlass gibt, zumal es einen Veränderungsprozess dokumentiert, der in seinem Ausgang völlig unsicher ist. Gesellschaftliche Entwicklung und die Entwicklung der Studentenbewegung laufen hier insofern auf fatale Weise parallel, weil sich hier wie dort massive Tendenzen zur Prekarisierung zeigen, ganz abgesehen davon, dass neue Formen der Herrschafts- und Machtausübung das Geschehen überschatten. Der Wunsch nach fortschreitender Demokratisierung ist nicht zu übersehen, obwohl sich doch zeigt, wie die Gewalt in der Gesellschaft zur Gewalt an der Hochschule führt. Allerdings deuten sich auch gegenläufige Entwicklungen an, wie sie im Engagement der Studierenden für soziale Aufgaben sichtbar werden. Politische Kommentatoren, aber auch seriöse Historiker und Sozialforscher haben gleichwohl auf die schon angesprochene Gefahr in den arabischen Gesellschaften hingewiesen, dass sich gut ausgebildete, akademisch qualifizierte junge Männer politisch radikalisieren: Sie sind ihren Herkunftsmilieus entfremdet, enttäuscht über ihre Hochschulausbildung und den Mangel an Arbeitsplätzen (übrigens insbesondere für Ingenieure), haben die Hoffnung auf Demokratisierung aufgegeben, verlieren ihre religiösen Bezüge, um Religion dann jenseits aller Ambiguität zu fassen; eine gefährliche Mischung, die sich an den Daten zeigen lässt, die Nasser Tolba vorlegt. Dass er sich weiterreichenden Interpretationen und Empfehlungen verweigert, zeichnet ihn als seriösen Wissenschaftler aus, der keine Dramatisierung vornimmt.

4. Als zentraler Befund zeigt sich, dass und wie sich doch innerhalb kurzer Zeit die leitenden sozialen und politischen Orientierungen und Werte der Aktivisten verändert haben. Allerdings bleibt ein bitterer Beigeschmack. Denn sowohl in objektiver Hinsicht wie in der subjektiven Wahrnehmung und Sinngebung der Akteure haben sich dann doch Repression, Grausamkeit und Rigidität als Kontrapunkte zu politischer Freiheit durchsetzen und gleichsam in die Mentalitätsmuster der Beteiligten einschleichen können. Dabei lassen sich drei Ebenen unterscheiden, die für die weitere Dynamik des Geschehens wichtig werden: Einmal entsteht eine neue Konstellation zwischen den Studierenden – übrigens aller Gruppen – und der Universitätsleitung, die aber als volatil gelten muss: Während zunächst eine Entwicklung zur Demokratie, zu Mitbestimmung und Kritik einsetzt, wird diese doch rasch administrativ und im Zusammenspiel mit den politischen Mächten, den Sicherheitsbehörden, wieder ausgesetzt. Man kann das wohl verallgemeinern: Bündnisse zwischen Studierenden und Hochschulleitungen sind fragil, man sollte besser nicht auf sie setzen oder vertrauen, wenn soziale und politische Änderungsprozesse angestrebt werden. Oder noch schärfer formuliert: Hochschulen und Hochschulleitungen bleiben den Instanzen von Macht und Herrschaft verpflichtet. Eine zweite Betrachtungsebene ist damit wohl verknüpft: Wenn von studentischer Kultur die Rede ist, muss man davon ausgehen, dass zumindest auf Dauer keine homogene soziale Bewegung erwartet werden darf. Es kommt sehr schnell zu Ausdifferenzierungen und Spaltungen, abhängig davon, ob und wie weit einzelnen Gruppen selbst den Machtapparaten nahe stehen oder näher kommen. Diese Differenzierungsprozesse kontrastiert allerdings – dritte Ebene – eine die einzelnen Gruppen übergreifende Tendenz, sich sozialen Problemen außerhalb der Universität

zuzuwenden und dort unmittelbares soziales Engagement zu entwickeln, mithin Solidarität etwa mit Armen und Hungernden zu zeigen, zuweilen explizit, manchmal eher verborgen. Ausgelöst durch die Revolution vom 25. Jänner 2011 hat sich doch ein tiefgreifender Wandel in der Studentenschaft ergeben, der letztlich nicht mehr rückgängig gemacht werden kann; man darf davon ausgehen, dass hierin ein Potenzial für weitere soziale und politische Entwicklungen liegt und liegen wird.

Freilich bleibt ein Vorbehalt: Es ist gänzlich unklar, in welche Richtung die Entwicklungen gehen werden, nicht zuletzt ist eine mehr oder weniger kapitalistische Modernisierung im Sinne neoliberaler Strategien möglich, zumal in Verbindung mit hochgradig autoritären Strukturen. Manche soziale Bewegung hat dem Vorschub geleistet und tut dies noch. Aber das wird sich zeigen.

5. Mancher wird dem Buch von Nasser Tolba methodische Mängel vorwerfen, zumal sich im Bereich der qualitativen Methoden ja heute geradezu ein Präzisionsfetischismus durchgesetzt hat, nur um mit den sogenannten quantitativen und statistischen Verfahren gleich ziehen zu können. Das ist übrigens albern, weil die Zugänge jeweils über unterschiedliche Leistungsfähigkeit verfügen, sich einander ergänzen müssen und sollten. Vor allem aber muss man sehen, dass und wie explorative Untersuchungen in einem offenen und dynamischen Feld, das durch menschliche Handlungen konstituiert wird, immer ein gerüttelt Maß an Ungenauigkeit enthalten können. Wir wissen oftmals nicht, wohin sich Verhältnisse oder Entwicklungen neigen und wie sich Dynamiken entfalten werden, oftmals spielen Kontingenzen eine Rolle oder sogar Einzelpersonen; die jüngsten Entwicklungen in den USA oder in England belegen dies, wie sehr man auch im Hintergrund Strukturen oder Klassenverhältnisse erkennen mag.

Sofern es um die Annäherung an ein komplexes und dynamisches Handlungsfeld geht, sofern eine Praxis erst exploriert werden muss, lassen sich methodische Wagnisse kaum vermeiden. Weder saubere Berechnungen, noch klare und distinkte Daten lassen sich erwarten – die soziale Wirklichkeit erlaubt keine Sicherheit und Gewissheit. Ob sich Tendenzen erkennen lassen, bleibt zumindest offen; manchmal wünscht man sich das gar nicht. Historisch können die Ereignisse zu einem Ausgang führen, der noch nicht einmal ahnungsvoll antizipiert werden kann. Dabei darf man sich nichts vormachen: Die Entwicklung könnte dramatisch und grausam ausfallen. Immerhin wären dann die Untersuchungen doch als eine Vorahnung des Schlimmsten zu lesen – eine Aufgabe wäre damit erfüllt, die Ulrich Beck als entscheidend für die kritische Sozialforschung festgehalten hat.

All das wird und kann man konzedieren. Und dennoch spricht dies für die vorliegende Untersuchung, zeichnet sie als das aus, was vor vielen Jahrzehnten einmal Wilhelm Flitner als Merkmal einer wissenschaftlichen Beschäftigung mit der Pädagogik festgehalten hat. Sie ist reflexion engagée, wissenschaftlich, empirisch und theoretisch fundierte Auseinandersetzung mit den Bedingungen des Lebens und der Entwicklung junger Menschen, ein Beitrag, um Bildung zu ermöglichen, nicht nur den einzelnen Subjekten, sondern allen, zumindest möglichst Vielen. Sie ist Beitrag auch, politische Bildung zu initiieren und zu begleiten, nicht an Parteien gebunden, wohl aber an die ethischen Grundsätze, die für jene gelten, welche sich der Freiheit und einer vernünftigen Vergewisserung verschrieben haben, im Bewusstsein, dass diese durchaus konflikthaft verlaufen kann.

Nasser Tolba hat eine kluge, kenntnisreiche Untersuchung vorgelegt, mit explorativem, aber dennoch exemplarischem Charakter. Sie eröffnet einerseits die Möglichkeit, einem zeitgenössischen und durchaus involvierten Beobachter über die Schultern zu blicken, der mit Empathie am Geschehen beteiligt ist, aber doch nicht in die Falle einer teilnehmenden Aktionsforschung gerät, die dann parteilich wird und unversehens normativ geleitet eingreift. Diese Falle hat der Autor vermieden. Dennoch kann man sich der Faszination kaum entziehen, die mit der scharfen und zugleich doch hinreichend distanzierten Beobachtung und Analyse eines aktuellen Geschehens einhergeht. Im Grunde muss eine Bildungsforschung so angelegt sein, die den realen Bildungsprozessen der Subjekte nahekommt, ihre Entwicklungsprozesse anhand der Deutungen erfasst, die sie selbst für ihre Situation vornehmen. Tolba hat damit eine Untersuchung zur Situation in Ägypten vorgelegt, zugleich aber auch einen Beitrag zur Jugendforschung geleistet, der so bislang nicht verfügbar war. Nicht zuletzt aber trägt die Arbeit zur internationalen Verständigung bei, indem sie über die jüngere politische und gesellschaftliche Entwicklung in Ägypten informiert, wie dies wohl an keiner anderen Stelle in solchem Maße realitäts- und vor allem akteurs- und handlungsnah geschieht.

*

Ein PS sei erlaubt: Subjektive Äußerungen sind im wissenschaftlichen Kontext eigentlich unzulässig oder wenigstens zu vermeiden. Ich verstoße ausnahmsweise gegen dieses Gebot, gerne sogar, und bekenne, dankbar dafür zu sein, dass – so persönlich darf ich dies hier sagen – Nasser Tolba den Weg zu mir und dem Institut für Bildung und Kultur der Universität Jena gefunden hat; und ich gestehe, dass es mich glücklich stimmt, ihm heute in freundschaftlicher Kollegialität verbunden zu sein.

Chapter I: Basic Concepts

1.1 Introduction

Societal changes are one of the major characteristics of human societies. These changes may consist of political, cultural, social, and economic changes which deeply affect societies (Cox, 1974; Lawler, 2010; Liping, 2008). Egyptian society is similar to other societies, witnessing a profound societal transition towards freedom, democracy, and political participation. These societal transitions come as a consequence of the January 25th Revolution of 2011.

It is important to mention in this context that revolution is an essential and effective mechanism for getting rid of the chains and misconceptions of the past. It also brings about freedom from the causes of oppression, exploitation, and tyranny (Arendt, 1963). It is a unique tool to overcome underdevelopment and encounter the challenges and obstacles that beset communities, whether developed or undeveloped. The notion of revolution means a radical change in every part of life in a community which must have profound implications that are broad and extended. However, revolution, in the modern sense, does not apply to just making superficial changes in the overall picture of life and it is not limited to just one part of life. Rather, changes must extend to all parts of the society in a deep way (ʿAmar, 1964, p.10).

Moreover, the January 25th Revolution of 2011 is considered to be one of the important revolutions in the modern history of Egypt for many reasons. It was a popular and peaceful revolution which arose to demolish negative phenomena in Egyptian society. The reason behind this revolution was that the political system was marked by corruption in all parts of its institutions, such as: forgery, fraud, manipulation of the law, greed, and a decline of solidarity. Further, talented and skillful people could not get ahead in Egyptian society, while inexpert and unqualified people who had connections with authority gained benefits and promotions. Finally, education was undervalued and science and scientific research were neglected (ʿAli, 2012). Therefore, the Egyptian revolution came to be established on the principles of dignity, freedom, democracy, and social justice. It accurately expressed the hopes and aspirations of Egyptians in order to accomplish these demands (Marzouk, 2011). This revolution destroyed the towering walls of injustice, oppression, and despotism and it stopped the robbery of rights that had continued for more than thirty years.

Egyptian youth are conspicuously deemed the instigators of the January 25th Revolution (Al-Gamiry, 2012). They first triggered the protests by their use of modern communication tools and the Internet through using social networks (Facebook, Youtube, and Twitter), which assisted them to communicate their ideas about freedom, democracy, and social justice to wider society. Furthermore, they made the utmost sacrifice for achieving the aims and principles of the revolution, as it was indicated by the fact that more than 85% of the victims of the revolution were between 18 and 30 years old (ʿAli, 2012, p.16). Consequently, this revolution brought about tremendous changes in all facets of Egyptian society. In the social sphere, it helped to develop mechanisms to reduce poverty and strengthen social justice through the introduction of a minimum and maximum wage, as well increased the availability of health insurance for the poor. In the economic aspect, the new administration attempted to improve workers' conditions, eliminate monopolies, and transform the structure of the Egyptian economy into a more industrialized model in order to reconsider its privatization policies. In the political aspect, there was a change in the balance of political forces, a return of legitimate authority, the end of the reign of a single party, and expansion in political participation of all groups of the Egyptian society (ʿAli, 2012).

1.2 Questions of the Study

The system of higher education in Egypt includes all public and private universities and institutions. Public universities provide free education to all holders of secondary education while private universities provide it with extremely high tuition fees. The overall number of universities and institutions is 208. This number is distributed as follows, 24 public universities, 26 private universities, and 158 private institutions. The number of the faculty members (Professors, Lecturers, and Teaching Assistants) is 122,577 members. The number of the enrolled students is 2,700,000 students (The Egyptian Ministry of Higher Education, 2017). These universities and institutions are affiliated to the government in terms of planning and supervision. Further, Egyptian universities suffer from many issues such as: low income for faculty members, problems of academic freedom, issues of redistribution, and funding scientific research and linking it to the state's development plans, in addition to the inflation of the numbers of students and problems of authoritarian administration within departments, colleges, and university's council. This comes in addition to the worn-out infrastructure at most public universities (ʿAli, 2007).

The changes that have occurred in Egyptian society as a result of the January 25th Revolution of 2011, directly impacted universities in general and student communities in particular. For example, university leadership is now selected through elections and the ways students claim their rights and commit to their duties have changed. For instance, the students of the College of Engineering at Cairo University made demonstrations to releasing the students who were arrested by the security forces during demonstrations at the university (Rabiaʿ, 2013). Moreover, the students at Fayoum University demand more freedom and political activities in their university. They request to be represented in the college council. All these changes took place after the January 25th Revolution in Egypt. Therefore, the students have become more positive and effective members of their community.

While these changes are obviously clear at both social and economic levels, they are also visible at educational, cultural, and moral levels. The changes that the revolution brought about led to the emergence of new values such as citizenship, positive initiative, respecting the opinions of others, and self-esteem. This is highly related to the situation of university students, their status, and their current and future roles as a reflection of the community transformations experienced by the Egyptian society. They will maintain with changes valued at the local level. However, universities do not function in a vacuum since they are especially related to their societies in the Third World. That students are also attuned to societal developments and their political activism in most Third World countries is directly related to broader political forces and trends (Altbach, 1989). In this sense, the research of student culture has significant importance nowadays. For that reason, the study problem is represented in the following question:

How has Fayoum University student culture changed with the January 25th Revolution of 2011?

In the light of this main question, the need appears for an in-depth study of many topics that contribute to deepening our understanding of this vital subject:

1. What is the concept of university student culture? And what are its most important elements and dimensions?
2. What is the January 25th Revolution of 2011? And what are its goals and trends?
3. What are the most relevant factors that shape student culture at Fayoum University?
4. What is the essence of university student culture after the January 25th Revolution of 2011 at Fayoum University?
5. What are the specific changes that have occurred in the university student culture after the January 25th Revolution of 2011?

1.3 Purpose of the Study

This study aims to explore the subsurface values, beliefs, social interaction, and basic assumptions that constitute Fayoum University student culture. Also, it attempts to determine the factors that shape university student culture. Moreover, the study aims to determine the most important changes in student culture after the January 25th Revolution in Egypt. The study also provides a theory that interprets the changes in student culture at Fayoum University after the January 25th Revolution of 2011.

Moreover, this study is essential for several reasons. It is the first study that discusses the Egyptian revolution after it occurred from an educational prescriptive. Furthermore, the study investigates the impact of the revolution on university student culture and tries to understand the changes that happened in their values, norms, and beliefs in order to continue assisting students in accomplishing their academic and personal goals. Furthermore, this study contributes a live case study of student culture in post-revolution in Egypt. Finally, the results and suggestions that this study provides may be useful for the decision makers in Egypt.

1.4 A Note on Language Used in This Text

In the fifth chapter which addresses the findings of the study, I purposely note that the interviews are conducted in the Arabic language because the students are not able to speak English very well since Arabic is the students' mother tongue. Also, they can express their experiences and inner feelings through their own language both standard and slang. The researcher translated the interviews into English and a language specialist revised them. The researcher used ALA-LC Romanization symbols to write Arabic words to Latin script via transliteration. Thus, this conversion makes it easy to read and write. Appendix number (A) contains a table for ALA-LC Romanization symbols for Arabic letters.

1.5 Definition of Terms

Student culture constitutes a miniature society with its own complex intra-and inters relationship with other segments within and without the campus environment. It consists of attitudes, values, expectations, ideas, and behaviors which the students bring to the university campus at which point the trajectory of the development of these constituents extremely rests on the character of the official or institutional culture. Students as individuals and in groups develop a particular identity with the university ethos (Nkomo, 1984, p.90).

Revolution is a "profound change in the structure of the political authority and the social system in society"(Tanter & Midlarsky, 1967, p. 265).

The January 25th Revolution of 2011 is a peaceful revolution led by the Egyptian youth against social injustice and widespread of corruption in the state. Additionally, it was a diversified movement of demonstrations, strikes, marches, non-violent resistance, and labor riots and strikes which led to throwing the regime and causing significant changes in Egypt ('Ali, 2012).

Societal Changes There is no specific definition of societal changes, but there are many characteristics that describe it. Through the writings of sociologists, we can define societal changes as:
Profound and powerful changes in the structure of society, which have a significant impact on the economic, political, cultural, and social systems. Violence and terrorism threats may accompany it.

Qualitative Research is "any kind of research that produces findings not arrived at by means of statistical procedures or other means of quantification" (Strauss & Corbin, 1990, p.17)

Qualitative Research is a form of social inquiry and multimethod approach that focuses on the way people interpret their experiences and the whole world in which they live in and interact with. (Denzin & Lincoln, 1994, p. 2).

Chapter II: Student Culture, Past and Present

There have several research studies that describe the changes in student culture after great events like revolutions and societal transformations that entirely change society. This review aims at covering the changes that occurred in student culture in Egypt after the January 25th Revolution of 2011 in comparison with the changes that have taken place in student culture in countries that have witnessed revolutions. This literature review demonstrates the role of revolution in changing the elements of student culture at the university.

There are four subsections in chapter two (1) university student culture, (2) student culture in Egypt, (3) university student culture after revolutions, and (4) university student culture in Egypt after the January 25th Revolution of 2011. The first section surveys the notion of student culture and its components such as: values, beliefs, traditions, and social interaction. The second section reviews student culture in Egypt with a historical background from the beginning of the first higher education institution in Egypt (Cairo University) till the January 25th Revolution of 2011. It also states the factors and sources that shaped student culture in Egyptian universities.

Moreover, the third section overviews the changes in student culture after revolutions in many countries such as Cuba, Iran, China, Czechoslovakia, Russia, Italy, and the United States of America. It critically describes the most changeable aspects of student culture and the impact of these changes on the university. The last section examines student culture in Egypt after the January 25th Revolution of 2011. Thus, it investigates the changes in student culture at Egyptian universities and compares it with these changes in student culture in different countries.

2.1 University Student Culture: A Critical Outline of Key Debates

To determine a specific definition of student culture is not an easy task at all, due to the diversity of its members and the interference with the culture of both university and society. Within literature, there has been much confusion among many terms which have been used in the studies of a university and student affairs. These concepts overlap with student culture. These terms are campus culture, youth culture, and institutional culture or university culture. Therefore, this review of the literature, especially in this part, endeavors to present different definitions of student culture and the elements that constitute it.

First of all, culture is a slippery term (Brake, 2003; Geertz, 1973; Inglis & Hughson, 2003). Until now; there is no agreement on the definition of culture between Sociologists and Anthropologists. The notion is widely used in diverse disciplines and in different contexts which has increased ambiguity and inconsistency of the term (Bennett et al., 2005; Kuper, 1999). Kroeber and Kluckhohn (1952) collected 160 definitions of culture (p.12). Most of these definitions consider culture as the main source of human behavior and it consists of activities, ideas, behavior patterns, customs, values, religion, and common traditions which are transferred over time among members of the same group (Eagleton, 2000; Kneller, 1968; Kuper, 1999). Therefore, culture includes what we feel, think, and do. It companies spiritual and materialistic aspects of human beings (Inglis & Hughson, 2003, p.18). Although, the vagueness of the term culture and the difficulty of studying it, we experience, learn, and transfer culture. It shapes our lives and affects our decisions (Al-'Adly, 1981).

Besides, there is a strong link between culture and society. Culture only exists in a human society and a society cannot survive without culture. Raymond Williams (1989), the pioneer of cultural studies in Britain, pointed out that every human society has its structure, goals, and meanings. The human society expresses this uniqueness in its institutions, arts, language, and education. The construct of a society means, first of all, the search for common meanings and trends that comprise all members of this society. Therefore, the core of culture is developing a unified identity between members of a specific group or a society. This illustrates the power of culture.

Consequently, culture is connected to human as it is a product of his active interaction with the environment. It represents a system of values, beliefs, traditions, trends, and standards that determine people's choices and behaviors within the social system in a certain society. Culture encompasses all areas of life (philosophical, religious, moral, economic, social, educational, and political, etc.). It is important to distinguish here between culture as a concept that includes all aspects of life and culture as a term for a particular group in a society. Therefore, each society is divided into several parts called sub-communities. Each component or part has its own values, customs, traditions, genetics, and trends, as a small society within the original society. This culture is called "sub-culture" which is a part of the macro-culture of the society.

It is important to mention that the strong link between culture and the idea of lifestyles has resulted in an enormous number of notions such as mass culture, high culture, low culture, sports culture, consumer culture, and visual culture...etc (Bennett et al, 2005). Moreover, the vagueness of the term culture impacted all other definitions related to it such as; political culture, school culture, youth culture, university culture, the culture of democracy, and the culture of change. Given the fact that the notion of student culture is derived from the definition of culture, it is, therefore, still vague and overlaps with other terms and definitions.

The term youth culture was the first step towards the emergence of student culture. It comes from the writings of the German philosopher and educator

Gustav Wyneken in the last 19th century (Lipset, 1972). The term coincides with the German Youth Movement which tried to constitute a new identity against the parental guardianship and the conservative society. Then, the definition of youth culture was developed after the World War II for many reasons as Wilson (1969) described "Youth culture has thus been largely created by the entertainment industry and the gap between generations has been made increasingly manifest" (p.71). As well as the political and social events which occurred at the western world at that time such as wars, social system changes, and new philosophical theories had been represented as a complementary factor for the development of youth culture (Brake, 2003). This culture concentrated on music, entertainment, having sex, drug taking, fashion, consumerism, and personal freedom without limitations (Johansson, 2007).

For the first time, attention has emerged in studying student culture in the mid of the last century. Kleinberg pioneered the study of what he called the phenomenon of "student culture". In his comparative study, he wrote that there is such a thing as student culture, but it is not easy to be described because the qualities and characteristics of this culture are not represented in all members of the group (Kleinberg, 1979). Furthermore, Kuh and Whitt (1988) mentioned that there was not much literature assure how culture is used to understand college and university life. The need for studying culture in higher education institutions came as a reflection of the Japanese management principals at the eighties of the 20th century (p.19). It was concerned much more with industrial organizations, including universities, as a research tool (Silver, 2003).

However, the studies of Kuh and Whitt were more related to the organizational culture of the university (university culture) than involved in studying students' lives and behaviors, but it shed light on the concept of university culture. It is noted that writings about student culture were significantly limited and this has impacted the development of the notion. Furthermore, the problem of the definition of culture contributed to the late discussion of the term student culture. Also, Kleinberg and other researchers at that time studied student culture through a positivistic view which affected the interpretation of the phenomena of student culture. However, in a later stage, serious contributions to studying student culture were made. The researchers attempted to propose a specific definition for student culture.

Nokomo (1984) pointed out that "student culture constitutes a small or miniature society with its own complex intra- and inter-relationship with other segments within and outside the campus environment" (p.90). He also declared that student culture consists of attitudes, values, expectations, ideas, and behaviors which students bring with them from different socio-economic backgrounds to the university campus. The development of these components relies on the character of the official or institutional culture and the interaction of students as individuals and in groups to develop a particular identity with the university ethos. Moreover, he assumed that the campus milieu (climate) enable or prevent the development of student culture. In the same vein, Cole (1982) assured that students in American colleges shared a common baseline of values, experiences, behaviors, and expectations between them.

Additionally, Nokomo adopted the non-materialistic view of student culture. However, he referred to the symbolic markers used by students to distinguish themselves from other groups in a society. However, he accidentally neglected the materialistic side of student culture such as rituals, art, and social organizations which are extremely important in understanding student culture at a university. On the contrary, he added an important dimension to realizing the influence of the institutional culture at a university on student culture. Besides,Van Maanen and Barley (1984) mentioned that the occupational group community is "a group of people who consider themselves to be engaged in the same sort of work, whose identity is drawn from the work who share with one another a set of values, norms, and perspectives that apply to but extend beyond work-related matters and whose social relationships meld work and pleasure" (p.287). Thus, it seems that the definition of Barley and Van Maanen connects with the definition of student culture introduced by Nokomo. This is simply because students also see themselves as a small and separate stratum with their own values, customs, and traditions which are entirely different from the outside society. Moreover, they attempt to constitute a centralized-identity for them at the university.

Studies on student culture have accelerated. For example, Kuh and Whitt (1988) studied the culture of American universities and colleges and they endeavoured to give a simple integrated and comprehensive definition of university culture. They stated that culture "is the summation or end-product of all the social and personal values and the consequences of those values that operate within the institution" (p.15). Kuh and Whitt give values the most important contributions in shaping the culture of American universities and colleges. Although the proposed definition by Kuh and Whitt related to the whole culture of the university, it implicitly considers students as an effective actor and a member of the institution community. Furthermore, Bishop et al., (2003) stated that student culture is a blend of norms, attitudes, behaviors, and shares common properties including the peer pressure, "Cliques" and "Crowds".

After reviewing the history of the definition, it seems that the term student culture is considered one of the loose terms which overlaps with some other terms such as university culture, youth culture, and campus culture. Despite the differences of the term student culture from the previous definitions, it is partially connected with them. For example, student culture is similar to youth culture as it belongs to students who attend university and are aged between 18-22 years old (Moffatt, 1991). Additionally, youth culture focuses on relations of friendship, love of music, partying, and unlimited freedom which is also what distinguishes student culture at university. As Nichols (1993) stated that partying is spreading among most of Denison University students even among students who are politically active. The partying culture, according to his study, includes drinking, dancing, and socializing with each other in groups. The difference between student culture and youth culture is that student culture is more mature than youth culture as it is based on some academic issues that pertain to students at a university. Furthermore, it is linked to political and moral issues which concern the community at large.

The term student culture overlaps with the term university culture or "institutional culture" of which students are members. Therefore, they live within the general culture of a university and it affects them. University culture represents a system of ideas, values, traditions, rituals, and behaviors that are shared among all members of a university (Simplicio, 2012). Therefore, it is a system of social relations and a system of meaning (Hays, 1994; Smircich, 1983). It exists among students, professors, administrators, and staff members. However, student culture distinguishes from university culture as it spreads only among students who are members of a large university community. Also, it concentrates on creating an identity for that group at the university. On the contrary, university culture converges to build a character or a personality for the whole institution to achieve its goals. It relates to achieving the administrative and organizational aims of an institution. In contrast, student culture is a subculture of society culture and university culture. This culture is linked to students and a variety of student cultures may exist at just one university culture. For example, a culture of white students, a culture of black students, and another culture of Chicano can exist in American universities (Kenneth, 1999; Nelson Laird et al., 2004).

However, the term campus culture is a general framework in which university styles and customs are found (Harman, 2002). Campus culture is characterized as an open or as a closed culture. It may also contain many cultures and represent an umbrella under which all these cultures exist (Douglass, 1966; Harman, 2002; Lafore, 1964). However, student culture differs from campus culture; it is part of this culture that characterizes campus. Additionally, campus culture may be characterized by tolerance or narrow-mindedness, welcoming or hatred and aggression. It also facilitates or blocks interactions and activism among student groups. Therefore, it has a deep influence on student culture as some studies have clearly shown (Kenneth, 1999; Reyes, 2015).

Although there have been many attempts to describe student culture, there is no common definition of the term. However, it could be defined as a collection of values, perceptions, expectations, ideas, rituals, and behaviors that spread among students and transfer from one generation to another. Moreover, it shapes their views and it is considered as a reference source for their behaviors and judgments.

2.1.1 The Elements of Student Culture

In previous definitions, Nokomo and Cole mentioned that student culture is a small community that has complex and varied relationships between its members. Moreover, they clarified that student culture consists of values, attitudes, expectations, norms, ideas, and social interaction. Student culture is an independent ecosystem working to do its job together, but we divided it in order to make it easy to study. Therefore, the components of this culture are as follows:

First, values are the fundamental element of student culture. It can be defined as "the regard that something is held to deserve; the importance, worth, or usefulness of something" (Oxford Dictionary, 2016). Berry (1954) also defined it as anything that is a subject of interest and benefit to human (p.13). Besides, the term is used to indicate the process of assessment performed by a person who ends with a judgment on a subject or a situation. This process of judgment is based on the standards of a person's moral system. Thus, values are a distinctive feature of subcultures within the society itself as it guides an individual's behavior and judgments in a sub-culture. Moreover, it determines what is desirable and what is undesirable.

Consequently, university students have their own value system that displays the unique character of this group. Their value system consists of various kinds of values; such as social, economic, political, personal, and religious values (Bishop et al., 2004). Thus, researchers have studied student value system and concluded based on their observations about it. They reported that values have a clear influence on student behaviors at university (Astin, 1998; Engle, 2002; Levine & Cureton, 1998). Furthermore, they stated that value systems are constantly changing over time (Berry, 1954; Shilito & Marle, 1992). Therefore, research studies must continuously adapt to explore the extent of change that occurs. Besides, it is noted that most of these studies addressed the change of value system for students in deferent times. The majority of studies have used the quantitative approach when dealing with student values. In addition to this, the change in student value system is different due to the impact of the contemporary issues that highly affected on the student community at the university.

Second, attitudes, beliefs, and norms are considered the basic component of student culture. Attitudes can be defined as "the way you think and feel about someone or something" (Mariam Webster, 2016). Breckler and Wiggins (1989) defined attitudes as "mental and neural representations, organized through experience, exerting a directive or dynamic influence on behavior" (p.409). Therefore, it is the tendency of something such as an idea, a person or a situation and this predisposition is to urge people to think and behave towards this idea, person or situation. Attitudes may be affirmative or pessimistic, positive or completely negative and usually changed through a process of persuasion. Attitudes are essential for student culture as it represents a driving force for behavior.

Additionally, beliefs are defined as "an acceptance that a statement is true or that something exists" (Oxford Dictionary, 2013). Beliefs are a motor of behavior and are considered a vital part of student culture. Most research studies have tried to describe and measure student beliefs including (political, social, religious ....etc) in a quantitative way. Norms also can be defined as "a standard or pattern, especially of social behavior, that is typical or expected of a group" (Oxford Dictionary, 2013). Therefore, they are behavioral expectations or rules for all students. These norms inform us concerning how students are expected to behave towards each other and other persons or situations on the university. Norms are developed by students, covering most students' behaviors and applying to all situations all the time.

It is significant to mention that the direction of research on studying the components of student culture have changed from just describing attitudes, norms, and beliefs of students to understanding how these attitudes and beliefs are applied to important issues posed by these studies. For example, most scholars have investigated the attitudes of students towards different subjects of student life such as charity work and volunteerism, learning, and teaching in a university and joining to political parties (Barhoum, 1983; Chung et al., 2001; Elizabeth & Marie, 1991; Emme, 1943; Furnhum & McManus, 2004; Gray & Saracino, 1991; Miner, 1971; Wallace, 1966; Warnath, 1961). However, other studies thus far have linked beliefs with some social, educational, and political issues such as dating, friendship relations, liberalization, and the work of women (Bishop et al., 2003; Mutlu, 1996; Wallace, 1966; Warnath, 1961). Results prove that attitudes and beliefs contribute strongly to student behaviors and direct them. The shortcomings of these studies come from investigating every element of student culture individually. Furthermore, they try to quantify all elements of student culture, but this did not provide a complete and a comprehensive picture of student culture overall.

Third, customs and habits represent an essential component of student culture. On the one hand, customs are defined as "an action or a way of behaving that is usual and traditional among people in a particular group or place" (Mariam Webster, 2016). On the other hand, habits are defined as "a tendency or a disposition to act in a particular way" (Collins dictionary, 2016). They are also considered as essential facets of human conduct (Baldwin, 1988). Students, at university, have a particular set of customs and habits which appears on campus. They have habitual ways of talking, writing, eating, treating friends and strangers, solving problems, and carrying out different daily tasks. Many scholars seriously attempted to explore student habits and customs in order to understand these vital elements of student culture at university (Bishop et al., 2004; Moffatt, 1991; Nichols, 1993). The customs are represented in arranging parties, festivals, and wearing special clothes in specific events, such as Halloween festival at the US Colleges and Universities.

Fourth, social interaction means participating in relationships with people who have common interest and goals inside one group. Many sociologists have confirmed the influence of the structural and social milieu, in which a person is a part, on the behavior and social relations that exist among its members. Therefore, the social context of a peer group interaction in a university determines student behaviors and patterns of interaction among students towards each other and towards their professors (Katz & Kahn, 1979). Considerable scholarly work has been directed to investigate student social interaction in university between students themselves, between students and professors, between student race-groups, and between student interaction online groups and in multicultural settings (Byrd, 2014; Caplan, 2003; César & Kumpulainen, 2009; Change, 2005; Hurs et al., 2013; Hutcheson & Chapman, 1979; Kuh & Shouping, 2001; Lacy, 1978). Results, for example, proved the role of interpersonal relations between members of a group on campus and their impact on patterns of student interaction and changes in their behavior (William, 1978). The official interaction between students and professors affected students' grades in a way that encouraged students to allocate more effort to other educationally beneficial activities during college (Cole, 2010).

Consequently, the unofficial interaction between students and professors are both limited in scope and rare. It was determined by a combination of elements. For students, determining factors were interest in interacting with professors and their level of free time or activities that they are involved in. For professors, determining factors were personality, the amount of time spent on campus, and interest in interacting with students. Additionally, university infrastructure, such as the size of the campus, facilities, and offices also played a role in interactions between students and professors (Cotton and Wilson, 2006).

Fifth, student organizations are considered one of the characteristics of student culture at university. They include formal and informal organizations which have been formed by students. These organizations serve as important agencies in students' life. Researchers have studied student organizations intensively. Although formal student organizations are important for students, informal student organizations have a profound influence on student behavior. This is due to the accessibility of the informal organizations and their role in meeting students' interests and common needs. Moreover, the official student organizations are represented in the groups studying a particular academic specialty, per-semester groups, as well as political organizations of the Communist Party and other political orgnizations. The non-official organizations were represented in the students who belong to the network of one city hometown, fraternities, sororities as well as communities and student clubs, peer group, and male-female groups (Arnold & Kuh, 1992; Englesberg, 1992; Kimbrough, 2003; Kuh, 1995; Milem, 1998).

Finally, political participation is a vital element of student culture at university. It gives student culture a dynamic and an effective picture for all members of a society. Usually, students aimed at changing their reality by involving in political actions and engaging in society's issues. University students have a prolonged history of political participation (Altbach, 1991; Levin & Cureton, 1998; Lipset, 1972). The essential era of student political participation was the sixties of the past century, which saw a wave of student political engagement which took place at most Western universities and extended to all universities in the Middle East and South America. Researchers are interested in studying political participation of university students as a manifestation of student activism. Many topics are related to political participation such as student demonstrations and participating in governmental elections, their ways to claim their demands, and joining to political parties (Altbach & Cohen, 1990; Horowitz, 1986; Konings, 2002; Levine & Keith, 1979; Levy, 1981; Lipset, 1964 ; Sheppard, 1989). Through the previous presentation of the concept of student culture and its elements, we can conclude the following:

– Student culture is considered a subculture within the culture of a society in which a university exists. Also, it includes ideas, values, behaviors, and symbols that distinguish students as a social and cultural group within the larger community.

– The function of student culture is represented in considering it as a reference for the behavioral patterns of its members. Furthermore, it represents a dominant force in their conduct and helps students to make sense of these behaviors.

– Student culture is not only a set of values, attitudes, ideas, and vocabulary, but it is also an interaction between all of them which produces a set of behavioral patterns. Moreover, student culture shapes student way of life as each element of student culture has its place in a hierarchy of values. Students arrange these elements so that some have significant strength and others have less. The elements and structure of student culture are dynamic, not static.

– The term student culture extends to the intellectual and materialistic products of a student group. The intellectual side includes habits, traditions, beliefs, language, and customs which are transmitted from the older students to the later students. As for the materialistic side, it includes tools, clothing, publications, and organizations used by student group at university.

– Student culture intensively reflects the aspirations of students, their hopes, their pain, their desires, and their frustrations. However, students often do not find channels to express their culture, because the political authority seeks to block and limit it to its social sphere. This is because it is always confrontational and anti-authoritarian.

2.2 Student Culture in Egypt

Although Egypt has known higher education since ancient times, the first university in the modern sense was established at the beginning of the twentieth century. The pharaonic civilization constructed many scientific institutions that attached to the temples all over Egypt ('Ali, 1996; Shann, 1992). "Onn" or "Heliopolis" and "Alexandria" were among the first universities in the human history (Adieb, 1990; Shann, 1992). Moreover, the Islamic civilization in Egypt established al-Azhar Mosque in 970 A.D which served as a mosque for praying and an educational institution for teaching Islamic studies (Mahmoud, 1986, p.8; Shann, 1992, p.226).

Historically speaking, University of Fuad1 (Cairo University now) was the first higher education institution in modern Egypt. This university was established in 1908 (Al-Jimy'iy, 1982). At first, it was a non-state university and it was funded through gifts and donations from princes, merchants, and wealthy people. This supports the claim of the social class formation of the university. Besides, the shortage of funding impacted the educational process at the university. This was a strong reason for changing the university's status to become a state university (Najjar; 1976; Reid, 1990). The class formation of the university, the the political participation of students and faculty members, the governmental control over the university, and the events that the university witnessed such as the Revolution of 1919 and other social transformations have been reflected on the advancement of this institution in Egypt. In addition, the idea of the university in Egypt had developed from the concept of the institution which sanctifies and teaches knowledge only for the sake of knowledge and for people whom are mentally able to learn "the ivory tower universities" to a new kind of university which makes an investment in education and serves the surrounding community ('Abdallah, 1985; Al-Jimy'iy, 1982; Mahmoud, 2008). All these factors highly influenced student culture at Egyptian universities for a long time.

2.2.1 Sources of Student Culture

Universities are not isolated to the rapid changes that have occurred in both developed and undeveloped societies. They have influenced and reformed student culture as causal factors for change. These factors are represented in revolutions, the development of mass media, political issues, and cultural events in the Egyptian society. The university itself has become a main source for forming student culture by way of its environment, activities, and social interaction among students, faculty members, and university administration (Tanṭawi, 1992). This section sheds light on the primary sources that constitute student culture at Egyptian universities.

2.2.1.1 First: Sources within a university. Universities are not only institutions for teaching and learning, but they are also social communities which have much integration and many interactions among their members. Student culture is formed in Egyptian universities through different sources that interact together to constitute the structure of this culture. The historical heritage of students is a significant factor in forming student culture. It has a longstanding balance of experience, rituals, and events which represent a historical legacy of this group. Thus, students have maintained their own unique culture for an extended period.

Additionally, university students are a social group and they have an ancient cultural heritage as members of a social organization within a university (Haferkamp & Smelser, 1992; Katz & Kahn, 1978; Wallace, 1966). It represents a summary of the essential experiences, events, and standards of behaviors appropriate for them which have been approved by the previous generations of students. This heritage is transmitted from the old students to the new students and through the accumulation of a cultural property which is considered one of the attributes and characteristics of culture. Moreover, the students at Egyptian universities have a vast cultural heritage which is transmitted from the older generation to the latest generation after a continuous process of revision and alteration for the elements of this heritage. This source includes the elements of student culture which have proved their worth and power for the social group on campus. The cultural heritage of students at Egyptian universities includes righteous elements that enhance student culture such as co-operation between student agencies, ideas about freedom and social justice, notions about typical and acceptable behaviors, and engagement in the political life of the society. Furthermore, it includes respect and collaboration with university administration and their solidarity with oppressed groups that suffer from social and political injustice (ʿAbbas, 1995; ʿAbdallah, 1985; Reid, 1990).

On the other side, some negative elements affected student culture such as the development of the political Islam movement (Abu-Al-Ftuwh, 2010), the feelings of alienation from society, (Ahmed, 1987) and the sectarian tensions between Muslim and Christian students. This was a result of political and social factors which fostered the establishment of many universities all over Egypt without scientific planning or any sufficient infrastructure (ʿAli, 2008). This is represented as an aid factor for increasing the number of students (with limited learning abilities and different social backgrounds) enrolling in universities. The sum of these events has critically impacted student culture at Egyptian universities.

The idea of university also served as the second major stream for forming student culture at Egyptian universities. The pioneers Mustafa Kamel, Jurji Zaydan, Sheikh Muhammad Abdouh, and Qasim Amin, had specific ideas when they founded the Egyptian University (Cairo University Now) in 1908. These ideas were represented in considering the university as a beacon of science and knowledge in Egypt. Moreover, there was a strong link between the emergence of the university and the Egyptian National Movement which sought to support the establishment of a liberal university for spreading knowledge among Egyptians (Al-Jimy'iy, 1982; Mughiyth, 2009).

Numerous studies have argued that the Egyptian university has been derived from the European model of the university at the beginning of its establishment. Mahmoud (2008), for example, mentioned that the founders of the Egyptian university had taken the western idea of the university. From his perspective, it was not appropriate for the nature of Egyptian society at that time and it had affected the development of the concept of university and its functions. Also, he pointed out that Egypt, at that time, was in need for a university in order to contribute to developing the society and expanding its educational services to all Egyptians, especially those who were poor and illiterate. Additionally, many scholars claimed that there is a range of problems that have accompanied the evolution of the concept of university in Egypt which has fiercely influenced the university's inputs and outputs. They believed that the problems that arose during the establishment of the Egyptian University are still influencing the university education and student culture (Ahmed, 1993; Mahmoud, 2008; Sakran, 2001). The influence of this classical idea of the university is represented in giving the the process of teaching much attention as the priority must be given to activities inside the university, not outside.

This view contributed to isolating the university from society and its inability to lead the process of change. These are called "closed-campus universites". Moreover, the spread of the elite's ideas among faculty members and even among students since the establishment of the Egyptian university had influenced student culture. It was perceived as an "ivory tower," which included the elite of society who were characterized by intelligence and culture, possessed critical and creative thinking, and had a prestigious social position in the society (Ahmed, 1993; Mahmoud, 2008). This classical idea had influenced the establishment of the newer universities on the same pattern. Newer universities have featured older, closed academic departments. It enhanced what was advocated by the medieval universities which separated between theoretical and applied knowledge. This was clear when you compared the numbers of theoretical colleges with practical college and the number of students in each type of college. This led to conflicting academic cultures at universities (theoretical versus practical, humanities versus natural sciences) which led to increasing intolerance and rejection of the other (Mahmoud, 2008, Shann, 1992).

All these problems which have been associated with the evolution of the Egyptian university since 1908 to the present have a significant impact on student culture in Egypt. Students consider themselves as a social class because the amount of knowledge they receive will give them more opportunities to have high social status in outside society than their colleagues who learn at vocational schools. Moreover, the skills of making open discussions with others who have different perspectives did not exist. This is back to the absence of teaching methodologies based on discussion and active participation.

Student Activities is the third basic source of student culture at Egyptian universities. These activities have an important position in university life because they play a dynamic role in the formation of students' personalities and developing mental, psychological, and social aspects (Muhamad, 2012). The philosophy of student activities at Egyptian universities is derived from the philosophy of higher education, which represents the general framework for all universities to work in the light of its principles and goals (Tanṭawi, 1992). The general functions of student activities help to direct student's energies in an acceptable social way. Besides, they provide appropriate space and channel for expressing an opinion and social interaction through seminars, magazines, and conferences. They also help students to use their free time in order to develop their abilities and skills as well as supporting their self-development (ʿAbdel-Satar, 2016).

Student Activities at Egyptian universities are varied; they combine social, cultural, literary, sports, and scientific activities which give a real opportunity for social interaction and for gaining positive attitudes and behaviors (Sayīd, 2008). Through these activities, new values and behaviors are growing and negative behaviours which are no longer suitable to communicate with others are disappearing. ʿAbdel-Wahed (2005) stated that student activities enhanced social values among university students. Besides, they are developing students' awareness of the society's problems, enforcing the notion of citizenship and belonging to the country, and increasing volunteering works (ʿAli, 2009; Muhamad, 2012).

Despite the variety of student activities at Egyptian universities, the numbers of students who practice these activities are still limited (Al-Mahdy, 2015). This is simply because the availability of activities is less than the number of students. Moreover, there is a shortage of funding and limited infrastructure for these activities. Besides, there is no time available to practice these activities because study schedules are full and students are busy in attending lectures and laboratories (Al-Sabaʿy, 2016; ʿAli, 2009; Sīliym, 2014). Consequently, the participation of students in activities gives them opportunities for interaction and acquisition of proper behavior. Accordingly, student activities have become an essential tool in shaping the culture of student community in Egyptian universities through indirect influence on the acquisition of desirable values, behaviors, and attitudes.

2.2.1.2 Second: Sources outside a university. Family is the first group in which an individual receives the foundations of social, moral, and religious education (Morin et al., 2015). This is because it is the first source of information, knowledge, and concepts through the prevailing relationship among family members. Furthermore, it helps in the formation of individuals' identity and their social status. Thus, gaining membership in a first group will reflect in the way student join to other groups. As it increases his activity and expands the scope of his interaction with the community (Shīrīff, 2006). Moreover, the family's social, economic, educational, and cultural situation has a significant impact on university students (Biraimah, 1994; Brimeyer et al., 2006; Eargle, 1963). Students go to university carrying different behaviors and values based on the social milieu of where their families live. These behaviors and values are derived from the family and represent an undeniable source of shaping student culture at the university.

A campus full of students from disparate social origins interacts to negotiate a common set of acceptable behaviours, as long as each student participates in the mechanisms of student culture. A student's family class status continues to affect them at university. Students who come from low social classes become more active and participate in university activities and this gives an excellent opportunity to use their behavior, ideas, and values brought from their families. In fact, Egypt is a country with a long history of social and class differences which have existed since the era of Pharaohs (Petrie, 1923, p.44). Then Muhammad Ali laid the foundation for the modern class system in Egypt. For example, Mamluks were replaced by landowners in Egypt (Al-Rafaʿy, 1989, p.544). Historically speaking, Nasser came after 150 years to create social justice through the Agrarian Reform Law which redistributed land for low-income families and led to social mobility through demolishing the class of landowners. Some people from the lower class moved up to the middle-class and many of lower class moved to the layer underneath the middle that may represent a vast majority of Egyptians now (Abdel-Hamed, 1994; Hussanen, 1981).

Additionally, this social mobility changed the family's socioeconomic status which was reflected in increasing the numbers of students enrolled in universities (Shann, 1992). For example, the number of students enrolled at universities rose from 3,368 in 1925 to 42,494 students in 1952 (Boktor, 1963, p.100). Many parents wanted to send their sons to a university and this inspired a diverse cultural atmosphere at Egyptian universities. Although large numbers of students went to university, many disputes took place between the poor and the wealthy students. This atmosphere helped to create the Islamic Movement (The Muslim Brotherhood and Al-Jama'a Al-Islamiyya) inside universities. After the War of October 1973 against Israel, the new regime adopted new economic policies "al-Infitah" in Egypt (Bush, 2007; Gray, 1998; Tucker, 1978). This led to the appearance of a new class consisting of (stock exchange speculators, businessmen, and brokers) and those people are transferred from the lower class to the upper class due to these economic policies. These newcomers sent their sons in order to raise their families' social status which bringing negative habits and values such as consumerism, adverse morality, and bad manners.

Societal events and shifts are the second source that shapes student culture at Egyptian universities. Many researchers confirm that there is a strong conections between a university and the society in which it exists. It is difficult to isolate a university form what is happening outside it in society. Political events such as demonstrations against ruling regimes and social movements that stand in the face of corruption in society are considered some of the most important events which have impacted student culture. Moreover, social and economic setbacks and crises influenced students. All these events have profoundly affected the culture of students at a university.

Egypt has witnessed many revolutions and transformations throughout its history. For example, the Revolution of the 1919 and the Revolution of the June 23th of 1952, which overthrew the king from power and announced Egypt as a republic, were critical events in Egypt (Goldberg, 1992; Stevens, 1969; Tignor, 1967). Those revolutions instituted some radical social and economic policies that affected Egyptian society in reshaping the social and economic structure. These changes impacted students at a university regarding participation, enrolment rates, and value changes. In the Eighties, Egyptian society witnessed an economic transition to the free market policies. These economic changes were followed by social and cultural changes in Egyptian society which impacted university students. Thus, students were influenced by the political atmosphere in the society before the revolution.

Tools of modern communication and technology are an important source in shaping student culture at Egyptian universities nowadays (Hussien, 2007). They have a significant impact on students' behaviours, values, and attitudes. Additionally, they increase students' social interaction and participation (Al-Asdudiy, 2012; ʿAbdel-Muwguwd, 2014; ʿAbdel-ʿaal, 2015; Nusīr, 2013; Shimey, 2016). Due to their easiness and the speed of communication and interaction, these modern tools led to the transmission of indirect values, trends, tendencies, and desires rapidly as compared to other sources. For instance, the Internet represents a rapid means of modern communication and technology. Social networking such as Twitter, YouTube, and Facebook are considered an essential tool for gathering students on the cyberspace. According to Shīrīff (2006), social networks have become an outlet for university students; because those tools are not governed and not nearly as authoritarian way as the students themselves are. Students share their views and express their opinions in a free and democratic way. The reason behind this is that students are close in age and inclination, hobbies, and it is easy to promote culture in general and any subculture in particular using social networks. Considering the importance of these technologies in redrawing social relations in a society on new foundations, scientists have adopted the concept of "virtual community", which is a synonym for peer group, but with a new perspective. The only factor that brings participants together is their interaction with virtual communities which provide them with a range of information, knowledge, and beliefs. This information and knowledge play a significant role in the formation and building of values, attitudes, and behavior within student culture at university as they are more subscribers in these virtual communities.

Moreover, mass media is the fourth source of student culture. Without any doubt, we are living now in the age of media. The media machine has simplified and controlled cultural arena by its enormous potential use of advanced technology and diverse messages influential in shaping public opinion (McQuail, 1987). Mass media, radio, TV, and newspapers are considered some of the primary sources which constitute student culture at Egyptian universities. The political, economic, and social issues which are addressed by media and the broadcasting of talk shows which analyse societal issues and present different views and new intellectual trends have a deep influence on values, behaviours, and attitudes of university students.

Recent studies have mentioned that there is a relationship between student culture and media because supplies the culture with a great deal of its facts and information, impacting society, and modifying the view of its members for life (Abu-'Omer, 2015; Farhaat, 2015; Radwan, 2016; Ṭanṭawi, 1992). Moreover, media provides a considerable opportunity for transferring ideas, facts, and interpretation and expanding the circle of debate as well as participation among social groups especially students at universities. Added, the media also spreads values that maintains the solidarity of the society and rejects ideas and traditions that harm society. This along with what it does as an education tool for spreading knowledge and refining the public taste. Despite the critical role of all kinds of media, it has a negative impact and severe repercussions on student culture. It negatively affects the culture of students because it broadcasts strange ideas and values that are not suitable for Egyptian society.

However, the current situation in Egypt reflects that mass media clearly has contributed to the absence of awareness and shredding of social cohesion across the spectrum of Egyptian people, especially university students. Mubarak's regime used media as a tool to whitewash the regime's image and discredits the oppositions' image. Moreover, the media in this era broadcasted superficial topics and stayed away from the issues that affected citizens who had ideological and intellectual opinions. This resulted in the existence of pseudo-intellectuals as well as cultural illiteracy among young people.

2.2.2 The Elements of Student Culture at Egyptian Universities

The definition of student culture which was previously mentioned in the first section applies to student culture at Egyptian universities in terms of substance and composition. Student culture in Egypt before the January 25ᵗʰ Revolution of 2011 was static especially during the previous twenty years (Mubarak Era) because the political regime in Egypt attempted to control every part of the state. He especially aimed to dominate universities since they are the beacon of knowledge and liberal thought that made dictators afraid. Thus, the ruling regime regularly tried to suppress any political, social or cultural activities at universities. As a result, students became apathetic citizens (Gumʿah, 1984).

The values of university students barely changed over this time. Mahmoud (1991) noted only small differences and limited changes in values system of students between the late fifties and eighties. The changes were in moral, social, economic, and personal values, but there was no change in intrinsic or cognitive values. The social, economic, and political conditions in Egyptian society impacted the university student values. There has recently been a change in public policy from a socialist influence to a more capitalist influence, which led the president to adopt an open market policy. This made significant changes in the structure of Egyptian society, such as the rise of corrupt, parasitic businesses; as well as rising incomes, increased activity of foreign investors seeking a quick profit and state neglect in the management and direction of economic activity. These results were compatible with the studies of Kashif (2001) and Habashy (2012) that found there were small changes in students' religious values, followed by social values, economic, political, and aesthetic values.

According to Helmy (1981), university students before the revolution had a moderate degree of positive values such as co-operation and volunteerism. However, they also had a low degree of values like perseverance, social awareness, leadership, public service, working in new cities, manual labour, and political awareness. Therefore, the changes in the value system were small before the revolution and scholars are all in agreement on this. However, there are no studies that used qualitative methods, which would have been helpful in studying these changes and might have created a better understanding of the factors and mechanisms that caused this change.

Additionally, Egyptian scholars tried to study the attitudes of students towards various subjects and crises in Egypt. Sakran (1989) identified the positions that university students held on some contemporary issues raised in the international arena and the Islamic and Arab world in order to detect the extent of their awareness of the issues of their community and world issues around them. The results showed that there are varying degrees of student interest in the issues under study and therefore different attitudes in terms of their opinions. A large proportion of students believed that the private sector must work together with the public sector in Egypt and they disagreed with the domination of the public sector by the private sector. Also, they disagreed with the policy of economic openness and there is an increase in students' awareness of the importance of Islamic solidarity and Arab unity. Finally, their awareness of the Iraq-Iran war and the Israeli-Arab conflict was improved.

University students have the ability and attitudes to prepare for problems and issues facing them, but they confront their problems by just talking about them, rather than acting (Mahmoud, 1991). This means there were positive attitudes for solving problems but in the way of determining problems not try to solve it. This arose from the nature of Egyptian society which still has a parental power over sons even at the university. This comes in addition to the autocratic and authoritarian pattern in the Education system which still exists at universities. Cook (2001) attempted to understand the attitudes and opinions of students about the role of Islam in public universities sponsored and funded by the state. The results indicated that most students look at the education system as dominated by Western style. Furthermore, the university students wanted to increase the Islamic characteristics in the university and everyday life. Most respondents believed that Egyptian society wanted an educational system that preserved Islamic values and traditions. More than 70% of the students thought that Islamic-oriented universities would be more desirable because they thought that it would enhance their education.

As for social interactions, Egyptian universities have a varied and a wide range of social interactions between students each other within the same group and between different student groups, but it seems to be limited between students and professors. Professors do not give students the opportunity to contact them inside or outside classes. This mainly related to the large numbers of students, the workload of professors, and the conservative nature of the university campuses especially in Upper and Middle Egypt (Sakran, 2001). Furthermore, there is limited interaction between male and female students especially at the universities in Upper Egypt. This is due to the conservative customs and traditions of people in Upper Egypt, in addition, to the role of religion in the students' life at most of these universities.

Despite the rich social interaction between student bodies at Egyptian universities, students have suffered from alienation from their home country and have not had any sense of belonging or social responsibility towards society (Ahmed, 1987). Also, they have created their own language for expressing themselves. This language is characterized by swearing and expressions derived from Pop Culture. This reflects their isolation from their society (Egyptian Cabinet, Information and Decision Support Center, 2006; Jadallh, 2011).

Student voluntary and charity activities inside and outside Egyptian universities were limited. Many studies stated the low participation of university students in providing this kind of activities in most Egyptian universities such as in al-Azhar University and Cairo University (Al-Bana, 2011; Ghonimah, 2008). This reflected students' pressure of time in attending lectures as well as the feeling of pessimism and alienation among student groups.

Student political activities have been one of the important features of student culture since 1919. For example, students participated in political activity against the British occupation in the beginning of the 20th century and against changing social and economic policies in the 1980s ('Abdallah, 1985; Hussein, 1972; Ramadan, 1998; Reid, 1990). However, in the last 35 years, student political participation at Egyptian universities has been insufficient ('Ali, 2008; Qandil, 2003; Mughiyth, 2004; Naṣr, 2005) as a result of suppression of freedom which was practiced by the political regime. The students were prevented from participating in political activity at universities (Gumʿah, 1984; Mughiyth, 2009). For example, wall magazines have been prohibited. The Political Committee of the Student Unions has been dissolved ('Ali, 2008).

Moreover, Student Union elections were rigged by the Office of National Security. Moreover, individuals who discussed ideas that contradicted the regime were persecuted ('Ali, 2008, p.116). For all these reasons Adieb (2009) clarified that student political culture was weak and superficial. This was exblained by the absence of activities that supported the political culture in conjunction with an education that did not support critical thinking and creativity and ignore any political discussions. These results are compatible with Harb's study (2001). She stated that there is a weakness of political awareness among university students for political and societal issues. The reasons for the low political awareness are a limitation in the role of political parties in the development of the students' political awareness, avoidance of discussing political and social issues in studying halls at the university, and the traditional way of teaching instead of critical teaching approach ('Attallah, 2012; Harb, 2001).

It is noted that the weakness of political awareness among students was a result of the repressive practices pursued by the authority in the Mubarak era. The regime tried to restrict students and prevent any political activities within universities. Students felt alienation from their community which caused them to pay little attention to the issues rose. Students observed the weakness of the political parties, as a result of the parties' ambivalence towards the problems of the masses. The rate of student participation in Assembly election was extremely low. Their participation in political parties was under 10% percent of the overall number of members ('Abu-alʿla, 1984, p.16). Consequently, the case of state control over the media led to the absence of awareness for citizens. As media has led the society according to the vision and ideas of the regime, students saw that this media was manipulated and then watched the foreign media instead for information. This illustrates the pressure exerted on university students and has led to an attempt fault finding and awareness. It is clear from what we have discussed above that student culture at Egyptian universities before the January 25th Revolution of 2011 was characterized by negativity and weakness. Moreover, university students were isolated from real participation in social, political, and cultural activities at universities as well as in society.

2.3 University Student Culture after Revolutions

It is worth noting that revolutions are considered one of the major influential factors in changing the prevailing stereotypes and conditions of a society. They also give a degree of democracy and freedom within the context of a human society. Many countries have witnessed revolutions that brought about tremendous changes in societal and political structure. Consequently, these changes and transformations positively reflected on university student culture through radical and profound changes.

Suchlicki (1969) studied the student political movements and protests in Havana University before and after the Cuban Revolution. Students had participated in political action since the beginning of 1920 as a result of injustice and oppression practiced by the political regime in the era of Machado and Batista. Furthermore, Suchlicki showed that students participated in the Cuban Revolution in Latin America. Many changes occurred in university when Castro took power, such as the prevalence of Communist ideology and using education as a tool to build a communist society. The private universities were abolished or nationalized. The Castro regime introduced technology to all universities and emphasized practical education rather than theoretical and liberal education. Furthermore, according to the Marxist pedagogy, the students worked and studied at the same time to engage in a productive work.

Additionally, a scholarship system was created for university students based on loyalty to the political regime. Also, the students were required to be involved in a large amount of military service during their studies in university. Furthermore, the students' political participation was low after the revolution because the Communist party directed the student activities and universities. The student opposition has been contained primarily by the coercive strength of the Castro regime (Suchlicki, 1969). Therefore, Foran (2009) came to conclude that the Cuban revolution failed to achieve democracy in the state's institutions including universities. I suppose that the study of Suchlicki lacks references to documented data, such as reports, photos, and documentary films to support the writer's claims. It also neglected to address the negative impact of the Castro regime of the students' political awareness and their participation in the university affairs.

However, the changes in student culture had a different form in Russia. Lane (1973) investigated the impact of the Bolshevik revolution on the recruitment of Russian students by analyzing their social origins and political party affiliation in various institutions in the higher education sector in the first eleven years after the revolution. The results clarified that although there were radical changes in class composition that occurred in the student body, the social gradation of institutions and employee chances of selection persisted. This was because recruiters valued loyalty to the political party above everything else.

Therefore, loyalty to the Communist party was a correlate with social origin and type of educational institution. This means that there was no social mobility and the students of workers and peasants were encouraged to work in a lower level of jobs after graduation. Thus, this revolution seemed to support class discrimination in Russian society and negatively impacted the students.

Additionally, the students in Communist societies suffered from alienation and marginalization. The student movement also lacked independence and effectiveness. In comparison, the political and social transformation that occurred in the sixties of the previous century in many capitalist societies had a tremendously positive impact generally on the student culture and particularly in the students' political participation. For example, in the USA Petras (1965) studied the student movements at Berkeley University. The students revolted against the bad study environment in addition to the free speech issues. Besides, the students protested against the Multiversity which considers students as materials for the industrial society. In other words, universities did not accommodate students' demands and desires to study as human beings wanted to gain knowledge and liberal arts and they wanted not to be a tool to serve the industrial society.

The student movement staged a sit-in at the building of the university administration in order to force the university administrations to make real educational reforms. Besides, students suggested building a free university which meant liberal education and programmes based upon the students' interests. Those interests including solve the problems of community and poor people and related to the individuality of students. After 800 undergraduate students were arrested, the administrations agreed to the educational reform. This movement was supported by students and faculty members as well. The students represented a social movement for change. Educational policy considered a university to be a factory. Students were deemed only as material for fitting the industrial society, against the students' own desires. This presented an enormous awareness about students' rights, especially academic freedom. The change in student culture has been represented in an excessive political activism, study boycotts, and rebellion. The rebellion shifted from Berkley to other campuses. Moreover, radical ideas spread among student groups. The New Left and Marxism have attracted many students (Horowitz, 1986).

In South Korea, Stone (1974) studied the students' revolution at the time of April 1960 and tried to analyze the causes and repercussion of that activism. He considered two main factors for interpreting these events. The first is that the students had been pushed to make these events as a result of repression in Korea and they were aware of their situation. The second factor is the socio-economic changes that occurred in the Republic of Korea and according to Karl Douche theory about social mobilization, a new behaviour starts to constitute after these changes. Others argue that the causes of student revolution are the inferior educational services and the high rate of unemployment in Korean society, as well as the authoritarian regimes and suppressions of speech.

In Italy during the sixties, the student movement turned to violence. It dissolved into different student groups with varied political orientations. The Red Brigades arose and started to attack other student factions at universities. They interfered with the elections and kidnapped many politicians. These groups adopted extremely radical ideas about change in social and political structure of the Italian society (Statera, 1979). This was a result of the decadence of social and economic conditions which impacted the student attitudes towards desirable change. This is in addition to the social inequalities of the industrial society at that time which increased student anger. Additionally, a similar wave of violent behaviours among students was reported in Japan in sixties. The student groups changed from cooperation between one another to a bloody conflict between them. Moreover, totalitarian behaviours had spread among student organizations. The new student movement became anti-university and anti-society as well. The poor social and economic conditions after the war were the leading cause of that dramatic change in the students' behaviour at Japanese universities (Michiya Shimbori et al., 1980).

Scholars have recounted new student uprising throughout the seventies. Levine and Keith (1979) stated the changes in the political activity of American students in 1970 came as a result of the Vietnam War and deterioration of the economy in the United States of America. These factors made profound changes in American society, which initiated new forms of student activism. This activism was represented in demonstrations, strikes, boycotts, lobbying, and the increased presence of special-interest groups on college campuses. These forms represented a fundamental change in the style, direction, and form of student activism since the 1960s. I speculate the writer did not adequately address the violence event that happened during this period, because the students organized many demonstrations and strikes in order to achieve their demands. Basically, during this political unrest, many clashes with the police were expected to happen and victims had to fall from the two sides.

Numerous studies investigated the change in universities after recent revolutions in Eastern Europe and Asia. Mauch (1994) identified the crucial changes and transformations that took place in the higher education system and universities after the Velvet Revolution in 1989s. He discussed the German-Austrian effects on the education system in Czechoslovakia, which led to the modelling of Czech universities on the German universities' model. Policies, administration, management, regulation, and the kind of knowledge which was provided were all highly affected by German influence. Mauch also clarified the situation of higher education and universities during the 40 years of Communist rule and attempts by the government to reshape higher education in Soviet-style. Consequently, results show that the legislation in 1990 after the Velvet Revolution gave colleges and universities a maximal amount of power to control its affairs. Furthermore, there was more devolution of power and independence of universities in the higher education system. The level of students' enrolment at universities increased after the revolution. Some radical changes were instituted in curricula and an increase in the resources available to universities was allotted. An increase in the proportion of freedom and democracy in the university community has also been noted.

The study proved that there are some systems, colleges, and academic departments resistant to change even though the education system itself has changed (Mauch, 1994). The study outlined the changes in the university in post-revolution through quantitative statistics. The study also lacks the analytical view of these changes at the university and its impact on student affairs. Cermakova and Holda (1992) stressed that the change in the value system of students after the Velvet Revolution was limited. After a short period of time, students gradually returned to routine study, stereotypes of behaviours, and reduced their interest in public issues. This return to the political regime came after the revolution, which did not achieving the aims of the Velvet Revolution. This led to the feelings of disappointment among students from not achieve change in their social and economic conditions.

Unlike the study of Mauch, Mashyekhi (2001) provided a sociological analysis of the student movement in Iran after the 1979 Revolution by focusing on student organizations on campus, especially the Office for Consolidation of Unity. The new changes that occurred in the culture of the student political movement have allowed them to adapt to the daily complex political challenges in Iran. Many changes have been noted, for instance: the political and organizational links between the Office for Consolidation of Unity and the Islamic Left are an increasing liability that prevents some student groups from addressing the long-term interests of students. Furthermore, there was no open dialogue or cooperation between student groups with different ideologies, especially between the Office for Consolidation of Unity and Liberal students. The reactionary conservative outlook did not value equality for all students. Furthermore, authoritarian attitudes persisted among male activists and despite the increasing numbers of female students, women did not find a sympathetic and accepting environment in Islamic societies.

The elements of student culture tend to change after societal transformations. Jerome (2001) investigated polish students' beliefs before and after the democratization process in Poland (in 1985 to 1991) in the light of Rotter's Locus scale of control. This scale of control is a leading notion of the social learning theory. It measures the degree of belief for polish students about what was happening to them, is to build on their disposal or as a result of possessing relative properties or skill or competence or mental capacity which made them feel that they could control what may occur in the future. This kind of confidence is called internal control. Others with external control believe that what was happening to them was a result of luck, chance, and destiny or the influence of others. This study applied the quantitative method with extensive use of statistical tools to achieve results. 100 female and male students in 1991 were chosen as a sample for the study. The sample was much closer to the sample of 1985. The results clarify that the study sample of 1991 showed less internal control and political control subscale than the sample from 1985. Furthermore, there was no variation among the two groups in the personal control scale. The author said that there was a higher tendency towards internality for the political control subscale from 1985 to 1991. This backed to the changes in the political sphere in Poland. The authoritarian Communist government was abandoned and the democratically elected government was installed in its place. From this evevdence its clear that the changes in the political sphere of Polish society affected the beliefs of the university students. The students became more aware of the democratic process and felt that they could reform their lives.

In China, Shan and Guo (2011) tried to investigate the reasons and factors that led to the emergence of groups of angry youth protesters. They analyzed the forms of expression of a group of young people called the "angry youth" on the Internet. Strong patriotism and nationalism characterized their expressions. Shan and Guo made content analysis for the articles and topics that were published on the internet by those groups of people. The study determined that the main causes for the rise of this group of young people to be the progress of telecommunications networks and modern technology, the development of popular culture in the new century, the rise of Chinese nationalism in recent years, and the adverse effects of internal social and political problems. The angry youths were mostly comprised of young people who grew up in privileged circumstances and had a good education and the time to pursue their political interests.

In conclusion, revolutions brought about profound changes in universities, especially in student culture. In Cuba, the students' attitudes, expectations, and political participation changed, resulting in decreased political participation. Furthermore, as Levine wrote, American university students' ways of expressing their dissatisfaction changed to include violence and resistance against the government. Likewise, in Japan and Italy, the student groups tended toward violent behaviours against each other. In Iran, deep changes occurred in student culture regarding social interaction among different student groups especially among Islamist and Liberal students. Although many studies addressed university students after revolution, none of these studies addressed the changes that happened in student culture in an integrated approach.

2.4 University Student Culture in Egypt after the January 25th Revolution of 2011

The January 25th Revolution of 2011 was a peaceful revolution by the Egyptian youth against social injustice and widespread corruption in the state by the ruling regime. Moreover, it was a movement consisting of demonstrations, labour strikes, marches, and non-violent civil resistance, which led to the toppling of the regime and caused significant changes in Egypt ('Ali, 2012, p.30). Undoubtedly, this revolution created a condition of democracy and freedom in Egyptian universities. This was positively reflected in the university students through clear-cut changes in their values, attitudes, social, and political interactions, in addition to changes in their ways of expressing their demands. Kolar, (April 23, 2012) in a higher education blog, clarified that the higher education sector in Egypt had reflected the national revolution events in a "wave of campus activism sweeping Egypt". Furthermore, she mentioned that students wanted to pressure the government to make changes and purge corruption from universities.

Now, seven years after the revolution, students and faculty members at Egyptian universities across the country remain involved in the process of national transformation. Egyptian Student Union, with support from allies in the labour force, called for a general strike to be launched February 11, 2012, to demand that the Supreme Council of Armed Forces relinquish power to civilian rule. The strike did not widely spread, Mahmoud Nawar, a student at Helwan University, claimed that "The student movement is reviving and those who called for the strike on 11 February are now aware that they need the workers." While Egypt's future peospects reman unclear, one thing is unmistakable: the current generation of Egyptian students is not ready to stop fighting for reform, both on campus and off. (Kolar, paragraph two).

Many newspapers covered the university students' ways of expressing themselves and claiming their rights after the January 25th Revolution. For instance, al-Azhar University students demonstrated for the dismissal of the university administration after 228 students in university suffered food poisoning from a dining hall in a students' dorm (Al-Hadiddy & Rif'at, 2013). The students of the College of Veterinary Medicine at South Valley University protested and closed the college doors in objection to the lack of educational services, such as laboratories, teaching hospital, and transportation from the province of Assiut to the university to attend classes (Abu-Nuwr, 2013). This is also what happened similarly, in the College of Pharmacy at Cairo University (Akhbar Altaalim, 2013). Furthermore, the democratic and fair Student Union elections witnessed an increasing student turnout for the voting for choosing their representatives. This is considered among the prominent aspects of change in the student community after revolution. For instance, Fayoum University Student

Union elections were done in a democratic atmosphere and the students held election campaigns and conferences at the university ('Azaam, 2013). As well, there was a notable change in the students' values such as citizenship, social responsibility, tolerance, and acceptance of each other (Abu-Khres, 2015).

In conclusion, the changes in student culture in Egypt are similar to American university students after the Vietnam War because they both used demonstrations in which they expressed their rights and demands. By contrast, the changes in Egyptian student culture were different from the changes that happened among Cuban students. Political participation decreased in Cuba, but in Egypt, it increased. In contrast with Iran, the students in Egyptian universities were more liberal and open-minded while the Iranian students were authoritarian. Moreover, there is dialogue and cooperation between different student religious, political, and social groups in Egyptian universities, while this did not exist between Iranian students, especially between the Office for Consolidation of Unity and liberal students. Lastly, students at Egyptian universities have had democratic elections and a large degree of freedom which did not exist with other students in third world countries which witnessed revolutions.

Finally, most of the previous literature was focused only on changes in students' political participation. This makes this study different from previous studies because it will investigate the changes in student culture in general after the January 25th Revolution in Egypt in an integrated approach. Moreover, this study produces a theory that interprets the change in student culture in a post-revolution era in Egypt. Through my exploration of the literature, there are no previous studies provide any substantive theory for explaining the change in student culture after revolutions. Thus, this gives a good indicator for this study which introduces the change in student culture as a live case study.

Chapter III: The January 25TH Revolution: Causes, Aims, and Obstacles

This chapter explicates the aims, events, and causes of the January 25th Revolution of 2011. Moreover, it discusses the achievements of the revolution in many fields such as in the political, social, cultural, and economic spheres. Finally, it briefly refers to the basic challenges and obstacles which are still facing the January 25th Revolution and prevent it from achieving its aims.

3.1 The January 25TH Revolution of 2011

Revolution is a unique and complex sociopolitical phenomenon (Arendt, 1963; Foran, 1993; Goldstone, 2001). It aims at changing the current situation with all its shortcomings to a new condition which achieves the demands of all society members. Also, it represents extraordinary moments in nation's life after depleting all peaceful means and violent pressure on the political regime in order to bring about change (Bu-Nuʿman, 1994). Revolution, in a modern sense, occurs only in the context of a political, economic, and social system that is called state. Moreover, it is a temporary situation because there is no society that lives in a permanent revolution. It should shift gradually towards stability (Bu-Nuʿman, 2012, p.15).

The January 25th Revolution is viewed as a momentous revolution amongst those critical revolutions in the modern Egyptian history (ʿAli, 212; Qayati, 2013). It has the main characteristics of the successful revolutions such as; popular support, changing the regime, social and protest movements which calling for political change and establishing a new democratic state. This revolution was not violent, but it was peaceful demonstrations which originated from the suffering of the middle class in Egypt (Amin, 2011; Beissinger et al., 2015). It aimed at changing the miserable reality and demolishing the corruption which has spread in all the state's institutions and became a distinctive feature of it. In the January 25th Revolution, all social strata of Egyptian society took part and lined up on one aim to overthrow the political regime and transmit Egypt in a democratic track. Consequently, the Egyptian revolution has exceeded the shapes and frames of the traditional historical revolutionary models (Mustafa, 2011). It connected the real and the virtual; the spontaneous and the organization of the various sects, and intellectual and political trends in Egyptian society, which makes it unique in its aims and events (Chalcraft, 2012; Tawil-Souri, 2011).

The global attention that accompanied the Egyptian revolution did not only come from being made against one of the most authoritarian and dictatorial

Arab regimes in modern times, but also its maintaining pacifism, firmness, and steadfastness even accomplishing its main aim from its first day, which was to overthrow the regime (Al-ʿAzabawy, 2012 ; Northedge, 2011). Furthermore, the revolution erupted after forty years of political stagnation in Egypt and after the convalescence of the old political movement such as the Egyptian Communist Party *"Al-Ḥizb Al-Shiau'iah Al-Miṣriry,"* the delegation Party *"Hizb Al-Wafd,"* and the Nasserist Groups *"Al-Nasserieen"* (Amin, 2011). Under these circumstances, the Egyptian youth realized the need for change and struggled to restore the freedom that they had lost. In the past, they did not have the opportunity to practice their rights in the real world. While their rights were absent from their world, they watched and spoke about it in their own virtual space.

Given the nature of the Egyptian revolution, it was noted that all social groups (workers, women, peasants, poor, and marginalized people) participated in this revolution, but the youth had a leading role in sparking it (ʿAbdel-Rahman, 2015; Al-Bashary, 2014; Heikal, 2013; Qayati, 2013). These groups participated in demanding change for their miserable social and economic situation. This was reflected in the revolutionaries' demands for improving wages, health system, and reforming education, which was represented in the slogans of the revolution for social justice, freedom, and human dignity (Kayla, 2013; Shehata, 2011). All in all, the Egyptian revolution was marked by a set of prominent features:

- It was a popular and youthful revolution, carried out by all strata of society, but the youth were the first group who faced the regime and expressed their willingness to sacrifice themselves for freedom and human dignity for all the people of Egypt. As a result of that, more than 85% of the victims of the revolution (Arrests, Casualties, and Fatalities) were between the ages of 18 to 35 years old (ʿAli, 2012, p. 16).
- The January 25th Revolution was characterized by spontaneity and suddenness (Clarke, 2014). Although, what was done by the social movements (Kifaya, The 6th April movement …etc.) created an atmosphere in Egyptian society where it was possible to criticize the regime and demand for usurped rights, it was not expected that the revolution would happen so rapidly and cause the downfall of the head of the regime.
- Political parties did not take part in the revolution. There was no central political party leading and directing this revolution, or even delineating plans for the coming period. Although the parties did not have any role in the revolution, they took part in the revolution after they were certain that the regime neared collapse.
- The Egyptian revolution began with slogans and demands for change in the existing regime (Mubarak's regime), but quickly the demands climbed to the overthrow of the regime and the establishment of a state of freedom and democracy, which would be based on justice and citizenship.

- It was marked by massive peaceful demonstrations and protests in order to pressure the regime to achieve the revolutionaries' demands.
- The January 25th Revolution was distinguished by proliferation of modern tools of communication (Facebook, Twitter, and YouTube), which illuminated the society's reality and problems of injustice, corruption, oppression, and tyranny (Alexander & Aouragh, 2014; Aouragh, 2012; Hirschkind, 2012).

3.2 The Events of the Revolution

In January 25th 2011, thousands of Egyptian youth rallied in Cairo's Tahrir Square to protest against Mubarak's autocratic rule. The protests coincided with the yearly celebration day of the Egyptian Police. The revolutionary youth demanded their rights as citizens in opposition to the corrupted regime. The idea of dropping the regime from power was not clear in the protesters' minds, but their demands were limited to repeal of the emergency law, dismissal of the Minister of Interior, and some other legitimate demands. In response, the regime dealt harshly with the revolutionaries by using tear gas, rubber bullets, and other brutal methods (Shehata, 2011). These events increased the will of the youth to complete revolt. They proclaimed the Friday of Rage "Gomaat al-Ghadaab" on January 28th, 2011, which shook the pillars of the regime (Winegar, 2012). The renunciations began by the regime after the fall of victims. The protesters' demands quickly escalated to a common demand to bring down the regime (Mustafa, 2011). This was due to some complicated factors related to the Army and power in Egypt. The Army, alienated from the regime, was no longer willing to defend and protect it. Therefore, Mubarak stepped down from the power or was forced to resign (Bradley, 2012, p. 58). He handed the power over to the Supreme Council of Armed Forces (SCAF) to take charge of governing the state (Farag, 2013; Hussien, 2015; Zahran, 2012).

It is notable that there are multiple reasons which motivated the Army to take the side of the revolution. First, Mubarak relied on a new class of capitalists in agriculture and industry, who threatened the economic privileges of the Army that maintains a huge economic empire. Second, the Army implicitly refused the anticipated political succession since Mubarak was attempting to make his son succeed him as a president. Third, Mubarak increased his support to the police and he attempted to restrict the political influence of the Army chiefs at the same time (Barany, 2011; Marshal& Stacher, 2012; Martini & Taylor, 2011; Naṣif, 2012). Therefore, the Army found the revolution as a chance to restore its power and keep its privileges.

After the downfall of the regime, the revolution entered a new stage of suffering to achieve its aims. A technocratic government led the country during the transition period, but the SCAF acted against it. This period was not long; the Prime Minister Eṣam Sharaf resigned as a result of the problems of security, poor economic conditions, and obstacles placed in front of his government by the SCAF (Al-Sharkawy, 2012). Hammad indicated that "much solid evidence has been provided that the Military Council has taken away the authority from Sharaf's government" (Hammad, 2013, p.102). The Military Junta moved slowly in providing genuine trials for the former regime members. It seemed that the SCAF was in support of Mubarak at that time and did not want real trails for him (Barany, 2012, p.32). The hidden aims for this complicity were to keep the whole regime from collapse.

As for the Military Junta after taking power, it attempted to monopolize its authority in Egypt. The SCAF issued the Constitutional Declaration which gave it the absolute authority for legislation in that time. It was clear that the Military Council did not prefer democratic rule. Military Trials were carried out for more than 7000 persons including journalists, activists, and protestors (Martini & Taylor, 2011, p.128). Additionally, it attempted to impose its guardianship over people to a degree that it did not accept any criticism, advice or objection to its policy (Al-Bashary, 2014; Ferjani, 2011). It seemed that the Army was the key stakeholder in this regime and it was ready to sacrifice the demands of freedom and social justice, which were the major aims for the revolution, in order to stabilize its rule (Teti & Gervasio, 2012, p.102).

It turned out that the Army, after assuming direct control, had deliberately begun a process of morphological change in the structure of the ex-regime to reproduce it again while inserting some groups and new faces to prove that the regime has changed (Kayla, 2013; Bradley, 2012). According to this claim, the SCAF did not allow the transition period to occur and prevented social groups and the revolutionary youth from engaging in real political parties which would reflect the demands and aspirations of the whole society. Consequently, the problems swept the country under the leadership of the Supreme Council of the Armed Forces. The tension and conflict between the SCAF and the revolutionary youth led to the influence of radical forces on the revolution and power in Egypt. This situation significantly affected the state's power and the presence of moderate forces disappeared (Hammad, 2013).

However, all these contradictory events led to the election of the most powerful and organised force at this time, the Muslims Brotherhood, which had rich experience in the electoral process (Heikal, 2013; Kayla, 2013). The power of Islamists grew in this period and they began preparation for the elections rally to enter the parliament through the adoption of some Constitutional Amendments which were rejected by the revolutionary forces. The purpose of the Muslim Brotherhood was the parliament's majority. Therefore, they informally allied with the Military Council by not supporting the demands of the revolutionary forces which pushed for the departure of the Military Council from power (Al-Talidy, 2012; Hammad, 2013). In return for that, the Military Council approved to run the parliamentary elections on time. This period was highly marked by bloody events such as Muhammad Mahmoud, the Council of Ministers, and Maspero which claimed the lives of hundreds of victims (Madi, 2015).

Within two years; Egypt moved from the dictatorship of Mubarak's rule to the tutelage of the Military Council of Armed Forces and finally settled under the rule of the Muslim Brotherhood. The political bureau of the Muslim Brotherhood corrupted the political and constitutional sphere through issuing the Supplementary Constitutional Declaration and dismissed the Attorney General. Furthermore, they attempted to repeal the judicial decision regarding the dissolution of the Assembly Parliament. Additionally, there were many other economic, energy, and security problems which were not solved (Yassien, 2013). The Muslim Brotherhood also failed to solve the basic problems which were, in fact, economic problems. Furthermore, they tried to adjust the democratic process (Supplementary Constitutional Declaration) to maintain its authority in a counter of those who wanted a profound change in the political, social, and economic structure in Egypt. As a result, the Army and the secular groups rose up on the 30th of June 2013 against Muhammad Morsi's regime (Al-Bashary, 2014). This led to the overthrow of the Muslim Brotherhood from power and appointing a new government directed by Hazem El-Biblawi. The Muslim Brotherhood staged a sit-in at Al-Nahdah and Rab'ah Square for about two months. The security forces have finished the strike with more than 817 victims (Human Rights Watch's Report, 2014, p.4). Then, the Egyptian revolution has entered in a dark tunnel of bloody events after Rab'ah and Al-Nahdah.

The experience of the January 25th Revolution taught us that there are only radical solutions to these problems. It was normal that once the regime of the former President Muhammad Morsi tried to impose his control, including protecting himself from judicial accountability, the reaction was radical, namely, demanding the departure of his regime after only one year of rule. Since Egyptians were recent to democracy, they did not accept the idea that Morsi should complete his term, even if he failed. This idea was supported by the masses that came down on the 30th of June 2013. Unfortunately, the price paid by Egyptian people for their radical stance, which did not accept compromises, was merely to eliminate the most significant gains of the revolution; i.e. (the beginning of the democratic process in Egypt). If the Egyptian people had experience in the democratic process, it would have been possible to accept the continuation of a regime that came to govern by fair elections, even if it showed a manifest failure, similar to what we witness in the United States of America and Europe when it came to power regimes that were rejected by a plurality of people but that the ballot boxes would judge.

In my opinion, the unforgivable sin for any regime that required it to leave under the pressure of a popular movement is that the regime breaks the democratic process through the abolition of the Constitution and articles defining the period of the President and declaring a state of dictatorship. Many Egyptian people believed that the Brotherhood regime was trying to reach this stage, but actually, it did not take any steps to manipulate the Constitution. Morsi's attempts to protect himself by Constitutional Declaration necessitated a democratic reaction by voting against him in the coming elections, but what has happened is that people took proactive action convinced that if the Brotherhood regime continued, it would certainly amend the Constitution. However, there was no evidence for that.

Most of the political elites, such as the left "Al-Yassar", the Delegation "Al-Wafaad" and the Liberals "Al-Liberallieen" such as Muhammad Al-Barad'y, have fallen into this false assessment of the political situation in Egypt. At that time, no real political institution in Egypt had a real presence on the street. It was normal that the Armed Forces governed Egypt at that time because it was the only institution that had a presence and leadership and was the ideal institution for any citizen seeking any form of stability. Besides, the events of the 30th June 2013 were simply a step towards giving up the democratic process, which would have lasted for years to be integrated, in exchange for the stability of their time under military rule for fear of the collapse of the country during transition to democracy. The price for Egypt has been a return to square one to search again for a new beginning of a new democratic process.

3.3 The Aims of the January 25th Revolution of 2011 in Egypt

The aims of the 25th January Revolution of 2011 were represented in youthful words which have expressed the aspirations and demands of all Egyptians. These goals have shortened in four basic words Bread "'Aish", Freedom "Haurriyya", Social Justice"'Adala Igtima'iyya" and Human Dignity "Karama Insanyya" (Mittermaier, 2014). The four main aims can be interpreted to a defined set of goals, which have reflected the demands and slogans of the revolutionaries at Tahrir Square:
- Repealing State of Emergency law.
- Dismissing the Minister of Interior.
- Determining the duration of the presidency.
- Establishing a minimum and maximum wage rate (Wahba, 2011).

With the increasing numbers of protests and support of all social strata to the legitimate demands of Egyptian youth, the demands rose for the protesters and reached on the following:
- Overthrowing the ruling regime.
- Dissolving the Assembly Parliament and the Consulting Council.
- Constituting an Interim Presidential Council or a transitional government without the former regime members for conducting affairs.

- Holding new elections for the Presidency and Parliament under the full judicial supervision.
- Working on writing a new constitution for Egyptians to ensures their rights and achieve their hopes.
- Choosing the Attorney General by the members of the judiciary through election.
- Making trials for the symbols of corruption (former regime members) in the state and the responsible for killing the revolutionaries.

Since the revolution's aim was bread, this had deep meaning including the need for real development to ensure the fundamental rights of work, production, and self-fulfillment (Hamza, 2011). The aim of social justice is not only to prevent injustice, fight against poverty, or reform the wage system but also, it means equal opportunity to enjoy life without any discrimination. Human dignity represents the final aim for people to live in a civilized state which respects human and consider them the valuable resource that it has. Moreover, one of the pragmatic goals of the 25th January Revolution of 2011, along with the slogan of bread and social justice, was the departure of Mubarak's regime and the achievement of a real democracy. Despite the fact that the January Revolution is fell, the practical goals of the revolution have already been achieved. Mubarak's regime has indeed been abandoned, even if it has been replaced by a more repressive regime, and the first genuinely pluralistic democratic elections have been held.

Therefore, the revolution succeeded in achieving some of its goals such as overthrowing the head of the regime, abolishing the State of Emergency law, improving the wage system, and writing a new Constitution (Al-Bashary, 2014). However, the revolution could not achieve its other goals because it did not have a clear political vision for post-Mubarak era. It also did not have a political leader to determine the compass of change and draw a roadmap with long-term objectives. Furthermore, the Military Council which negatively affected the transition period through its attempts to restrict the peaceful transition of authority is considered the fundamental obstacle in front of achieving the revolution's aims.

3.4 The Causes of the January 25th Revolution of 2011 in Egypt

The reasons for the January 25th Revolution are varied and interrelated. It included political, social, and economic reasons as well as the social and protest movements which prepared Egyptian society for revolt. All these reasons have served as a starting point for the revolution.

3.4.1 First: The Crises of the Egyptian Reality.

The revolutionary ideas which accompanied the January 25th Revolution did not reflect the ideology of a specific group of people or orientations of a particular political party. It rather reflected the frustration, resentment, and enormous energy of anger which emerged from the womb of the social construction as a result of the status of a large percentage of Egyptians of deprivation and extreme destitution. These inhumane and atrocious conditions affected a large segment of young people, who expressed their aversion to the regime and their desire to bring it down. Many social, economic, and political factors led to the widespread frustrations and explosion of the January 25th Revolution. They will be presented as the followings:

3.4.1.1 The political reasons.

The prevalent set of policies during the reign of President Mubarak was regarded as one of the worst policies in Egypt's history, whether on the external or the domestic level (Bradley, 2012). **Externally,** the Egyptian global role has declined and Egypt has lost its leadership among Arab region and African territory. This is simply because Mubarak's administration has deliberately neglected the strategic aims of the Egyptian state (Shaaban, 2013). Moreover, the regime has slackly responded to the national and regional issues, which represent an essential dimension to Egypt as the leader of the Arab nation. The regime has abdicated its initiative to resolve the Arab and African conflict issues in support of Americans and its allies as well as keeping the peace agreement with the Zionist entity (Farag, 2013, p.82). For example, The Egyptian regime sacrificed the Palestinian case and did not act to make justice and comprehensive peace for Palestine. Moreover, it did not formally oppose the invasion of many countries such as Iraq by the United States of America and did not show any sorrow for what occurred in Lebanon from strife and infighting which became substantially aggravated. Furthermore, the regime did not give any attention for the dividing of Sudan's lands into two states that would affect Egyptian territories.

There is much profound evidence indicating the decline of the Egyptian role. The most remarkable evidence was the attack of some young Palestinian on the Egyptian Ambassador Ahmed Maher during his prayer in Al-Aqsa Mosque in Palestine. Moreover, Lebanese protesters have put coffins in front of the Egyptian embassy in Lebanon as a symbol for the death of the Egyptian role in the Arab region. Additionally, there was a growing dissatisfaction at Egypt's foreign policy which neglected the rights of the Egyptian people abroad. The most notable example was the crash of the Egyptian plane carrying 75 military experts during its return from the United States of America (ʿAli, 2012).

As for the **internal policy,** it was not in the best-off to the foreign policy, but it was crueler and more dictatorial. The features of the authoritarian state dominated Egypt during Mubarak's era. The ruling party "the National Democratic Party" "*Al-Ḥizb Al-Waṭanī Al-Dimūqrāṭī*" had all the authority, which overwhelmingly led to the monopoly of power and all levels of the state's institutions (ʿAli, 2012, p.31). The corruption reached major institutions such as; the Parliament, Consultative Council, and local governmental circles. This resulted in a widespread of corruption throughout the whole system (Farag, 2013; Teti & Gervasio, 2012). Besides, electoral fraud was one of the prominent policies that contributed to the explosion of the revolution. The former regime deliberately manipulated elections, whether the parliamentary elections, the local elections, or the syndicate elections in order to control the state and put down any opposition to its policies. The regime was used to falsifying elections, but this time in the last elections in 2010, the fraud was extremely obvious. The oppositions in general and the Islamist groups in particular (the Muslim Brotherhood) were prevented from achieving any success in these elections. The National Democratic Party has achieved 99% percent of the numbers of the parliamentary seats in these elections (ʿAli, 2012; Farag, 2013; Heikal, 2013; Qayati, 2013; Shehata.2011).

Moreover, the tricks of political and constitutional reform were aimed to have Hosni Mubarak's son, Gamal Mubarak, succeed him as the new president. The regime implemented many constitutional and legal changes towards that end. For example, the candidate for presidential elections would have to get two-thirds of the parliament votes. However, it was impossible to be achieved by any candidate who was not affiliated with the ruling party (The National Democratic Party). Therefore, these changes were, in fact, to pave the way for the prospective succession and to prevent any political force from getting the nomination requirements for the presidential elections (Farag, 2013).

The relationship between the regime and opposition was disturbing. The regime adopted the policies of repression and torture against the rejectionist groups. It also closed the channels of expressing opinions and it exercised gross violations of human rights (ʿAbdou & Zaazou, 2013;ʿAli, 2011; Meringolo, 2015). The most obvious indicators for confiscation were at freedom of expressing opinions, persecution of journalists in general and the journalists who discussed the events that affect the public sphere in particular. "The regime arrested many of the opposition journalists such as; Ibrahim ʿIssa, Wael Ibrashi, and Anwar Al-Hawary for allegedly insulting the symbols of the regime" (Shaaban, 2012, p.52). The regime antagonized journalists and considered them the main reason for the deterioration of its reputation in the international forums.

Furthermore, the political regime aimed at marginalizing the political opposition and turning it into a decor in the political life without any role except as part of the political game (Heikal, 2013). This impacted the opposition parties through losing their credibility in the street. They appeared as a worthless protrusion and margins inside the Egyptian political life. In the meantime, the opposition has followed the deceptive democracy slogans launched by the ruling regime. They have sought to take a foothold in the Parliament. These actions have drifted them away from the street and from the suffering of the people under the authoritarian rule that has prevailed over the Egyptian society (Kayla, 2013; Albrecht, 2005). One of the main reasons that contributed to the absence of the political parties from the Egyptian political reality was falling as a captive to its locked Gazette and party's headquarters. This negatively impacted the effectiveness of these parties as a real opposition. Moreover, the split between political parties has weakened and affected its vision for the current issues in Egypt. Consequently, their role has ended at the point of the denunciation and rejection.

The alliance of power with wealth created a formation of a gang (Mubarak and the elite of the National Democratic Party) which hideously attacked the country's wealth and resources. This alliance resulted in great tragedies such as the sinking of the ferry Al-Salam 98 and the death of 1033 of its passengers in the Red Sea. The owner of the ferry, Mamdouh Ismail, the member of the Consultative Council received a decision on acquittal in that case (Yassien, 2013). Furthermore, there was the case of the contaminated blood bags of the Haeddlena Company which has been owned by Hani Sroor, the member of the National Democratic Party and the Parliament Assembly. He also imported the contaminated blood bags, which infected thousands of people with blood and virus diseases. He received innocence from the charges against him (Shaaban, 2012, pp.158-161). Moreover, Egypt's rank on the scale of transparency became the eighth among the Arab countries in 2005 after it was the third in 2000. In addition to the number of financial and administrative corruption cases reached 63,269 cases in 2005. The number of embezzlement shifted from 54 cases in 1981 to 7,000 cases in 2009 (Laylah, 2012, p.35).

The emergency law, which has been implemented since Sadat's assassination in 1981 with an exception for 18 months only in the early Eighties, was considered a cause for the revolution (Northedge, 2011). Under this Act, the authority of the police has expanded, suspended the constitutional rights, imposed censorship, and prevented any political activity; such as organizing demonstrations, unauthorized political organizations, and the prohibition of any officially not-registered financial contributions. The law has given the government the right to incarcerate any person for a non-specific period whether he is accused or not. The prisoners cannot defend themselves and the government could keep them in prison without trials. Consequently, more than 17,000 people were detained. The numbers of political prisoners at the highest estimate was 30,000 prisoners (Ramadan, 2012).

3.4.1.2 *The economic reasons.*

The economic crisis and the collapse of the overall economy must lead to a change (Chaney, 2013). The previous statement corresponds to the economic situation in Egypt before the revolution. The economic transformations (Economic Reform Program) that have begun in the eighties of the last century, which were represented in the overall liberal transformations followed the programs of the structural adjustment and privatization policies, has a negative impact on Egyptian society. These policies have led the Egyptian economy to become revenue-generating economy after disposal the primary tools of production (industry and agriculture) as a pretext of losses with a reliance on the nonproductive economy based on tourism, banking, and taxation. This has increased the rate of poverty in Egyptian society (Al-Ghubashy, 2011; Al-Sayīd, 2002; Kayla, 2013).

The era of Mubarak's rule witnessed an unprecedented economic collapse starting from the nineties until the time of his departure. His government implemented economic policies which destroyed the tools of production. Privatization was one of the failed policies which have been applied by the Mubarak regime (Farag, 2013; Heikal, 2013; Ramadan, 2012; Roccu, 2013). This policy was represented in selling the state assets of the public-sector companies for a pittance price. The losses of privatization policies exceeded an estimated of 40 billion Egyptian pounds, according to the Egyptian Center for Strategic and International Studies. The state has failed in managing its resources and met the needs of society. This represented a significant loss in oil, media, and telecommunications sectors which consider the highest income sectors for all countries (ʿAli, 2012; Yassien, 2013).

Moreover, the regime attempted to postpone the Anti-Monopoly Law, which contributed to the increase of practicing monopoly for goods and commodities. The most apparent example was the company of Ezz Steel which had been owned by the businessman and Secretary for Policies at the National Democratic Party Ahmed Ezz. He greedily monopolized the industry of iron and steel in Egypt and controlled the prices with continuous increasing every month and the government did not give any attention to these monopolistic practices. Additionally, the government sold the state's lands with the lowest prices to the cronies of the regime (ʿAli, 2012; Shaaban, 2012; Yassen, 2013).

In 2005, the government issued the new Tax Law which is considered against social justice. The law imposed a fixed tax on the individuals who have a yearly income of more than 40,000 Egyptian pounds, including millionaires. Moreover, the government has legalized many laws under the pretext of encouraging investment which exempts projects from taxes for ten years. Besides, it exempted stocks and bonds stock market from taxes, which support the bias towards Egyptians bourgeois and foreign businessmen who were interested only in swift profit (Yassien, 2013). These economic policies have increased the inflation rate from 4, 2% in 2006 to 16%, and 30% in 2009 (Al-Nagar, 2009, p. 58). The regime has also marginalized large sectors of society, increased suffering of people, and expanded the gap between rich and poor in Egypt. It also reduced the growth of the economy and increased unemployment, recession, and inflation.

3.4.1.3 The social reasons.

Despite the negative impact of the economic transformations on Egyptian society, the political regime has deliberately ignored the basic needs of Egyptian people. Egypt suffered from increasing levels of social inequality, poverty, unemployment, slum housing, and suicide during the last ten years before the revolution. The absence of social justice was the Egyptians' main problem. The economic transformations that happened in the last century aimed at getting rid of the social and economic role of the state in providing free education, health, employment, and the balance between wages and prices in order to ease the burden on the state. All of these policies have demolished social justice and equality among members of the society (Farag, 2013; Kayla 2013). Moreover, the regime consciously ignored applying the policies of social justice in every sector, especially in income and wages. There was a notable wide gap between ministries budgets and individuals' income under the name of productive ministries versus service ministries. Moreover, the inequality in the distribution of services and more tax revenues directed to urban areas at the expense of poor-rural areas (Amin, 2011).

However, the failure of the economic policies led to several social changes in the structure of social classes in Egyptian society. These changes had a negative impact on large segments of society, especially the low-income and middle class. The elite, however, were able to raise their incomes and gain high profits than the rate of inflation in the country (Amin, 2011; Bradley, 2008). A large proportion of the middle class fell into the poor and destitute class. The total number of Egyptians under the poverty line has reached 35 million people representing 40% of Egyptian people (Shokr, 2011, p.10). The number of people under the extreme poverty line has reached to 4.5 million people. The poverty rate among youth was up to 85% of the total youth population, which makes us conclude that poverty in Egypt is a youth phenomenon (Laylah, 2012, p.34).

This was clear from the number of the five million employees in the state's administrative apparatus live below the poverty line ('Ali, 2012). Egyptian society is divided into two main classes. The wealthy class is saturated with money and has strong relations with the authority which has given them the protection to steal the country's resources. The marginalized and impoverished class which has suffered from the bitterness of their quality of life and a small slice represents the middle class that also suffers from the rigors of social and living conditions in Egyptian society (Kayla, 2013).

Under the pressure of massive demand, the lack of housing, and services, slum houses have spread inside the Egyptian state with more than 400 slums containing up to 8 million inhabitants. Although Egypt was ranked 119th among 135 countries regarding poverty, the number of millionaires doubled in the last year of Mubarak's rule in 2010 by 47% to reach 10421 individuals, with a combined net worth of 5 trillion American Dollars ('Ali, 2012, p.115). The spreading of poverty belts around big cities in the form of slums and tomb housing such as Manshiat Nasser, Al-Duwaiqa, Al-Sayadih 'Aisha, and Turab Al-Ghafiir was a prominent feature of the urban cities. People live a primitive life in these slums. Although they exist on the edge of urban areas, they live without water, electricity or sanitation in their houses which are made of tin and wood (Shaaban, 2012). On the opposite side, a minority of Egyptian people (the elite) were closely related to the regime and acquired greater part of the country's wealth, while large sections of the people lived in abject poverty and needed (Lesch, 2011, p.36; Al-Ghubashy, 2011, p.3).

Unemployment in Egypt is a social problem with an economic dimension. Kayla (2013) and Yassien (2013) have stated that social and economic policies pursued by the former regime led to marginalization of large sectors of Egyptian society. It increased the numbers of unemployed people and demographic blocks that had no place in the non-productive economy. Laylah stated that the rate of unemployment reached 9.5% in 2009 within the community; particularly young men who reached 17.5% unemployment and young women who reached 23.5% (Laylah, 2007, p.45). These neoliberal policies have impacted the labor market in Egypt which resulted in the decline of job opportunities especially for newly-educated young men ('Abdel-Rahman, 2015). These massive proportions of unemployment illustrated the size of the crisis which has had the most considerable influence on the youth rebellion and anger from the political regime in Egypt.

Moreover, these social and economic factors also led to the phenomenon of street children, which reflected the collapse of the social system in the era of Mubarak (Farghaly, 2012). The number of street children has reached to 594,000 children representing a ticking time bomb in Egyptian society. These children were between 12-14 years old ('Ali, 2012). Therefore, they have been regarded as a threat to the social security of Egypt. This had already happened before, during the January Revolution of 2011 in the events of the Council of Ministers, and Muhammad Mahmoud. The Counter-Revolution has used them in demonstrations and violent events towards police. This phenomenon reflects the absence of the state's role in protecting children and caring about the human element. Also, it highlights the problem of social solidarity within Egyptian society.

Additionally, suicide rate rose during Mubarak's rule as a result of desperation to get a job and to live a better life. The suicide numbers reached 104,000 cases during 2010; only 6000 cases survived. Among the most famous cases of contemporary suicide was the case of Abdul-Hamid Shetah, who committed suicide in 2002 after he was rejected from working in the Ministry of Foreign Affairs because he was not socially suitable for this job due to being a son of a poor farmer. Another was the suicide of Amr Abdel- Latif in 2010 who put his neck on the power lines in Kasr Al-Nile Bridge because he could not get a job to survive. Additionally, a father put poison in the meal to his wife and children, because he did not have a job and could not buy food for them ('Ali, 2012).

3.4.2 Second: Social and Protest Movements

The revolution which erupted on the January 2011 was not only the result of the moment but it was also the outcome of the events and protests built up over long periods of time. Al-Ghubashy (2011) mentioned that "For at least a decade, Egyptians have been working in kinds of social grouping and movements, which gave them experience in that old type of politics" (p.3). Many scholars reported that the social and protest movements in Egypt were one of the basic reasons for the revolution because they removed the culture of fear towards the regime (Birkholz, 2013; Clarke, 2014). Egyptian society has witnessed many protests and uprisings. Some of these movements were political in their nature such as; the Kefaya Movement, the April 6 Movement, the Movement of March 9th, and the Egyptian Association for Change which focused on the political reform issues in Egypt. Others factional movements and labor strikes have attracted attention to certain issues such as; wages, workers' rights and the consequences of privatization on the economy. Finally, the last group was the students at universities and colleges who have represented the critical mass in those protests.

3.4.2.1 Kifaya movement (Enough).

The Egyptian intellectuals and politicians have founded Kifaya movement at the end of 2004. It was the first national movement that stood in the face of the regime as a result of political and economic corruption. The movement focused all its attention on rejection the idea of re-electing Mubarak and political succession after him to his son, Gamal (Clarke, 2014; Farag, 2013; Qayati, 2013; Northedge, 2011; Shaaban, 2012; ṣiyam, 2009). The movement issued a document in the constituent conference held on 22, September 2004; it purposefully coincided with the National Democratic Party congress to inform the Egyptian society that there were many political forces refused the political bequeathing to Egypt (Idris, 2011).

Kifaya demanded in its constituent document to create real political change and to end all kinds of social injustice and monopolies of wealth that led to the prevalence of corruption, unemployment, and rising prices. Moreover, it called for upholding the rule of the Constitution and independence of the judiciary. In addition, the Kifaya movement wanted to restore the role of Egypt which had been lost since following the United States of America and signing the Camp David Agreement with the Zionist entity (Kifaya, 2014). The movement has taken the slogan "enough" *"Kifaya"* as a way to demonstrate frustration against the ruling regime. The word Kifaya referred to "enough" to rule and regime by Mubarak and his family. It mobilized the first demonstration in winter 2004 in front of the High Court to denounce the rule of Mubarak. The movement used new methods to express its views, connect its ideas to the people, and to the political regime as well. These methods were represented in using drums, coffins, and candles as metaphoric tools against the excesses of the police for demonstrations in front of the Journalists Union on the 25th of May 2005 and on the presidential election on 7 September 2005 (Shokr, 2011).

Moreover, the movement suffered from an extensive campaign of distortion and abuse from the media which was in support of the regime. The members of the movement were accused of treason, working according to foreign agendas, and were targeted for arrest by members of the security forces. Despite the dangerous situation that the movement worked in, it remained steadfast against the corrupt regime until the revolution had started (ʿAli, 2012, p.111).

3.4.2.2 *The popular democratic movement for change (Al-Harakah Al-Dimauqratiah Al-Shaʿbiah lill Taghiir).*

This movement was founded in 2005. It has had many aims especially making profound reforms of political, economic, and administrative sectors in the Egyptian state. Therefore, the campaign activists held many conferences either individually or with other movements such as Kifaya to discuss the deterioration of the political situation in Egypt. Besides, this campaign collected within its membership many intellectuals, politicians, and human rights activists from different political parties such as the Progressive Unionist Party (*Ḥizb al-Tagammuʿ Al-Taqadomi Al-Wahdawi*), the Egyptian Communist Party (*Al-Ḥizb Al-Shiauʿah Al-Miṣriry*), the Muslim Brotherhood (*Al-Ikhwān Al-Muslimīn*), and Al-

Ghad Party. The overall target was to make a real political reform and to prevent the political entailment ('Ali, 2012).

3.4.2.3 The 6th April movement (Harakat 6 Apriil).

It is a national political movement founded by young conscientious people on social media (Facebook) in 2008. It has shown solidarity with Al-Mahalla Al-Kaubrah workers' strike due to the lack of motivation and their poor living conditions (Beinin, 2011). Also, the campaign has used its Facebook webpage to raise awareness of the idea of strike and to spread demands (Clarke, 2014). These demands included better education, medication for all patients, fair judicial decisions, security, freedom, and reduction of high prices along with the elimination of the police excesses against citizens.

However, it was obviously clear that this movement had attracted the youth, especially university students. Before the revolution, more than 80% of its members were students at university level (Al-Sayid, 2015, p.8). The movement adopted the idea of peaceful resistance and non-violent striking. This movement does not follow any specific political or ideological prespective. The total number of people that had interacted with the movement was more than 70,000 people on the movement's Facebook web page ('Ali, 2012, p.119).

Despite splits between the members of this movement concerning some political issues such as participation in the presidential elections, it still has an active existence in the street after the revolution (Al-Sayid, 2015). Currently, the number of the active members is deficient, because of the suppressive policies of the current regime.

3.4.2.4 The 9th March movement (Harakat 9 mariis).

The 9th March Movement is a social movement aimed at protecting the independence of Egyptian universities and preventing any interference or control of the state in their affairs. The movement took the name of 9 March which refers to the day that Ahmed Lutfi Al-Sayid resigned from the presidency of Cairo University as an objection to the authority's decision to dismiss Taha Hussien from the university. The movement included in its membership many famous professors and activists in Egypt, such as Muhammad Abu Al-Ghar, Ahmed Al-Ahwani, Shadiah Al-Shishiny, and Hany Al-Husseini.

Moreover, this movement believed that the university should be independent in all of its affairs in order to restore its position and role in the society. It also discussed issues such as acts of administrative authoritarianism, appointing teaching assistants only after security approval, and preventing many politicians and intellectuals from participating in scientific meetings at universities (ʿAli, 2012). Besides, the March 9th Movement was not only interested in university issues, but it also called for political reform and supported Egyptian judges in their struggle against the Judiciary Act to ensure the independence of judges (The Movement of March 9, 2014).

3.4.2.5 The Egyptian campaign against entailment (Al-Hamlah Al-Miṣriyah ḍiid Al-Tauwreth) "Mayhkomsh."

This campaign was established in 2009 and its mission was directed at what they viewed as an underdeveloped political system. According to the constitutive statement, the regime was the reason behind the country's failure for decades. Thus, this call was against the political system, not against any particular person. The pioneers of this campaign were Hassan Nafʿah, Ayman Nour, the founder of Al-Ghad Party, the Nasserite leader Hamdiin ṣabahi, and Muhammad Biltagiy, the member of the Muslim Brotherhood. The campaign has merged with a National Association for Change movement (Hamada, 2012, p.103).

3.4.2.6 The National Association for Change (Al-Jamʿiah Al-Wataniah lill).

Muhammad Al-Baradʿy established this association in April 2010 after his return to Egypt. The association gained its political weight from its founder. Political elites have been wrapped around the founder's political thought. The association declared in its first statement that it would serve as an umbrella for any movement that calls for change. It will also reflect the entire political spectrum without any distinction or discrimination. Thus, the primary aim of this association was working hard to reach a political system based on real democracy without disenfranchisement. The first step for these reforms was initiating free and fair elections involving all Egyptians without any discrimination (Clarke, 2014).

The demands of the movement along with fair elections included cancelling the law of emergency in Egypt, civil society organizations monitoring the election to ensure them, and the right to run for the presidential elections without any restrictions. Therefore, this association attracted the political elites and other social movements such as the 6th April movement, the Egyptian campaign against entailment, and other movements. This movement collected the signatures of more than 25,000 to support the demands of the movement for fair elections (ʿAli, 2012).

3.4.2.6 Revolutionaries Socialists' Movement (Al-Ishtarkiien Al-Thawriien).

This was one of the leading movements that prepared people for the revolution. It was marked by a vast network of members and levels of hierarchal leadership up to the executive bureau through elections. It was also a closed movement which did not allow ideological differences to exist. It was primarily located in in Cairo, Alexandria, and Giza, but after the revolution, it expanded to Fayoum, Port Said, Sharqiyah, and Luxor. Additionally, the members of this movement have commited in the revolutionary direction which aimed at revolting against the regime, destroying the national government, and reconstructing it on the basis of social justice and democracy. It has an increasing influence on the youth especially after the revolution (Al-Sayid, 2015). At present, movement's membership has decreased as a result of the state's suppressive policies especially after the events of the 30th June 2013.

3.4.2.7 Youth for justice and freedom (Shabab Men Agil Al-ᶜAdalah wal Hurriah).

This movement calls for restoring the national rights and the necessity of change in the political regime. Also, it has a political bureau which promoted the responsibility of normative circles chosen through democratic elections. A central planning and non-central implementation characterized this group. It existed in Alexandria and Tanta. The movement stopped after the events of June 2013 (Al-Sayid, 2015).

3.4.2.8 We Are All Khaled Said "kullina Khaled Said."

We Are All Khaled Said was a Facebook webpage and the most important virtual social movements in Egypt at all. It took the name of Khaled Said, who was tortured to death by the police (Birkholz, 2013 & Northedge, 2011; Shehata, 2011). The movement attracted about 1.7 million Egyptian on its Facebook page. The most important roles of this movement in the revolution were to call the members of the group on the Facebook to go down on January 2011, to rally in Tahrir Square (Kullina Khaled Said, 2013).

It is thoroughly clear that social and protests movements have had a deep influence on the culture of Egyptian society in general and student culture in particular. It has removed the wall of fear that prevented Egyptian people from enjoying their political and social rights and contributed clearly to shaping the future of their country. Moreover, it contributed to spreading a culture of political proactivity and ending the domination and restrictions of security forces, because it opened up new horizons to claim rights and worked to achieve them through pressing on the regime. Furthermore, some movements used new methods in collecting people through social media such as the 6th April and we are all Khaled Said movement, other movements have utilized traditional methods of criticizing the political regime such as the 9 March and the Egyptian Campaign against Entailment. In sum, these movements were essential for the January 25th Revolution in Egypt.

3.5 The Achievements of the January 25th Revolution

The Egyptian revolution has fulfilled many significant results. These achievements are represented into two major categories; the internal and the external level.

3.5.1 First: The Outcomes on the Local Level.

3.5.1.1 Judicial trials for the former regime figures.

The trial of Mubarak and his regime figures was considered one of the noteworthy results on the domestic level. It was unprecedented in the Arab region that people prosecuted their president for his crimes. Egyptians have expected a maximum punishment prescribed by law for President Mubarak, but what happened was entirely different. The court has acquitted Mubarak of the accusations against him, which has made the people of Egypt feel frustration and distrust of the court's rulings (Bradley, 2012). Moreover, the Minister of Interior, General Habib Al-ʿAdly, and his top six security officials have been acquitted of murdering protesters. Also, Ahmed Ezz, Safwat Al-Shīrīff, and Fathi Sroor have been released from prison. Despite these judicial rulings, which were not appropriate for the crimes of the former regime, sending them to the prison and made judicial trials are considered a success for the revolution. The factors that have led to these inequitable verdicts are not necessarily due to the revolution, but they are connecting to other conditions related to the ruling power at that time.

3.5.1.2 The return of the authority's legitimacy.

Most of the Arab uprisings came as a direct result of the absence of a regime's legitimacy. The political legitimacy is not the sole criterion for people to accept regimes, but also people should be convinced of their president's abilities and his vision to achieve the demands of his people. When a regime works for its own profit, it will lose its legitimacy. Therefore, people have been able to bring down the legitimacy of President Mubarak and removed his regime. This represented the return of stat's legitimacy.

3.5.1.3 Change the Constitution and end the totalitarian reign.

One of the main accomplishments of the Egyptian revolution was the change of the old authoritarian Constitution to a new one that will accomplish the demands of the protesters for freedom and human dignity because the old Constitution contained 300 acts which restricted freedoms and political activities ('Ali, 2012, p.332). Moreover, Egyptians have prepared the new Constitution through democratic mechanisms and a founding committee that representing all social strata. The new Constitution has eliminated all acts that did not correspond with the aims of the January 25th Revolution. It also has determined the duration of the presidency and defined the powers of the president, the legislative, and judicial authority. Thus, the restoration of Constitutions that patch up over decades has been finished (Heikal, 2013).

Unfortunately, the new Constitution has been demolished after the events of the 30th of June 2013. The current regime has suspended the work according to the new constitution. It made many amendments to the Constitution. A committee known as the Committee of the fiftieth "Lajnat Al-Khamssin" was assigned to achieve amendment of controversial articles in the Constitution, especially in the section of the system of governs. It just took only 60 days to finish these amendments.

3.5.1.4 Dissolve the state's security apparatus.

"It was a police state because the security apparatus was the chief administration's arm to the state" (Al-Ghubashy, 2011, p.4). The state's security agency "Amn Al-Dawlah" had controlled all the state's institutions. The regime implemented it to follow the opponents. Thus, it had a significant role in the suppression of freedoms and control over thought and culture. It had numerous powers which included the control over schools, factories, mosques, churches, universities, and civil institutions. Every place in the state was subjected to the power of this security apparatus even appointing ministers (Shokr, 2011).

Despite dissolving the state security agency, the current regime has established a new security agency which called the National Security Agency "Al-Amn Al-Waṭanī."It exactly has the same role of the previous security agency, but just the name has been changed.

3.5.1.5 Increasing political awareness.

After the revolution, the political awareness of Egyptians has extremely grown. The concern has been returned to the political issues and public affairs. This will significantly contribute to the creation of a social culture helping in the process of change that takes place in Egypt now. The political participation also increased after the uprising (Khatib, 2013, p.6). This was clear through the effective participation and the absolute numbers of people voting for referendum of the Constitution, presidential, and parliamentary elections. It was the most significant elections participation in the modern history of Egypt. This political awareness did not exist in the era of President Mubarak due to the suppression of freedoms and eliminating the political work at universities and other institutions of the state (ʿAli, 2011).

3.5.1.6 The balance between political forces.

A definite change has begun to appear in the political forces in Egypt after the January 25th Revolution of 2011. It has opened the way for all society factions for participation in a democratic sphere. The time of the single party has been ended. It began a new phase of real political pluralism through political parties, coalitions, and revolutionary movements. There were many political forces in Egypt such as Seculars, Marxists, Muslim Brotherhood, Liberals, Salafis, and non-ideological people (Al-Bashary, 2013).

Consequently, new political forces have become known, such as the Coalition of Revolutionary Youth, the Constitution Party *"Hizb Al-Dostour"*, the Centre Party *"Hizb Al-Wasat"*, the Party of the Revolution Tomorrow *"Hizb Ghad Al-Thawra"* , Youth of the 6th April Movement, The Dignity Party *"Hizb al-Karāma"*, the Egyptian Social Democratic Party *"Al-Ḥizb Al-Maṣrī Al-Dimuqrāṭī Al-Ijtmāʿī"*, the Socialist Popular Alliance Party *"Hizb Al-Tahalof Al-Shaeby Al-Ishtiraky"*, the Strong Egypt Party *"Hizb Misr Al-Qawia"*, and other parties that support the practice of democracy in Egypt. Additionally, the increasing numbers of independent workers unions and Non-Governmental Organizations existed (ʿAbdalla, 2013; Teti & Gervasior, 2012). They have a real political role because the presence of these parties will make a free and genuine competition in a democratic atmosphere. Consequently, it will contribute to constituting a strong parliament expressing all visions and orientations that have the power to account the government (ʿAbdel-Fatah, 2013).

3.5.1.7 Providing social justice among Egyptians.

After the January 25th Revolution, the state's public policies have changed towards more social justice and equality. Many policies have been designed to reduce poverty and to strengthen social justice between society's strata. For example, the minimum and maximum wage rate was implemented. The minimum
rate was 1,200 Egyptian pounds and the maximum wage was 42,000 Egyptian
pounds. Besides, the government has expanded the scope of health insurance
and social security pension for the poor and destitute. Moreover, it increased
the support of supply commodities for low-income people (ʿAli, 2012). All
these policies will seriously act to mitigate the gap between social strata in
Egyptian society. This makes us assume that we are going towards social equality among the members of community. Unluckily, with the economic crisis and
the high rate of inflation in Egypt now, the gap between the poor and the rich
is maximized. Additionally, many governmental positions in banks, investment, financing, and media, do not apply the maximum wage rate.

3.5.1.8 Increasing community participation.

The community participation has increased alongside with the government.
The popular security committees emerged during the revolution when the security forces were absent from the street. The people protected the governmental
institutions from destruction or steal. Also, the popular committees have had a
vital role in solving the problems of trash and bread distribution. Thus, this revolution has contributed to discovering the capabilities of Egyptian people not
only in participating in politics but also in participation in the issues of economy, security, and education (ʿAli, 2012; Mustafa, 2011). However, the activities
of the Non-Governmental Organizations have been increased in providing help
and services for poor and marginalized people. The foundation of *"Misr El
-Kheir"* has provided education and prepared youth for the labor market (Mis-
relkheir, 2015). Besides, the association of *"Resalah"*at universities has provided
books and clothes for the needy students and programs for literacy at Upper
Egypt.

3.5.1.9 Emergence of a new culture.

The January 25th Revolution has produced a new cultural atmosphere characterized by the intensive use of internet and social media for all people of different ages and high rates of buying books and newspaper. Also, many positive
values have emerged in the Egyptian character, such as; positively initiative,
sense of belonging, patriotism, sacrifice, and tolerance. On the other hand, neg-

ative values have disappeared such as opportunistic, fraud, and superstition (Mustafa, 2011, p. 23).

3.5.2 Second: The Outcomes on the External Level

The Egyptian revolution has many results on the external level. The foreign policy has abolished many agreements with the United States of America and began a new relation with Iran after more than 30 years of interrupting diplomatic relations. Also, the new policy has become clear in maintaining the rights of Egyptians abroad and expanding their participation in the presidential and parliamentary elections. The Egyptian foreign policy strongly began to solve the Palestinian case and worked to find a comprehensive solution. Also, it worked on the reconciliation between the two competing Palestinian groups Hamas and Fatah. Moreover, the Egyptian revolution had a significant impact on the revolutions of Libya, Yemen, Syria, and had an effective role in the acceleration of political and economic reform movements in many countries, such as Bahrain, Saudi Arabia, and Jordan (ʿAli, 2012).

3.6 The Challenges and Obstacles of the January 25th Revolution of 2011.

It is not easy for any researcher in the midst of these political storms in Egypt, since the outbreak of the vigils which begun in January 2011, to generate a complete picture about the ongoing transitions in Egypt, the surrounding events, and its final results. If we have a positive view for the transformations in Egypt since the January 25th Revolution of 2011, we must not forget the immense network of complexities and interactions that drive the revolutionary event into the chaos of communal strife, fragmentation of sectarian, and racist tendencies. Therefore, the most realistic perspective looks at the Egyptian situation as streaked with fog and wide open for all eventualities. There is a range of challenges and obstacles that are confronting the Egyptian revolution. They almost have limited its inception and affected the degree of achievement of its objectives.

3.6.1 First: Political Challenges

Some political issues threaten the Egyptian revolution from the beginning till the end of the transition period. The first challenge is the security problems which have been considered the essential political agenda for all governments after the revolution. These challenges were the leading cause behind the dismissal of several governments such as the Ministry of Eṣam Sharaf and the Ministry of Al-Ganzouri. Most of these governments were not able to provide the security dimension after the January25th Revolution. As a result of the security weaknesses, crime rates have doubled and reached more than 300% after the revolution with a number of 120 murder crimes per month. Additionally, thousands of armed robberies and attacks on public property were taking place during and after this revolution ('Ali, 2012, p.86).

As a consequence of these security problems during the post-revolution era, the state has lost its power and control over the rest of the country. Satirically enough, the thieves and criminals have exceeded their activities to the degree that they stole the car from the Security Command in Giza from the front of his house. They also kidnaped many political activists, such as Abdel- Moneim Abu-Fotouh, the head of the Strong Egypt Political Party *"Hizb Misr Al-Qawia"* ('Abdel-fatah, 2013; 'Ali, 2012; Bradley, 2012; Madi, 2015). Furthermore, criminals broke into prisons and Ministries' buildings. They burned the courts and security districts after the revolution and also after the dismissal of President Morsi. This situation portended significant seriousness on the social peace in the society and on the revolution path.

Moreover, political disunity is representing the second challenge. After this revolution, coalitions and political movements have widely spread and exceeded more than 240 coalitions and 25 new political parties. These vast numbers of political movements and parties have destroyed the unity of the revolutionary power which should guide the political process in Egypt ('Ali, 2012, p.439; Heikal, 2013, p. 209). Most of these coalitions and political movements have had its own political orientations which are different from those of others. This has created a political clash between them. This is actually what happened at a later stage between the liberals, Marxists, and the Islamist forces. Additionally, the convergence between the Muslim Brotherhood "Freedom and Justice Party" *"Ḥizb Al-Ḥurriya wal Al-'Adala"*, and the Supreme Council of Armed Forces facilitated making secret agreements for few political gains. All these conflicts affected the way of the revolution in achieving its aims (Kayla, 2013& Suliman, 2013).

The unity of political forces (Political grouping) in one party, including the revolutionary youth and the national political elites, was an essential case to achieve the revolution's demands. Otherwise, the former regime members and the anti-revolution will get benefit from this conflict at the revolutionary forces (Al-Ghamiry, 2012: Heikal, 2013) and this actually what happened after the events of the 30th June 2013.

The third political challenge is the Counter-Revolution. Mubarak's regime and his members have constituted and still represents a significant threat to the Egyptian revolution. The delay of implementing the law of political corruption has encouraged members of the former regime to corrupt the political life again ('Abdal-Fatah, 2014; Amin, 2011; Heikal, 2013; Mustafa, 2011). Those people represented the Counter-Revolution. "The leaders of the Counter-Revolution varied between businessmen, generals in the police, members of the National Democratic Party, and owners of the private media channels, who feared that the revolution succeeds in achieving its goals, discovered their corruption, and sent them to jail" (ʿAllam, 2012, p. 387). Rashwan (2011) stated that the suddenness of the Egyptian revolution, the lack of organizational leadership, and the revolution's general slogans and aims which have no vision or mechanisms to achieve it, were the loophole from where the counter-revolution comes through. The Counter-Revolution has worked to mobilize against the revolution through demonstrations denouncing for insecurity, the lack of essential food sources, and supporting the factionalism protests.

The Counter-Revolution also worked to differentiate between the revolutionary youth through hiring thugs who have been inserted between youth to make riots in Tahrir square. Additionally, purchasing gasoline and throwing it in the desert to create a crisis of energy as well as, supporting many political parties through money to impose their view and generate problems in the Egyptian political life. ʿAllam (2012) mentioned that many intellectuals and politicians believe that the Counter-Revolution constituted only the first fuse to obstruct the revolution. Then, it spread the spark to ignite the situation taking advantage of the contradictions of Egyptian society that has not entirely get rid of the old culture before the revolution. Accordingly, the anti-revolution was trying to make the revolution involved in bloody chaos leading to the loss of the priorities of the revolution pretext of maintaining security. This leads to the inability of the revolution to achieve most of its objectives.

The interventions of the Supreme Council of Armed Forces are the fourth challenge. Although the former president mandated the SCAF to manage the country's affairs, it was a step towards the country's stability; it also has imposed the Egyptian revolution in real trouble with aged officers. They have a mentality of issuing commands and that was not appropriate for democratic practices. The role of the SCAF was to "lead the transition phase through a solid and resolute political process that paves the way to a genuine democratic rule in response to the ideology and aims of the revolution" (Hammad, 2013, p.33).

Besides, the SCAF was unwilling to cede the power to a civilian rule and a democratic process. He wanted to preserve his power and ensure his privileges (Bradley, 2012, p. 58; Martini& Taylor, 2011, p. 129). This has represented a disaster for the revolution. He disrupted the transition, clings to the power, antagonized the revolutionary youth, and had made secret bargains with the Brotherhood for conducting the parliamentary elections on its time according to the roadmap (Teti, 2011). He also has prolonged the transition phase which helped the former regime symbols to restore their power and caused many problems such as burning the state security files, disrupt Mubarak's trial, and make it as a mock. Therefore, the Military Council harmed the path of the Egyptian revolution ('Abdel-Fatah, 2014, p. 37). Kayla (2013) clarifies that the Army has played a significant role during and after the revolution. It was used as a power to absorb the blast, which caused by the Egyptian revolution through its role in the morphologically peaceful transition for authority. This was employed for the benefit of the same old class.

Finishing the autocracy rule and transmitting to more democratic and institutional governance represents the fifth political challenge. One of the challenges that are facing the Egyptian revolution is the ideological and cultural transition from the idea of the ruling pharaoh, the son of God, to a state of institutions that respects law and provides pluralism and diversity. The culture of exalting and reverence for our heads at work still exists. They are creative people and innovators, without them, no one can manage the country and it will collapse. This has destroyed the capacity of young people and made them feel frustrated and bring the old men to lead all the government's institutions ('Ali, 2012).

When the Muslims Brotherhood took power, they worked to exclude all political parties and youth coalitions from the rule. It was clear that they did not wish to share power with other political groups. President Morsi abolished the rule of the Egyptian Supreme Constitutional Court about the Parliamentary elections without any respect to the judges. Moreover, he issued the Constitutional Declaration that fortified his decisions against cancellation. Therefore, the Muslims Brotherhood has paved the way for individual dictatorship (Bradley, 2012; Qashquwsh, 2013).

3.6.2 Second: The Social Challenges

Building a culture of citizenship among Egyptians is an essential case for the revolution. The most dangerous challenges which facing the January 25th Revolution are achieving the effective integration between partners from different affiliations in Egypt. The events of strife sectarian cracked the unity of the national ranks and distracted the revolutionaries from the revolution achievements by calling the Islamic dreadfulness in its Salafis' version ('Allam, 2012, p. 391; Bradley, 2012, p.57; Heikal, 2013, p. 219).

Moreover, the sectarian problems have appeared after the revolution between Muslims and Christians in Egypt regarding burning churches. For example, Sol, Rafah, and Atfih churches have been burned after the revolution. The strife events between Muslims and Christians in Imbabah are a profound example of the crisis. The distraction of a church because it did not have a permit in Aswan, in addition to the sectarian problems between Muslims and Christian in Minya and Assiut represents a serious challenge ('Ali, 2012; Shuwman, 2012; Tadros, 2011).

The citizenship dimension represents another challenge for the Egyptian revolution. Citizenship means equality of rights and duties among all people without discrimination regarding religion, ideological affiliations or political orientation (Heikal, 2013). Egyptian people are among the world most patriotic and belonging peoples. They are Egyptians before anything else (Bradley, 2012, p. 56). There is no difference between Muslim, Christian, Salafis, Communists or Muslims Brotherhood (ʿAli, 2012). There were also many problems related to the Nubians after displacing them from their land during the building of the High Dam to areas in Upper Egypt, but these lands or urban style was inappropriate to them. However, the Nubian leaders have protested against the Egyptian government to return them to the former territory around the Lake of Nasser. Furthermore, the Amazigh tribes were asking for their rights and for representing in the parliament as Egyptians (Abu- Sikiin, 2013; ʿAli, 2012). Although the people of Sinai are a vital part of Egypt, they are suffering from discrimination.

Eliminating corruption is another challenge facing the Egyptian revolution. Despite the removal of the regime head, which was the first step in the right way, the revolution has entered a new phase aiming to achieve its objectives through the removal of corruption in the state. Revolution has confronted with the lackeys of the former regime who fought against the revolution with all the power they have from the beginning of the Battle of the Camel *"Muwqʿat Al-Gaml"* during the first days of the revolution even fomenting factional protests and smuggling of petroleum products (ʿAbdel-Fatah, 2014). After the first phase, the revolution has experienced problems with eliminating corruption by reforming the corrupt administrative structures in the country and removing the rest of the former regime figures from various bodies of the state.

It is worthily to mention that providing job opportunities and eliminating unemployment is a crucial challenge for the revolution. Unemployment was conspicuously one of the main reasons behind the revolution. The economic problems and decline of the national production with high rates of inflation do not provide job opportunities inside the public or the private sector. This has affected people's belief in the revolution and increased the society's discontent as a result of the lack of work opportunities within the Egyptian economic system. Therefore, the unemployment's rate reached 13% among the youth at 2012 (Ghoneim, 2014).

The new political administration should work to change the structure of the economy in Egypt from a yield parasite economy depending on a real estate, tourism, services, and import into a more productive economy based on production and manufacturing. This is the only guarantee to accommodate these enormous numbers of young people. Besides, we are in need to end the monopoly and control of capitalism and trying to invest in small projects and funding to help young people to get jobs as well as building an economic system based on the integration between its branches ('Abdel-Fatah, 2014).

3.6.3 Third: Economic Challenges

The Egyptian economy has a unique historical experience based on the development of the economic monopolies through the Army and the so-called sovereigns. It is not a free economy, a mixed economy or a kind of directed economy. It is a different type of monopolization. The management of this economy is not in the hands of economists and does not follow the scientific methods of managing the economy. The fiscal policy is inoperative as the budget does not reflect the financial situation in Egypt. Undoubtedly, the indicators of the crisis in the Egyptian economy deteriorated after the January 25th Revolution of 2011(Bradley, 2012). As a result of the conditions of insecurity and the economic, social, and political chaos that followed these events and especially the events of the 30th of June 2013, the crisis was exacerbated. This was followed by the escalation of the crimes of terrorism which damaged tourism and economy. With the January revolution, many expectations represented in economic and social demands, both legitimate, and illegitimate, followed by a spate of disappointments that made matters worse; productivity and performance were low.

Due to political instability in Egypt, the Egyptian economy is still suffering from successive crises as a result of lack of foreign investments and weak demand for tourism. The government still borrowing billions of dollars from abroad with significant benefits from the International Monetary Fund in addition to the financial aids which have been received from the United Arab Emirates, the Kingdom of Saudi Arabia, and Kuwait (Ghoneim, 2014) Furthermore, the continuing rises of public debt reached to 1.7 trillion Egyptian pounds by the end of 2010. This means that 34% of the budget's amount automatically will be paid as benefits. Large sections of Egyptian society will not benefit from this budget which will witness a growing deficit doubling the size of the economic crisis experienced by the country. According to figures from the Central Bank of Egypt, in the last year, the external debt in June 2016 was 55.8 billion dollars, which reached 79 billion dollars in June 2017 increasing the debt ratio to 41% in one year only.

Consequently, domestic debt became 3.073 trillion pounds in March 2017, compared to 2.496 trillion pounds a year ago. Foreign investment fell to 17.8% in March 2017 compared to the last year. According to the head of the Central Agency for Public Mobilization and Statistics, the rate of poverty was 25.2% in 2011 and increased to 35% in 2017. The extreme poverty rate was 2.3% in 2011 and reached 7.8% in 2017. The foreign investment, especially in Egyptian stock market, often conflicts with the national interests and aims at achieving swift profits. Speculative will not establish productive projects or create jobs for young people (Abdou & Zaazou, 2013; Shaheen, 2011).

3.6.4 Fourth: Cultural Challenges

It is evident that the post-revolution confronted a reactionary and backward cultural heritage which has contributed many economic, social, and political crises. For instance, it has supported the creation of violence culture through confronting with the police and created sectarian strife between Muslims and Christians. There is also a fierce struggle between heterogeneous cultures in Egypt in post-revolution era. The conflict is between different political groups on the concept of the identity of the Egyptian state (Al-Bashary, 2014, p. 10). It represents a challenge to the Egyptian revolution because of its soci-ideological dimension which turned into a political conflict between Islamist background groups and the left-wing liberal trend. Consequently, disagreements over the identity and legitimacy acts within the constitution have emerged during the rule of the Muslims Brotherhood.

Therefore, it is necessary to work for providing a suitable atmosphere to re-solve the crisis through the consolidation of dialogue. It must avoid the intellec-tual terrorism (Al-Barbary, 2013; Shuman, 2012). Furthermore, there are many values and cultural practices that are still adhered to the Egyptian character, such as the weakness of a sense of belonging, intolerance, narrow-mindedness, formal compliance, and respecting the authority (Yassien, 2013). Additionally, there is an influence of media, which in turn helps in the absence of awareness of people. The TV channels do not follow professional and objective way in their presentation of all issues and topics, whether political, economic or social with a political background and it has taken certain stances with or against po-litical groups or ideological perspective.

In conclusion, after presenting the January 25th Revolution causes, conse-quences, and the main challenges and obstacles that the revolution experienced, it becomes obviously clear that the January of 2011 was a generic revolution which was exploded by the youth who were not affiliated to any political gath-erings, political elites, religious, or ethnic aggregations. Thus, Egyptians have as-sembled with the revolutionary youth to restore their rights that have been stolen by the ex-regime. There have been many reasons for the revolution which varied between economic, political, and social reasons. These reasons have pushed the youth to burst in the face of tyranny. Although the revolution achieved the fundamental goal, it is still facing many obstacles and challenges which limited its start and disrupted its path. Regardless of the seriousness of the challenges which the revolution afflicted, it has created clear-cut changes in Egyptian society in general and in the university community (students) in par-ticular and this is what we will discuss in the findings chapter.

Chapter IV: Methods of Measuring Student Culture

This chapter implements a qualitative research design to address the questions of the study. It also intensively describes the site, the population of the study, and the process of collecting data. Moreover, It explains the process of analyzing data . Finally, it deeply discusses the researcher's role, the way he entered this field, the time-frame for implementing the study, and the difficulties of the study.

4.1 Appropriateness of Qualitative Design

The primary aim of the current study was to identify the changes that have occurred in Fayoum University student culture following the January 25th Revolution of 2011, in terms of their political participation and modes of engagement in the university. Besides, it is a descriptive study of twenty students from Fayoum University. The changes in the structure of student culture with all its components are an example of a complex social process in a miniature community.

Moreover, the qualitative approach is derived from the philosophy of social constructivism, which considers knowledge as socially constructed (Crotty, 1998; Flick, 2009; Strauss & Corbin, 1998; Willis, 2007). Therefore, this reality has many dimensions and forms in peoples' minds (Fetterman, 2010; Heaton, 2004). Hence, it is difficult to understand meanings and symbols of any social phenomena or culture of a particular group away from the social context in which it appeared.

The qualitative design is appropriate to the current study because it uses a naturalistic approach in order to understand a specific phenomenon in a certain context or place (Flick, 2007; Guba & Lincoln, 1985). Moreover, it provides a variety of ways and research techniques to identify the changes in student culture closely and describing it from student's point of view. It also helps to reach a deep understanding of these changes through describing the nature of interactions among its members, the most important concepts and visions, ideas and behaviours that undergone change as a reflection of the January 25th Revolution of 2011.

4.2 The Choice of Ground Theory and Case Study Research Method

The qualitative research approach has many kinds of research designs and methods. Creswell (2007) referred to five main methods: biography, phenomenology, ethnography, case study, and ground theory. The aim of the study determines which method is suitable for the topic of a research. Glaser and Strauss (1967) described grounded theory as "the discovery of theory from data systematically obtained and analyzed" (p.2). It is also a comprehensive research strategy depending on the collected data in order to generate a theory. It is an inductive method consisting of many rigorous steps leading to the development of new conceptual categories (Charmaz, 2007). These categories are linked to each other in a compatible way as a theoretical illustration of an action or a social phenomenon.

The case study method is an approach which looks to any social unit with a comprehensive view accommodates the evolution and growth of this unit. It concerned with one specific case whether that case was an individual, a group or an institution. It gives an intensive oriented data and deep understanding of the phenomenon in a specific research site (Bray, 2008; Given, 2008 ; Yin, 2003; Schutt, 2006). Consequently, the current study is a grounded case study because; it looks to student culture as a sociocultural process and the student community at Fayoum University as a unique context for that culture because study aimed at exploring and describing the changes that have occurred in the student culture (values, beliefs, attitudes, interactions, assumptions, and political participation) after the January Revolution in Egypt. It also aimed at building a theory interpret the changes in student culture in post-revolution.

It is also a case study because it intensively describes and analyses one unit (student culture at Fayoum University). The grounded theory case study fitted the research's purpose and answered the questions of the current study. The combination of the two research methods was positive to the current study as Wells and et al. (1995) mentioned that "the case study methodology facilities theory building or the process of developing new prepositions and generalization about phenomena" (p.19).

4.3 Setting

Understanding the characteristics of the site in which events, interactions, and experiences of students take place, is essential for the process of data collection and data analysis in any qualitative research (Fetterman, 2010). Fayoum University, located at Fayoum city (about 130 kilometers south-west of Cairo). This public non-profit university affiliated to the Egyptian Ministry of Higher Education in funding and supervision. It was formerly a branch of Cairo University from 1975 till 2004. It was also founded as an independent university in March 2005.

4.3.1 A Public University in a Small Rural City

Fayoum University exists in a rural and agricultural part of Fayoum city. It includes eighteen colleges and institutes[1]. It has 25,000 students from all over Egypt. It has also about 2000 faculty members; appendix number (B) presents the major statistics of Fayoum University. Besides, the university offers a rich variety of accrediting courses and academic programs such as bachelor's, vocational diplomas, masters, and doctorate degrees in several areas of study. This 13-year-old university has a preferential admission policy based on pre-tests and students' past academic record. It started new and distinctive programs such as nanotechnology at the College of Science, agricultural business management at the College of Agriculture, and health management programs in medical schools (University's yearly book at the festival of science, 2014). Further, the university offers many kinds of vocational education and training.

Fayoum University

Fayoum University's logo has a symbolic nature. It consists of the letter (F) which is the first letter of Fayoum and symbolizes the great River Nile and its delta. The dome of the university is surrounded by a waterwheel which is one of the tourist signs at Fayoum. Inside the water wheels, green and blue colours have existed. The blue colour represents the River Nile and the lake of Qarun. Besides, the green colour represents the agriculture land which characterizes Fayoum (Fayoum University's website, 2014). The light energy, which covers the dome of the university, symbolizes for the knowledge which will be spread by the university in the vicinity of the middle and northern part of Egypt.

Additionally, the vision of Fayoum University is represented in its aspiration for excellence and leadership. It aims at becoming a high ranked university, according to the international standards of education, scientific research, and community service. The mission of Fayoum University is to prepare students for competing in the local, regional, and international labour market by en-

---

[1] The university's colleges are (College of Education, College of Agriculture, College of Science, College of Arts, College of Tourism and Hotels, College of Engineering, College of Medicine, College of Early Childhood Education, College of Specific Education, College of Archaeology, College of Computing and Information, College of Social work, College of Nursing, College of Dar al-Uloom, College of Dentistry, College of Pharmacy, Institute of Nile Basin Countries, and Institute of Nursing)

abling them to develop their knowledge, skills, and ability to think and work creatively (Post Graduate Booklet, 2014, p.6).

Fayoum University has a clearly defined hierarchical and administrative structure which distributes roles and responsibilities among university leaders. On the top of the administrative and executive committee is the university rector. He has all administrative, educational, and research authorities. The President of the state appoints the Prisident of the university. There are three Vice-Presidents for education and student affairs, postgraduate studies and research, and community service and environmental development. The Prime Minister appoints them after the agreement of the Minister of Higher Education. Moreover, every college or institute has a Dean and three Vice-Deans.

Fayoum University has many facilities which are essential to the educational process, student activities, and scientific research. It includes the main campus about 50 acres and includes all colleges except (College of Education, College of Specific Education, College of Early Childhood Education, and College of Medicine) which are existing outside the campus. The campus includes several buildings next to colleges such as; the buildings of university presidency, which contains the university President's office, the offices of the three Vice-Presidents, the Secretary General's office, and the Major Celebrations Hall. In the middle of the campus, the administrative and services' building is existed (Fayoum University's website, 2015). The Central Library is also situated at the centre of the campus. It is a large building with an area of 800 square meters consisting of four floors comprising a large number of Arabic and Foreign books in various discipline spreading over six halls for reading.

At the northern part of the campus, the University Hospital is located. It is a modern and a massive building with four floors and a capacity of 350 beds. It mainly seeks to provide health service for faculty members, students, administrative staff, and the surrounding community of Fayoum city (Fayoum University's website, 2015). In the southern part, the dormitories of male students exist with a capacity of 2100 student. At the west of the campus, the Project's Management Building is also located. It coordinates and manages the university research's projects and provides training courses for the faculty members. The Center of Student Activities is located outside the campus. It is a space of 15,000 square meters, includes a variety of open playgrounds for football, volleyball, handball, Olympic swimming pool, and fitness hall.

4.3.2 *Fayoum University and Community Service.*

It is important to mention that universities are the primary sources for developing communities through its human and scientific resources. Fayoum University has a prominent role in Fayoum Governorate. It provides different services to the local community such as; free health care at the university hospital, medical convoys at the poorest places in the city, as well as providing agricultural products for the local community in Fayoum.

On the educational level, it provides distance and online education for all who wish to complete their studies. The university is also attempting to solve the problem of literacy in the poor and far places of the governorate. Moreover, it founded a center for the children and students with a special needs. This center aims at providing scientific and technological services for the handicapped students in order to motivate them to continue their education (Post Graduate Booklet, 2014).

4.4 Participants

I did not accurately check what is subjective and what is objective when I chose Fayoum University as a research site. Among important reasons for choosing Fayoum University as a case study, it was a place for democratic practices during and after the revolution. Moreover, it was among the first three universities that have witnessed free elections for College Deans, Department Heads, University President, and General Student Union. This is in addition to various student groups and organizations which are existed at the university, especially the organizations of the political Islam (The Muslim Brotherhood and The Salafis). The university also had an intensive student activism during and after the January 25th Revolution of 2011.

Besides, Fayoum University site which is located in the northern part of middle Egypt is the main gathering place for students from the north, upper, and middle Egypt. This gives Fayoum University a cultural and intellectual climate, which significantly influenced the culture of student community. Moreover, Fayoum University was accessible to the researcher because he already works and studies at the university and lives in Fayoum city which made it easier to conduct the study and to extract the necessary approvals for conducting the interviews.

A purposive sample of twenty students was used (Fetterman, 2010; Flick, 2007; Hammersley & Atkinson, 2007). Ten Muslim Brotherhood students were chosen because they had an effective participation in the student activities and events at Fayoum University. Furthermore, ten independent students who were not affiliated to any political or social organizations were also selected. Appendix number (C) showed the characteristics of the study's sample. The sample included male and female students in the two groups. The number of female students was four and the number of male students was sixteen. The students had different educational backgrounds. They were enroled in various colleges such as College of Education, College of Arts, College of Engineering, College of Social Work, College of Agriculture, and College of Dar al-Uloom.

The privacy, anonymity, confidentiality, and safety of the participants have been taken into consideration (Flick, 2007; Heaton, 2004). The researcher attempted as much as he can to care about the participant's lives and not to expose them to any threats or problems. Besides, he attempted to preserve the confidentiality of the participants' personal information such as; participating in demonstrations or discussing topics which were not accepted by the society. Consequently, the names of participants will not be mentioned in the study and this was a pressing desire of the participants. The nicknames (codes) will be used instead of the real names.

4.5 Data Sources and Data Collection Procedures

After choosing the research site and selecting the participants, the puzzling questions have arisen. What issues will form the categories of data collection from the field? What is the suitable research tool for such case? Through the exploratory visits, talks with students, and quick observations of the students' activities and interactions, it seemed that some certain issues and topics can be addressed in the interviews. In addition to these visits and talks with the students, the researcher used a focus group which helped the researcher to identify the main issues and attitudes that concern students at Fayoum University and helped him to develop the questions that will be included in the interviews.

Due to the nature of topics which are likely to be addressed in the interviews; it might include students' perceptions of themselves and other student groups. Besides, their perceptions and points of view about authority, university administrations, and participating in demonstrations are also included. Therefore, the students' conversations are full of symbols, signs, and metaphors which are not suitable for a survey or questionnaires. Thus, the researcher employed the grounded theory method in order to draw a complete, holistic, and realistic picture of student culture at Fayoum University after the January 25th Revaluation of 2011, through a range of tools:

4.5.1 Participant Observation

Observation is one of the basic qualitative research techniques for collecting data from the field (Alexander, 1982; DeWalt & DeWalt, 2011; Flick, 2010). I conducted a participant observation for the daily activities and events of the study's sample. I joined the student demonstrations and strikes. I also tried to observe many aspects of student culture such as; the interactions of the students, how they organized demonstrations, seminars and workshops on social and political issues, and how they planned for charity and volunteering works inside and outside the university.

During the process of observations, I intensively took field notes. Sometimes I wrote the notes either in situ or as immediately following the observed event. The field notes included two types of data, descriptive and reflective. The descriptive data of the field notes were recorded in an objective way for the physical setting, the people involved in the interactions, account of the observed interactions, and behaviours of the sample in the setting. The reflective part of the filed note was from my thoughts, impressions, ideas, and feelings in this situation as a researcher. A typical daily filed note was about 6 to 10 pages of single space handwriting. The observations threw light on control, power, and dominance relations prevailing between the student groups at Fayoum University and between them and the university administration. Moreover, the field notes data clarified some aspects of the interviews and were extremely helpful in the process of analyzing data.

4.5.2 Semi-Structured Interview

The study employed a semi-structured interview as the basic instrument for collecting data (Eisenhart, 1988; Mason, 2002; Russell, 2006). The researcher developed an interview guide. The questions were bulid on the concepts and topics which arose from the focus group sessions. The questions were open-ended to cover a wide range of topics (Eisenhart, 1988, p.105). The guide generated discussion around the following topics: (a) the daily life activities of students at university after the revolution, (b) political participation at university after the January Revolution, (c) social interactions between student groups, and (d) perceptions of some issues that related to the revolution and practicing democracy such as student elections. Appendix number (D) provided a list of the questions in the guide. Three professors reviewed the guide at Fayoum University and Appalachian State University. The changes were made based on the review and protest.

The interviews were conducted personally and lasted between fifty to ninety minutes. Every participant interviewed at least one time during the time of the study. The interviews were conducted at different places such as; inside the campus, at the participant's house, at the researcher's house, and in far public gardens. This was simply because of the security circumstances and students' apprehensive to give any information regarding the events of the revolution or student activities within the university especially demonstrations.

Moreover, the researcher used a small recorder for the interviews. Most of the participants have accepted to record their speech, but a few students refused. The researcher respected the desire of the participants who refused to record their interviews and I wrote the dialogue manually after the end of the interview. Moreover, the researcher observed the students' hints and signs during the interviews. These observations concerned with the reactions of the participants, the expressions on their faces, movements of their hands, and other expressions towards the interview's questions and subjects.

During the interviews, I realized the uselessness of reading questions from a paper, because of the sensitivity of issues that may affect the credibility of the participants and their speech with the researcher. Therefore, the interviews took the form of crosstalk with the participants and the researcher deeply asked questions after the participants felt comfortable and satisfying to talk. In this case, the subjects take inflow and the human contact channels between the researcher and the participant were opened for more real, substantial data, and hidden feelings.

Additionally, I did not commit to being neutral in my speech to the participants. Sometimes, I gave a contrary opinion to the opinion of the participant in order to encourage him to continue talking and giving examples, arguments, and live experiences in his discussions. Other times, I joined the participant the same feelings and attitudes when addressing points which are sensitive to him in order to encourage him to show the repressed feelings, and ideas. The obligation of neutrality in those positions will impose a psychological distance between the researcher and participants during the conversation (Mitchell, 2010). Once the participants realize this distance between them, the communication channels will close. As far as the researcher is neutral, the participants will be neutral in their talking to him.

4.5.3 Documents, Records, and Photography

The researcher was able to get the new student regulations, which determine the student rights, duties, and activities. Furthermore, the researcher could get the Ministerial decrees, decisions of Fayoum University President and colleges' council decisions which related to the student activities at Fayoum University. The documents represented a rich and useful source to confirm or reject the collected data from the field (Flick, 2007). Furthermore, the researcher got many documents and motts from the Muslim Brotherhood's campaign and exhibitions at the university. Besides, the researcher collected many writings, slogans and phrases of the Muslim Brotherhood students at Fayoum University.

Photography and recording the students' conversations and discussions while conducting different activities provided a large amount of data which was significant for the study. These data reflected the profound changes in the students' ideas, opinions, social interactions, and political attitudes at the university. Thus, the researcher was able to capture many images of the students' writings on the walls of colleges, classrooms, and bathrooms. This is in addition to taking pictures of the important activities carried out by the students such as; demonstrations, charitable exhibitions, leisure time activities, and meetings.

4.6 Preparation and Organization of the Field Work.

The preparation for social entrance to the research site and reaching to the participants is an essential step for the success of any field work in qualitative research. The process of entering the field is a continuous process of negotiation between the researcher and the persons (Gate Keepers) who have the influence on this society or the group that he will study. I do not mention only the physical entrance to the research site, but also the involvement with the participants to get data, experiences, and hidden feelings about the phenomenon (Fetterman, 2010; Hammersley & Atkinson, 2007).

Moreover, the researcher has obtained the needed permissions from the university administration to conduct the interviews see Appendix no (E). These permissions provided the necessary protection for the researcher during his stay on campus conducting the interviews and participating in the students' demonstrations and riots because the period in which the filed study started was coincided with the state to counter violence with some extremist groups. Thus, the researcher had to be cautious about getting the permission from authorities. Also, the researcher prepared the equipment for the field work such as; camera, small recorder, and notebook to take notes and write daily reports of the field work.

Regarding the organization of the field work, the study of student culture at Fayoum University has lasted two years from May 2013 till May 2015. During this time, the researcher closely lived and studied the student community. This long period has included times for interruption as a result of the university holidays and examinations period. Mostly, the observations started from the beginning of the day at 10,00 A.M and continue until the end of the day about 5,00 P.M. During this time, the researcher was trying to participate in the students' activities, trying to monitor more data, and observations that help him in understanding the dynamics of cultural change within student culture.

At the beginning of the field study, the researcher hired some informants "students" who helped him to enter the Muslim Brotherhood student organization at Fayoum University. Moreover, they represented a functional link between the researcher and the student organizations. They solved many problems which faced the researcher. They were also a source of knowledge and clarified some of the symbols and terms that the researcher did not know. The researcher hired two students from the College of Dar al-Uloom and the College of Engineering. These informers have been characterized by their interest in the topic of the research and they assisted the researcher. Furthermore, they gave a lot of their time and their effort which has an effective impact on the field study.

4.7 Data Analysis

The qualitative work is not always organized systematically as empirical work. The process of analysis is concurrent with the process of data collection (Chamarz, 2007; Fetterman, 2010; Filck, 2007; Hamersley & Atkinson, 2007). It is an ongoing process started with the beginning of entering the site and remained to the end of the research. It was an attempt to get the meaning from the collected data and make a deep understanding of the phenomenon according to the living experiences from the field (Biber & Leavy, 2006). However, the quality of analysis depends on the effectiveness of managing data (Dey, 1993, p.77). In this study, the process of analyzing data started after the first interview and field note. I transcribed the recorded data to a written form in a texts editor program (word processing). I followed this systematic method with the interviews, filed notes, researcher diaries, and memos. Then, I read the entire data to understand it and to make sense of the general ideas. Afterward, I started asking questions on these data for better understanding. Further reading of data was made (line-by-line) and new questions have risen. What are the main ideas that related to the changes in student culture? Are these ideas are connected together? A further reading was conducted with writing notes and reflections about data (Dey, 1993; Flick, 2009; Marvasti, 2004; Saldaña, 2009).

Additionally, the researcher returned to the field to find answers to those questions. After an intensive reading of the collected data and answering the upraised questions, coding for data was made. The open coding process which is the first stage of analyses was represented in giving specific names and short titles for specific parts of similar data after a constant comparison (Chamarz, 2007; Flick, 2007; Strauss & Corbin, 1998). The open coding produced various codes and ideas which were considered the base for further analyses. I also attempted to provide primary explanations for the data at this stage. Afterward, I categorized concepts, linked, and organized them as themes by the relationship in a process called axial coding. This process provided coding families that became the major findings of the study through clear thems (Biber & Leavy, 2006; Charmaz, 2007; Flick, 2007; Fetterman, 2010). Conditions and dimensions developed and finally, the study themes emerged through an interpretive process called selective coding (Chamarz, 2007; Strauss & Corbin, 1998).

4.7.1 Narrative Writing as a Way of Knowing

The style of writing is substantially impacted the study's findings. Besides, it is considering the core of qualitative writings. The researcher intensively described all dimensions of student culture at Fayoum University supported by live examples. I also chose and quoted some parts of speech from the interviews that are essential and expressed the nature of the study. The quotes were selected from the participants' language and from their own words which were spread in the student community at Fayoum University. Furthermore, I tried to involve the voices of the participants in writings. In this case I tried to give them a chance to show their ideas and perspectives that the regime tries to prevent or block it.

4.7.2 Researcher's Position / Reflexivity

In the qualitative study, the researcher is considered as an instrument for collecting and analysing data (Bodgan & Biklen, 2007; Fetterman, 2010, Patton, 2002). Reflexivity is a self-awareness of the researcher's role, ideas, and values as he is a part of the social world that he studies (Eisenhart, 1988). The researcher's role is significant in qualitative studies because most of the collected data depends on the social relations between the researcher and participants (Flick, 2007; LeCompte & Goetz, 1982). In the current study, the researcher had a certain role as a participant observer. Also, I had developed many friendships with the participants and this gave me a chance to access their world and to know much vital data about them.

The students knew that I am a doctoral student and the data which I am collecting from the interviews will include in my doctoral dissertation. The students approved to make the interviews voluntarily and most of them accepted to record it. I felt that the participants were comfortable to talk to me. The conversations were relaxed and full of frankness. The Muslim Brotherhood students were more cautious than the independent students. This was back to the unstable political atmosphere at this time in Egypt. The female students were more open to talking and willing to give real examples of their participation in the student activism. Actually, I astonished by the females' frankness and clarity.

During my participation in the student activities, I was opened to the new ideas, explanations, and behaviours. I did not consciously ignore any information or events even if it seemed to be not related. Conversely, I was extremely interested to know the new behaviours and ideas and tried to search for the reasons that constitute it. However, I tried not to behave obtrusively; the students felt that I was a stranger from the group and not related to them. This pushed me to ask myself, Was I a good participant observer? Did I disturb the students while acting their activities? Did I get all the needed data?

Moreover, when I conducted the observations or the interviews, I tried to be a low profile to other students at the research site. I dressed casual clothes like students and behaved in a manner convenient to them. I contacted the participant via mobile. I did not want to make them feel pressure to respond to my request. At the end of the 2015 academic year, I left the field site after I reached the saturation point (Biber& Leavy, 2006). Therefore, I felt that the continuance of my stay in the field will not add further information, but it will repeat the information. Thus, I decided to leave the site gradually and to maintain the relationships with the individuals. Finally, I still have strong relationships with the participants and I am delighted to stay in touch with them.

4.7.3 Validity and Reliability Issues

Most scientific studies aimed at producing reliable knowledge. Quantitative and qualitative methods give the issues of validity and reliability significant attention (Bogdan & Biklen, 2006; Le Compte & Goetz, 1982; Patton, 2002). Unlike the quantitative method which uses statistics, correlations, and models of random samples to achieve validity and reliability, the qualitative research uses alternative ways which is suitable for understanding the complexity of social phenomena to achieve reliability and validity. However, there are several techniques to ensure validity of qualitative studies. The experience of a researcher and mastery of his area of study plays a significant role in achieving validity (Maxweel, 1996). Therefore, I studied the techniques of qualitative methods for one semester at the Department of Anthropology; Appalachian State University; United States of America. I also have some experiences in qualitative research as I participated in the Foundations of Educations Department's studies which some of them relied on qualitative methods.

Moreover, the data triangulation and the quality of collecting data supported the validity of the study (Biber & Leavy, 2006; Denzin, 1998; Fetterman, 2010; Flick, 2007; Golafshani, 2003). Thus, I used four techniques of data collection: interviews, focus groups, participant observation, and official document review to ensure the internal validity of this study. Further, I chose two groups of participants; one was the Muslim Brotherhood students and the other was the Independent students who also reinforced the study's validity. The accuracy of analysing data is also crucial for the study (Hamersley & Atkinson, 2007; Maxwell, 1996). The quality of coding data and generating patterns affect the validity issues. I gave the coding process much effort because it was the base of analysing data. I also remained at the filed for approximately two years. I left the field after reaching the saturation point. Moreover, I compared the study's results with the previous studies that examined the same phenomenon. These procedures aimed to boost the case of validity for the current study. As for the external validity, I had the participants' feedback on the study results (Flick, 2007). This was actually useful as it gave new insights into the data to present what the participants think of themselves.

To ensure reliability in qualitative studies, the researcher should examine trustworthiness through every step of the study (Strauss & Corbin, 1998). The quality of the research method determines the reliability of the study (Eisner, 1991; Flick, 2007). I used many ways to adhere reliability for the current study.

I rechecked the transcripts and by cross-checking the codes (Flick, 2007, P.102). Thus, I sent the transcript to two experts at Fayoum University to get feedback on the data and analysis.

4.8 The difficulties of the study

I encountered many difficulties and challenges while conducting this study. For example, many students procrastinated to conduct the interviews because they had many classes and laboratories to attend. This forced the researcher to go to the students' dormitories, public parks, and the participants' houses, or any place made the students feel safe and relaxed. These took a lot of time and efforts to conduct the interviews with the sample of the study.

Moreover, significant barriers related to the unsecured atmosphere in the field site, restrictions of the security forces and exposing to smoke and tear gas. I felt panic from being arrested by the security agencies as a result of my participation in the Muslim Brotherhood students' activities such as; riots and demonstrations. Besides, the scholarship, which I had been granted by the Egyptian Ministry of Higher Education, was postponed for one year. The Minister of Higher Education suggested sending my research proposal to many experts in social and political science in order to re-evaluate it because the title included the January 25th Revaluation and most leaders in Egypt were anti-revolution.

The experts gave the research proposal a high grading and suggested to implement the scholarship, but the Minister of Higher Education refused again. Finally, after one year, the Minister of Higher Education has been changed and a new minister approved to implement the scholarship with one condition which was changing the title and avoiding the January 25th Revolution at all.

Chapter V: Holistic Picture of Student Culture at Fayoum University

This study aims at drawing a realistic picture of the student community at Fayoum University after the January 25th Revolution of 2011. It also tries to identify the nature of changes in student culture (values, attitudes, activities as well as political and social participation). Furthermore, it conspicuously focuses on the impact of the January 25th Revolution and its successive events, whether positive or negative, on the identity of the student community and its activities from the perspective of the students.

This chapter displays several themes representing significant cultural features of student culture at Fayoum University in the post-revolution era. The first theme focuses on the daily activities of students at Fayoum University. The second theme tackles the features of students' perceptions of education system at the university. The third theme deals with student elections and political activity at Fayoum University as a critical element of student culture that has been influenced by revolutionary changes. The fourth theme represents the forms and patterns of social interaction among students at Fayoum University. The fifth theme highlights voluntary and charity activities of students at Fayoum University. Finally, the sixth theme tackles the linguistic symbols and expressions that emerge as an outcome of the January 25th Revolution of 2011.

5.1 First Theme: Description of the Students' Daily Activities at Fayoum University

Student life at university campus is full of details that constitute a significant stream for the formation of their perceptions and their awareness of many important issues and events in their life. It also has a widely impact on the way they acting their daily life activities (Brown, 1968; Moffatt, 1991; Robson & Sell, 1998). The details of daily life contain an important cultural pattern that contributes significantly to form a distinctive identity and culture for students at a university. Since the students' daily life is rich and diverse, the daily habits and behaviors are a vital part of student culture at Fayoum University. According to the study, the features of the students' daily life activities are their ways of organizing time, attending lectures, their style of clothing, selecting food, and spending leisure time. All these aspects have essential cultural connotations that increase our understanding of the nature of this culture.

5.1.1 Students' Habits and their Daily Behaviors

5.1.1.1 Time management.

One of human's important daily habits is having a certain schedule for sleeping and waking up. This habit also helps man to organize his day and perfectly make use of his time. Students at Fayoum University have harmful sleep habits, including waking-up and sleeping times, which seem to be unpredictable and random. Thus, the waking-up time is irregular and it is determined simply according to the time of lectures. If a lecture is at 10, 00 A.M., students wake up just one hour or half an hour before that time. This applies to students who live in cities, villages, and rural areas as well. Therefore, there are no specific times that the student is obliged to wake-up at. This is in addition to the lack of practicing sport in the morning or being involved in useful hobbies before going to the university. The form of organizing time was evidenced by what the Independent participants said:

> I wake up from sleeping according to the time of lecture at the college. If I have a lecture at 12, 00 P.M, I wake up at 10, 00 A.M., and if a lecture is at 9, 00 A.M., I wake up at 8, 00 A.M., and then pray, put on my clothes and go to the college (Participant, D 8).

> I wake up at any time, regardless of lectures. I wake up at the time that I want. I wake up after my body takes enough rest. Then, I put on my clothes and go to the college (Participant, D 5).

> Certainly, I wake up according to the time of the first lecture, at 8, 00 A.M, or 9, 00 A.M., and the first thing I do is to pray (Participant, D 9).

> I am like any other student; I wake up an hour before a lecture. Our lectures start at 9:30 A.M., and I wake up at 8:30 A.M. If I did not pray the dawn prayer "ṣalāt Al-Fağr", I pray it immediately as the first thing that I do after waking up (Participant, D 2).

> I am used to waking up an hour before the time of a lecture. I may pray "ṣalāt Al-Fağr" and then I become lazy to do the rest of the prayers. I wear my clothes and go to the university half an hour before the lecture's time (Participant, D 3).

It is obviously clear that the students do not have a schedule to organize their time. Moreover, the value of time is almost absent, for example the student who reported "I wake up at the time I want". This is also due to the lack of respect for time as a common societal value at Egyptian society. This negative value is shared across the university community, professors, staff, and students. There are no specific times for anything in the university community except for exams. On the contrary, students belonging to the religious groups (The Muslim Brotherhood students and the Salafis) have programs for time management that are particularly specific and make an effective use of time.

As for the study day, it begins after dawn prayer "ṣalāt Al-Fağr". I say the supplications "Dhikr"[2] and then I have two things, which I must do them daily. Reading the Holy Book is a priority. The Quran is the whole knowledge. The God said, "We have not neglected in the register a thing. Then unto their Lord, they will be gathered" (Surat Al-An'am, Verse 38). The Holy Quran's wonders never end. Besides, it is necessary for me to have a spiritual aspect because of the nature of our fast- paced life. It is essential that my soul is connected to the God. I begin reading and reciting the Quran every day and afterward, I read a part of the interpretation of the Quran "Tafsir". Then, I go out of the mosque to my room and start studying. I divide my time after the dawn. I start with the difficult study subject that needs more concentration such as rhyme and morphology because a human wakes up active and with a completely pure and fresh mind after I have taken a dose of faith and connected my spirit to the God. Then I go to the college and attend all lectures and then return to the student dormitory at 3:30 P.M (Participant, B 4).

Moreover, the Salafis students and the Muslim Brotherhood students have a comprehensive program of organizing times that is characterized by its religious form. Praying and reading the Quran is a high priority for those students. In addition to attending lectures and studying at specific times followed by the student and never deviate from them. The style of bringing up of the students of religious organizations often influences their lives and the organization of their times. Before they enter the university, they are exposed to a set of strategies that help them to successfully organize and utilize their time through committees emerging within these groups.

Therefore, the accurate identification of dates and the optimal utilization of time significantly help the Brotherhood students to increase the area of their community participation, because time management gives students freedom and space to practice hobbies and to play an active role in Fayoum community in which they live. This is an obviously clear indication of the strength of these religious organizations that students take them as a permanent reference to their behaviors and provides them with the broad lines to follow in their lives.

Consequently, the religious organizations have power and control over students, which beyond the perception of policymakers at the higher education institutions in Egypt. This is mainly due to the decline of professors' roles in the life of their students, as well as emptying university life from its political and societal content and limiting its role to just giving lectures and issuing certificates. We can finally conclude that the lecture times are an essential criterion for determining time of waking up and going to the university. The students who live in urban areas usually take about an hour to prepare themselves to go to the university. This is different for the students who live in far rural areas and who have to take more than one means of transportation to reach the university.

---

[2] It is religious statements recited after the dawn prayer. Religious people usually practice this dhikr.

Additionally, the lack of time organization is due to the vacuum experienced by the students and the lack of practicing hobbies along with sports since childhood. The failure of Youth Care Institutions to play its assigned role in absorbing youth's positive energy and opening up sports, artistic, and scientific fields in front of their abilities and talents, in addition to the decline of the university's role in preparing programs to develop students' abilities and hobbies, which is reflected negatively on the students' sense of the value of their time and the need to organize it appropriately.

However, some students have a specific program and a specific time for all activities of the day such as studying, attending lectures, and practicing hobbies. These students belong to the religious organizations as the Salafis and the Muslim Brotherhood students. Besides, these groups set a program to organize time by an extensive distribution of tasks and spectacular use of time in studying as well as attending lectures and practicing activities and hobbies. It is noted that the performance of praying and other religious events takes up a considerable amount of time for students in general and the students of religious organizations in particular. It also seems that there is a vast increase in the student religious practices in post-revolution. The mosque which exists in the center of the College of Education is often full of students at noon prayer "ṣalāt al-ẓuhr" and afternoon prayer "ṣalāt Al-ʿAṣr". This also applies to other mosques in different places of Fayoum University.

This is because religion takes a central value in the lives of Egyptians. Most of the participants pray immediately after waking up, even though, they have remained during the study day without prayer. Further, the absence of security from universities after the revolution has increased the student religious practices. Because the security before the revolution hired spies to identify students who are attending prayers regularly at the mosques inside the university. Then, that security arrested students in charge of gathering for protest and disturbing social peace at the university. Therefore, the students did not intensively pray at universities' mosques or showing their tendency to be religious before the revolution.

However, the students' interest in religious aspects has emerged through intensive attendance of meetings organized by the university or student families for the Islamic intellectuals who came to the university after the January 25th Revolution. Religion is a feature of the Egyptian personality and is, therefore, an important dimension of the analysis of any cultural component. Despite this religiousness, its contribution to modifying the behavior of individuals in Egypt is almost negligible. Is this a false religiosity? Alternatively, is it a wrong understanding and interpretation of the religion?

5.1.1.2 Attending lectures.

It is usual for a university student to be able to organize all the study syllabus and assignments he needs for studying at university. The students prepare in advance the scientific material for lectures because many professors explain only excerpts and give a general idea of a lecture. This greatly obliges students to attempt to read and understand the subject of a lecture before attending a lecture at the university. The students also prepare assignments and research papers required by professors to support their understanding of the study subjects. Professors usually evaluate the students' activity and abilities through these assignments. This is apparently clear through the phrases of the Independent participants:

> I usually prepare my stuff in the office at night. In the morning, I immediately put the things in my suitcase and then go to the university (Participant, D 8).

> I must know which lectures I have to attend tomorrow, the assignments, and what I have to study (Participant, D 4).

As for attending lectures, it is deemed as an essential issue that the students are supposed to adhere at the university. It is noted that the percentage of attending lectures among students is extremely low because of the inappropriate times of lectures and traditional methods of teaching. In addition to the monotony of the lecturer who does not use any interesting techniques in presenting the study subjects. Two Independent students at the College of Engineering and the College of Dar al-Uloom reported:

> Frankly, in the preparatory[3] year at the College of Engineering, we were young and we attended all lectures, but now, we attend some lectures and neglect others. We are always sitting under a tree in the garden of the College of Engineering (Participant, D 1).

> Usually, I go to the university and attend a few lectures, just for a few professors; such as Dr. *Muhammad Hassan ʿAbdullah* and Dr. *Wajih Al-Shimi*. These are specific professors whom I feel that they are cultured and educated. Thus, I like to listen to them and learn from them (Participant, D 5).

Additionally, the method of recording attendance and absence is undoubtedly a pressing tool that leads students to attend lectures. The students are almost afraid of deprivation of entering the examination or the decrease in their exam marks. Therefore, the students attend lectures against their desire due to their sense of futility and usefulness to them. Further, the style of a lecturer is often dull and tedious. It primarily relies on speech without any use of modern

---

[3] All Engineering Colleges at Egyptian universities provide the first year of study as preparatory for students. Students study different subjects related to all kinds of Engineering (power, architecture, mechanical,…etc.). Then, according to the grades in this year, the students are distributed to different departments of engineering at the college in the beginning of the second year.

means of educational technology. This leads to the aversion of students from both the lecture and the instructor as well.

On the other side, among things that attract students to attend lectures are the character of a lecturer, his style, his mastery over the scientific subject, and his way of presenting it. In addition, the close relationship of a professor with the specialization of students and the skills that students are expecting to benefit in their career after graduation is essential to them. There is a group of students who attend all lectures because they consider them useful in their specialization. Therefore, these students are usually from the language departments.

> I go directly to the college to attend all lectures which I have on my schedule. If I could not attend a lecture, I feel lost (Participant, D 8).

> Our department consists of a small number of students. Thus, the lecturer takes attendance and absence that is, of course, a useful thing. I attend all lectures. I am the only male and the rest are girls (Participant, D 2).

However, the students' expressions prove relatively that they attend all lectures. This may be due to their passion for specialization and their tendency to benefit from all lectures to continually improve their skills. Alternatively, the reason behind attending lectures may be back to the difficulty of the academic subjects which are hard to understand. The lack of commitment to the dates of a lecture by a professor gives students a negative attitude towards the subjects and, therefore, they refrain from attending lectures. A student said that lecturers are not committed and they prevent students from attending classes.

> We come from far places in Fayoum to the university. Then we want to attend our lectures. So, we are committed to attending lectures, but professors are not committed to the times of lectures. One day, while we are waiting for the professor to come to the lecture, he called our colleague via cell phone before the ending time of the lecture and said that he is sick and he canceled the lecture. The week after, I came late to the lecture; he refused to let me attend the lecture (Participant, B 7)

This is why students have their reasons for not attending lectures, which are primarily motivated by their awareness of their social and educational status within the university. The educational process was stalemated and lost its appeal to students. The weakness of the preparation of instructors and the dependence on old methods in teaching and learning, in addition to the accumulation of classrooms prevented students from attending lectures. Consequently, the administrators of the educational system should pay attention to the need for developing Internet-Based Learning Systems to access and communicate information to students in an interactive way that ensures participation. More flexibility in setting lectures' times are needed for students to participate in the scheduling of lectures to suit them. It encompasses a real involvement of students in the educational decisions that relate to them and their future.

5.1.2 Clothes

Clothing is one of the cultural symbols of any social group. The quality of clothes, the colors used, and the way of wearing it, has profound cultural connotations that highlight the uniqueness of this group. The students at Fayoum University have a unique view of the clothing and the quality of colors that are worn and this contributes significantly to satisfying their basic needs. Realistic evidence shows that in the last few years the quality of clothing and the manner in which it is worn have been markedly different regarding quantity and quality. According to different types, it is noticed that Fayoum University students tend to wear casual clothes. The common clothes among students are jeans and T-Shirt with English phrases written on it. Students may not understand the meaning of these phrases, but they wear them because their favorite star was wearing the same type of shirt. Students generally imitate actors and celebrities of what they wear in Egypt and Hollywood through their watching of the Arabic and English movies.

Moreover, the idea of imitating fashion lines of the beloved characters significantly affects students' choice of what they wear, as well as the imitation of students to each other. If one of their colleagues wears a kind of clothes that attracts girls, other students tend to imitate him and buy the same type of clothing. They believe that these clothes attract female's attention and establish relations of friendship between them at the university. However, few students wear classic trousers and shirts. They often follow the precepts of religious organizations such as the Salafis and the Muslim Brotherhood. These conservative organizations often prompt their members to wear this kind of clothes. The social environment, in which students are involved in and outside the university, affects what students wear. The presence of students in a conservative family is reflected in their type of clothes (the length of clothes and wearing of the head covering *"Hijab"* as well as dark colors). This is completely opposite to the students who grew up in a liberalized environment where they are more liberal in choosing the type of clothes and color used. Religious-minded groups, such as the Salafis and the Muslim Brotherhood, influence the clothing of their students. These students wear the clothes according to the group's will and, thus, it exerts unofficial pressure on its followers and members.

As for female students, I found the most significant denominator of students wearing *"Abayas"* (a long and flowing garment), especially what is known as *Al-Khaliji*. It is a long black dress and topped by black headscarves. Besides, this type of clothing is widespread among female students. This is due to the spread of the Gulf culture in clothing and the presence of large numbers of Egyptians are working abroad, who bring these types of clothes to their relatives and families as gifts. Also, the veil *"Al-Niqab"*[4] spreads among female students at Fayoum University where there is no group of female students without wearing *Al-Niqab*. This is especially true to the Salafis and the Brotherhood students. Many students have no affiliation with any religious groups and also wearing *Al-Niqab*. This is because the students are profoundly influenced by watching many religious programs on the T.V channels, which considerably affected the way they dress clothes. This is also due to the call of female students of the Muslim Brotherhood and the Salafis Movement to other students to wear the veil as chastity and purity for females.

Moreover, the standards, on which students of Fayoum University wearing clothes, are varied. Most students tend to wear what is ready for the study day. Some students wear certain types of clothes to meet their girlfriends and some wear clothes based on the prevailing weather. The Independent students stated:

> I wear clothes without any standards to choose from. Everything for me is okay. However, there are certain clothes I wear on a particular day, for the sake of the oksha[5](Participant, D 3).

> I wear according to the weather because this college is not the suitable place to wear your best clothes [6] (Participant, D 9).

> I divide my clothes, each shirt and Jeans for one specific day. I should choose the shoes with the same color of the clothes (Participant, D 4).

> I find out what I wore last week. I will not wear it this week. I always wear pants. I choose the clothes according to the day. If it is a long day, I will need to wear comfortable clothes that are trousers and t-shirt and it must be something ready and easy to wear. I wear it quickly and I go to the university. If it is an average day, only one lecture, I began to wear my veil in a new way. I may search for other clothes (Participant, D 8).

> I wake up from sleep and choose clothes according to my view (Participant, D 5).

> I am wearing my clothes according to the weather. There are specific colors that I wear and there are certain clothes when I meet the *moza*[7] (Participant, D 10).

Additionally, the fundamental criterion in selecting clothes is the ready-made ones, or according to the nature of the study day as well as the weather. This may be due to the fast- paced daily life, which significantly affects students. Ca-

---

[4] *Al-Niqab* is traditional religious clothes which female wears in order to hide her face. It has largely spread among female students at Fayoum University, especially after the revolution.

[5] *Oksha* is a term for a female student who has a romantic relationship with a male student. This is a symbolic expression invented by students in recent times.

[6] This student is at the last year of the College of Education and already shows through what he wears that he is indifferent to external appearance and the way to wear it is free from any harmony between colors or any other thing.

[7] *Moza* is an expression which describes the beautiful girl. It is spread among male students. There is also *"Moz"* which describes the beautiful male student and this expression is intensively used by female students at Fayoum University.

sual clothes, in addition to their aesthetically pleasing appearance for students, help them to feel comfortable. Additionally, they are light (sport shose) and do not need ironing to be ready to wear. Therefore, students prefer to wear them. Besides, it is noted that the sense of taste for students in selecting clothes and its colors is low. There is no consistency in colors between what male or female students wear. On one occasion, as I was passing from the university campus of the College of Agriculture to the College of Education, I watched a group of students wearing Jeans that were slipping from their bottom which shows the students' underwear. The trousers also have some malformations and holes, which show parts of the knee and thigh. They wear T-shirts that tend to be more feminine (rose, purple, and red colors).

This is mainly due to the lack of interest in aesthetic education and study of arts in primary and middle education stages. Thus, there is a decline in the general taste of the students in choosing the quality of their clothes, which often appear strange in their colors and designs. Additionally, choosing the styles of the western clothes indicates the influence of the western culture on students in post-revolution. Therefore, clothes are deemed as a cultural feature that shows many cultural things adopted by the student community at Fayoum University.

5.1.3 Food Habits

The students of Fayoum University are like any human groups that eat certain kinds of food in a certain way and at defined times and places. Most of what the students eat is fast-food in restaurants and cafeterias which is characterized by high prices and low nutritional value. In addition to the imbalance in the time of eating breakfast and lunch, which is often, vary according to the times of lectures in the study day. An Independent female student at the College of Arts stated:

> After my lectures, I usually sit with my friends in the university's yard and we eat breakfast at 3, 00 or 4, 00 P.M. We eat potato sandwiches, burger, crêpe or anything like cake and chips, according to the choice of the group. We used to sit on the pergola in front of the university hospital or at the College of Tourism's cafeteria, or it is possible to sit beside the College of Social Work (Participant, D 8).

Moreover, female students often eat in groups and in various places on campus. Sometimes, they eat in the studying halls if there are no lectures. The students also eat in what the group of comrades known as "Shilah" [8] and this represents a kind of pressure exerted by the student group over its members. Although there is some freedom to choose food if a student does not like the food agreed by all

---

[8] *Shilah* is a term describes a group of students who have deep and strong friendship relations. The students of *Shilah* are close to each other. They have a baseline of similar perspectives, favorites, behaviors, and wearing particular kind of clothes.

other friends. Male students often want to eat outside the university in restaurants and sometimes at the hawkers who exist across the sidewalk. This is due to the low price of meals as compared to the university restaurant.

Abu Islam[9] is the most famous roving bean vendor around the university area. Students go for eating the bean meal in the morning or after attending lectures. There are various kinds of beans is offered to students such as hot bean, sweet bean with pieces of tomatoes, onions, radishes, and watercress for students. Students may find this bean vendor crowded in the morning. They eat bean on a table in the street without feeling guilty or shame. This is back to the economic factor, which is represented in the low price of the meal as compared to restaurants and cafeterias in the university.

> I usually sit in a cafeteria when a lecture is not important. Other times, we sit in a coffee shop. Sometimes we go to Abu Islam to eat our breakfast (Participant, D 3).

> After lectures, we go to the library to make a photocopy of papers and then we eat our breakfast at Abu Islam (Participant, D 4).

> At 7, 00 A.M., I usually take my breakfast with tea and afterward go to my university (Participant, D 2).

The Muslim Brotherhood students also share the same food habits with the Independent students, but they usually eat at the university's restaurant. A Brotherhood student mentioned that:

> I usually eat at the university's restaurant. The food is good with a reasonable price (Participant, B 6).

Besides, there are several reasons behind the preference of students to eat fast food meals such as Crepe, Burgers, Hot dogs, Macaroni, Beans, and Negresco in cafeterias or restaurants and refuse to prepare some foods and bring them to the college in the form of "Sandwich":

- The cynicism and ridicule stance from the students who bring food with them to the college or eat food in the central restaurant of the university where they accuse them of miserliness for not eating food in the cafeteria or restaurant. This is a hidden way of imposing pressure on these students to follow the habits of their colleagues.
- The spread of restaurants and cafeterias throughout the university that provide fast food with some offers of discount, which helps to increase the demand for its food. The advertisement of these cafeterias is an attraction for students at the university. In addition to its presence on the campus and near the university buildings and studying halls makes it easy to access.

---

[9] *Abu Islam* is a man who prepares beans on a wooden cart in the neighborhood adjacent to the university and prepares beans and presents them to the students on some seats in the street. There is a significant turnout due to the low price of the bean meal, which does not exceed three pounds. Many students go to him for breakfast almost daily.

– Social relationships between students at university are a reason for demanding fast food. Usually, some romantic meetings or discussions of study are held to talk about the studying subjects and to prepare research in the cafeteria inside the college. Students drink Tea, Nescafe, Cappuccino, and eating some types of fast food such as Crepes, Hotdogs, Fries, Chips, and Spaghetti. Because the female students often prefer this type of food, male students are interested in this kind of food. Additionally, bringing food from the cafeteria is a kind of social appearance, "Prestige", among students at the university.
– Lack of a healthy food culture among students at Fayoum University. Also the fast- paced of the modern life and the preoccupation of parents in work in the morning, students go to the university without breakfast, and go to the cafeteria to bring food.

5.1.4 Hobbies and Leisure Time

Leisure time activities are cultural symbols of any social group. Besides, spending and enjoying leisure time is especially important for students of Fayoum University where the students engage in hobbies and activities during their free time. The leisure time spent by students is divided into leisure time between lectures where food is eaten and leisure time after the end of the study day. The activities and hobbies that students do between lectures are different from those they do after the end of the study day or on the public holidays. This is clearly evident in the speech of the Independent students:

> Between lectures, I usually go to the cafeteria. I order Nescafe and sit with my friends. If there is something that I need for the study, I take it from the girls. I discuss the research project with my colleagues and spent the rest of the day with my friends. Then I go to home. Other times, I hang out with my colleagues outside the university to a café to use the internet. Before the Egyptian Football League stopped, we went to the stadium or played PlayStation (Participant, D 4).

The students usually take advantage of leisure time between lectures to complete some assignment or photocopying of lectures' materals from their colleagues. After the study day, hiking and watching football matches in the stadium are among the common hobbies of leisure and recreation time. Some students may go over to cafes and cafeterias to drink tea and coffee. Moreover, they often smoke Shishah[10], which is widespread among male students.

---

[10] Shishah is a waterpipe tobacco smoke machine which is used to smoked tobacco with some flavors of apples and grapes. Shishah consists of a bottle of glass with a long pipe, water and tobacco. The smoke is first drawn through a bowl filling with water. This will cool the smoke. After that suspended solids and are filtered in the waterpipe smoke when passing through the water. Shishah smoking is widespread among most of fayoum university students both males and females. This is because they mistakenly believe that shisha is less harmful comparing to cigarettes and that the passing of smoke on the water prevents many toxins.

> Between lectures, I go to the cafeteria. Other times, we shall sit in the café or go to play PlayStation or play cards (Participant, D 3).

> We talk about general topics. Or if there is a lecture has a specific comment, we talk about this thing. Also, we have the Wi-Fi in the college. We open it and search for websites and open Facebook. Furthermore, it is possible that we all go out with our friends and sit in the cafe and play cards (Participant, D 5).

The students also go to eat breakfast and go to pray noon *"ṣalāt al-ẓuhr"* at the mosque, depending basically on the available time between lectures. Some students take advantage of this period to go to the library and consult with their colleagues to find out what is difficult for them. Thus, they productively invest their free time. Thus, this usually related to the female students because the male often goes outside the university.

> After lectures, we may take a photocopy of papers and then we take our breakfast. After that, we pray. If there are lectures, we attend them. If there is an assignment that should be submitted or an exam, otherwise we go home. There are breaks between the lectures; in the first break, we have our breakfast and then the second break, we go to the library and search for books. After finishing lectures, we go home directly, because we have at least three lectures a day. After we go home, we play a match. If there are no matches, I watch another one on the television. If there is nothing on the T.V I prepare and study lectures. After that, we go out with our friends to have fun and then come back at 12, 00 A.M., to sleep to wake up early (Participant, D 9).

> During the time between lectures or after the lectures, I meet my friends in the department and talk about our study subjects, what we summed up, what we do not understand, which research assignments should be submitted and others that do not. We go to the professor and tell him how to study or to inquire about something in the course. Other times, we explain difficult subjects to each other (Participant, D 6).

As for students of the religious organizations such as the Brotherhood students, they rarely have a leisure time because they precisely follow a specific schedule of tasks that must be punctually implemented. Hence, they spend free time in reading or praying and reciting Quran. A Brotherhood student stated:

> Between lectures, I spend my time in two things; reading the Holy Quran, which is always with me. Or read in a book of general culture, such as books that speak about self-development. People need to remember their aims which they are seeking to achieve (Participant, B 4).

It is noted that there is a flaw in using leisure time. Most students spend their free time in useless conversations with colleagues, watching television or going out to the public places in groups. They do not have any idea about how to spend their leisure time productively. This may be due to the lack of objectives they seek to achieve in addition to the pressure of the study. As for the hobbies practiced by Fayoum University students, they vary from playing football, reading books or stories, playing basketball, and watching foreign films.

> My hobby is reading the English literature and the political books in English (Participant, D 3).

My hobby is playing, practicing, and watching football (Participant, D 1).

I like to write novels and stories. Also, I like watching TV, especially the foreign movies. I am listening to music, but not all singers. I like to listen to Amr Diab very much. I usually enter the kitchen and create some new dishes. My main hobby is watching television. I used to get out in the open and fresh air even for an hour, is better than staying at home. (Participant, D 8).

When I was in the high school, I practiced basketball, but in the college, I have no time to practice any hobby or sport (Participant, D 6).

When I feel bored, I usually play a football match or run on the track (Participant, B 10).

I like football and I am a goalkeeper (Participant, D 4).

Moreover, we can conclude that watching football matches especially the English Premier League and the Spanish league is the main leisure time hobby of the students at Fayoum University. Besides, many students are smitten in playing Play Station; however, it is dedicated to children. These hobbies are traditional and non-productive because they do not help in the physical, psychological, and mental integration of students. This is related to the economic and social situation of the family.

The family's interest in developing the skills and talents of their children contributes developing themselves and integration of their personalities. However, the majority of families belong to the working class in Fayoum Governorate. In addition to the low cultural and educational for some families, those imagine that hobbies are useless and time wasting. It will distract student's mind and keep him away from studying. Furthermore, the drop of the state's role in supporting Youth Centers in villages and small cities and in providing them with tools and devices that help young people to practice and develop their hobbies appropriately is another cause. Additionally, the hobbies are traditional and useless. There has been no significant change in the student attitudes toward useful activities. On the contrary, the area of non-productive hobbies has increased, which consume time and money. This pushes us to ask about the type of education that supports or prevents the practice of useful hobbies and activities in the Egyptian family? Does the curriculum help in various educational stages and encourage students to engage in valuable activities and hobbies or hindering them from practicing?

5.2 Second Theme: Students' Perceptions of the Educational System at Fayoum University

It is important to mention that students have unique perceptions of the education system at Fayoum University. The importance of this view is back to its realistic, as it has been formed through years of study and interaction at the university. The university's four-year study promoted students to comprise perceptions of the elements of the education system such as courses and programs, professor, administration, and university policies. Thus, the features of this vision support students' understanding of the educational reality at Fayoum University.

5.2.1 Academic Preparations for Students at Fayoum University

Students' perceptions of their academic preparation at the university are crystallized through their view of some elements of the educational system that contribute significantly to this. These elements are the university book, the quality of courses, and programs, teaching methods, university professor, along with the assessment, and examination methods and techniques.

5.2.1.1 The university textbook.

It is a basic element of the educational process at university. Although modern educational systems have advocated the importance of self-acquiring knowledge, Egyptian universities rely primarily on the textbook as the only source of knowledge for students. The students' perceptions about the university textbook are varied. They feel dissatisfied with the textbook policy at Fayoum University, which they called "the book trade." Professors are interested significantly in selling large numbers of books to get high profit.

However, this is even worse when a textbook is linked to the so-called *"Al-Sheet"*, which *it* is a set of questions that should be answered by student and delivered with the book reservation card to professors to obtain high marks in the oral and final test. Professors and lecturers aim to publish and sell more books for the highest profit. The college in which more than one professor join in teaching a single subject or curriculum, the number of textbooks in one subject or a course exceeds four books. This exhausts students both financially and academically. It is supposed that these four books are integrated into a robust scientific material. However, students perceive it as filler and have no significance and its only goal is the financial profit for professors. A Brotherhood student at the College of Dar al-Uloom stated:

> We have here, on the level of our College Dar al-Uloom, which I know; I do not want to judge other colleges. For financial status, the students suffer a lot. Everything is by money. Every student needs much money to get these books. The paramount thing for professors is the textbook. The book is linked to many things, as well as *"Al-Sheet"* and oral exam marks. It is exhausting, but not all professors do that. The majority wants to get high profit (Participant, B 2).

Additionally, the students feel financial pressures as lecturers forced them to buy the textbooks. They feel that the university's education had become commercial and for marketing. This affected their attitude towards the entire educational process. Many students who belong to poor families cannot afford buying all these books "One subject has four books". This is a heavy burden on families in addition to the expenses of study and housing.

> The college relies mainly on the idea of selling books and most professors force students to buy their textbooks. The subject or the content of a curriculum does not become necessary as buying a book. I can stay at home, study those books, memorize them, and get high marks in the exam, but what are the educational benefits which I have acquired? (Participant, B 4).

The students are aware of the weakness of the educational curricula, the prosaic of its language, and lack of cohesion. This happens because of the attempts of professors to prepare a book quickly in order to sell it to students. Because colleges such as Dar al-Uloom, Education, and Social Work have large numbers of students, this makes professors more eager to publish books regardless of their scientific content, durability, and novelty. The Independent students mentioned:

> You buy the handbook for the previous versions of an exam from the bookstore that include all the information and exam questions in the course that you are studying. The professor compels us to buy his book by force (Participant, D 4).

> There is a professor who teaches us an educational curriculum imposed us the entire book. Ok, we argue that we do not have time, especially since the book was just printed twenty days before the exam. He also said that there is no argument and no debate. "You must buy the book" (Participant, D 9).

Moreover, it becomes apparently clear that the university textbook is a severe problem for students at Fayoum University. They find it as a commodity and trade. Besides, professors take advantage of their authority to force students to buy the book otherwise it will affect the marks of students. Professors are also practicing all means of pressure on students by linking the book with a small card or "Al-Sheet". Furthermore, professors threaten students by delaying printing book because the book reservation was not completed for all students. These factors hurt students psychologically and diminish the professor's scientific status. The students are unanimous on the low quality of the university textbook and its content that was not commensurate with the paid value. In addition to the poor quality of papers which is used in printing.

The students now see universities as bourgeois castles, as a normal reflection of the structure of a capitalist society. They reject this exploitation by professors and try to resist it. They are photographing the textbooks or borrowing them from their former colleagues. This is, therefore, apparent resistance to the monopolistic practices of professors in the policy of selling the university textbooks. Thus, there has been a little change in the policy of book distribution in the university. In this way, it will not contribute to the advancement of the educational process or provide students with a new and vibrant knowledge. Moreover, students will be exhausted financially and academically through the high prices of books that reach to fifty and sixty Egyptian pounds for just one book.

Hence, the university textbook in this way will serve only the professor of the course and it distorts the educational process by providing knowledge for students in a desultory way. This will also lead to the decline of research skills among students. It is also devoted to the culture of hegemony, exploitation, and manipulation of minds by what a professor imposes on students. Thus, the professor imposes his ideology on students in this educational sphere and students cannot confront these images of exploitation for fear about their grades and their future in the university.

5.2.1.2 Programs, courses, and teaching methods.

Courses, teaching methods, and programs are essential tools in achieving the objectives of higher education in universities. Through these courses and its scientific content, students acquire skills and knowledge. Modern teaching methods contribute significantly to the unambiguous delivery of information and knowledge. In addition, using modern technology as an educational teaching aid and instructional material contributes to the simplification of facts and the establishment of scientific experiments through virtual labs. The students at Fayoum University realize that programs, curricula, and teaching methods have many shortcomings which do not adequately prepare them to acquire modern knowledge. Consequently, most of these courses are old and do not benefit students in their life or prepare them for the labor market. The expressions of the Independent students are consistent with their perceptions as follows:

> I see the College of Education is the only college which has an academic pressure on students. Why students study in the first two-year subjects away from their specialization. In private schools, there is a specialization even in the first years in language. College of Kindergarten constructed an English Teaching Department from the first year. Other colleges began the specialization from the beginning of the first year. Why does the College of Education not do that? The students at the College of Education are studying Geology and Mathematics that are not relevant to their specialization. The students wanted the academic regulation to be changed, but unfortunately, it did not work. The administration of the college stated, "This is the university system" and no one can change the law of the university (Participant, D 8).

The students are conspicuously aware of the gap between the courses they are studying and what their actual specialization at the university requires. Many courses are not related to their scientific specialization such as the "Basic Education Section" in the College of Education. For example, the students of the Department of English in the Basic Education Section are studying in first and second-year mathematics, chemistry, geology, and physics, although their major is English. The students believe that these curriculums will not work in their favor and will not entirely prepare them as specialists in their field of study. The Muslim Brotherhood students also have the same perceptions about the programmers and teaching methods at Fayoum University. A Brotherhood student at the College of Engineering mentioned:

> There is an absence of the needed skills to qualify students for the labor market. In our college, there is a shortage in practical training and the academic content of lectures is extremely old. Besides, all subjects have a vast theoretical background which is a big flaw. It does not enable students to acquire the needed knowledge and skills for the labor market. The lecturer prefers to explain information in a very theoretical and obscure way. Professors ask you to imagine the process or the component of a machine. The college does not provide any practical side which helps us to understand the subjects that have practical applications. It was possible for the university to contract with a company that trains us on the practical parts and, thus, will be able to qualify students for the labor market. We know at least the things we have in the college. We will be graduated as a half engineer. (Participant, B 5).

The students also feel that they need courses that qualify them for the labor market and that these courses do not exist at all. Furthermore, the teaching methods of some curricula are traditional and monotonous, in addition to the lack of laboratories, tools, and the necessary equipments to apply the practical part of the course. The students believe that professors do not adequately explain the study subjects. There are no explanations or comments from instructors on some parts of texts in most lectures.

However, this may be due to the large numbers of students attending in the studying hall, which do not give any opportunity for professors to interact more with students and allow them to participate effectively in the discussion, interpretation, and analysis of topics. This affects the supply of modern knowledge to them and it has influenced the student scientific competence and intellectual skills. Moreover, this has weakened the students' thinking and shrank their analytical and interpretive skills.

> The problem we have here at the College of Dar al-Uloom is that many curricula which are traditional and do not benefit us such as Hebrew and Persian. A group of students tried to ask for changing these courses, but they did not succeed (Participant, B 2).

> Oh, we need a modern curriculum for many subjects such as architecture and computer programs used in engineering designs. Because of most jobs required to be an expert in engineering programs such as CAD and SAT. However, in the college, the traditional way that I answer the questions in my exam paper and draw using my hand is prevalent (Participant, B 5).

It is noted through the expressions of the Brotherhood students and their perceptions; that they are not satisfied with the quality of courses they are studying in various colleges. This puts us in front of questions such as why students' opinions are not taken in the courses offered to them? Why do colleges not respond to the innovations of the era in every field of science and research? What harms will occur if teaching methods depend on discussion, dialogue, and interaction between a professor and his students? I think that it is very much related to what the regime wants from the university. A university that has educated, learning, and highly qualified generations is a source of concern for authoritarian regimes that do not want people to reveal their falsity and their manipulation of minds and feelings of the youth. Consequently, education in this form is a means of social stability and preservation of the social situation, which is characterized by inequality. Comparing public universities in which the students from low class learn with the conditions of private universities such as French, German, American, and Japanese, where the sons of the rich learn is entirely different. The accurate observer finds that the education system and curricula differ entirely from those found in public universities.

This asserts the common belief that the regime allowed educational opportunities for the sons of the elite to continue in their social strata from which they came. The sons of the marginalized and poor remain in the same socio-economic conditions, which ultimately serve the interests of the regime and the interests of the ruling class. Poor and low quality of education, as well as the authoritarian structure of the university administration, encourages students to rebel. Thus, the student unrest that swept universities in the 1960s was also a result of low educational services in universities (Peters, 1965; Levine et al., 1979).

5.2.1.3 University professor.

University professor is the mainstay of the educational process at university. This is due to his supreme status in front of his students as a model and an example for them. Besides, university professor has many roles and holds many responsibilities as an educator, advisor, an evaluator for students' performance, and participant in their activities along with other roles and liabilities. The students at Fayoum University have a particular view of professors and his roles. They give them a highly significant deal of respect and an aura of holiness for their scientific and literary standing in the hearts of their students. At the same time, they criticize many actions and behaviors of a few professors such as the injustice of students in exams, their permanent demands to buy the university textbook, and disregarding the views of students and ill-treatment of them as well as other behaviors rejected by the student community at Fayoum University. Therefore, the expressions of the Brotherhood students during the in-depth interviews expressed this view as follows:

> I want a real learning environment and preparing a professor who does not have absolute power over his students. We have a professor in our college who said to us "if they

do not get the book's card that proves reservation or *Al-Sheet*, you will see what I am doing with you". I will decrease all your marks in the exam. The professor is not a prophet or a king. However, he has to be censored to improve the educational process. It is possible that a professor being unfair to the students who have different political, ideological or personal perspectives from him. Then, he may make the student fail in the exam. This pattern of relationship never changed after the revolution, but it increased to the worst. How can I prepare a liberal student with a free culture in this oppressive atmosphere? (Participant B 10).[11]

We are the only students who confronted the professors who insulted us. A professor, who teaches us a particular course, knows my political beliefs and may cause harm regarding my grades. A professor said to a female student does not speak with this girl because she is a terrorist. However, students said how she is a terrorist? We interacted together and we are friends for four years in lectures, in campus, and we ate together. Thus, his words did not affect other students (Participant, B 8).[12]

There were several differences between professors and students. This professor has a specific political orientation and some students are against his perspective. They hate and harassing him and do not attend his lectures and vice versa. Other professors have no political orientation so if a student does something; he does not give any comment. If we can classify students as supporters, opponents, and neutral. The professors also divided supporter, opponent, and neutral. Currently, I prefer the neutral person for many reasons. If a professor is a supporter or an opponent of what is going on in the lecture, there will be a lot of clashes (Participant, B 2).

Additionally, the students feel the power of professors and they see that they use it in an unjustified way. The lecturer uses his authority in places which are not assigned to use it. He uses his power in forcing students to buy books or to impose his opinions, which may be contrary to the perspective of the majority of students. Not only at that point, but it also exceeds the intellectual conflict between students and professor, which may sometimes reach to a verbal clash between them.

Also, the students see that the work of a faculty member has many shortcomings. Therefore, the students are demanding for real academic and professional preparation of instructors in a way that considers the abilities of students and respecting their minds and opinions. This is completely consistent with the evidence of many studies that have identified many imbalances within the university environment. This is represented in the professors' desire for quick profits and his indifference to the value of knowledge acquisition and dissemination among students as well as pursuit work at the Gulf universities (ʿAmar, 1996). The Independent students announced that:

---

[11] This is a Brotherhood student at the fourth year at the College of Dar Al-Uloom, and he is distinguished ethically and academically. Moreover, he is within the top high grades at the college level.

[12] This female student is at the College of Education and is belonging to the Muslim Brotherhood group. The lecturer who taught her tells her colleagues to completely keep away from her.

Honestly, many professors are unfair; others are not. There are a few professors whose style of conversations with us is quite good. They give us a space for discussion and they respect our views. We get to be benefited from those professors. They give us enough time to meet them in their offices. Besides, they are patient and discuss everything with us. Other professors are subject to their vision and arrogant and they do not listen to us (Participant, D 9).

Many professors have their perspectives and political orientations, but they did not try to impose them in lectures. However, we are still aware of the way they spoke about a particular subject (Participant, D 1).[13]

Also, political debates have Thus, been brought into the studying rooms. Consequently, students and professors discussed many political issues that of course led to discord between them. The students are aware of the political orientations of their professors and realize that some professors may involve certain political ideas within lectures. The students do not respond to these political discussions at the moment for fear that they will be caught by the security forces which stationed throughout the day in front of the university. After the revolution, there has been much political discussion among students and professors. One of the discussions ended with the expulsion of many students by a professor because they disagreed with him concerning political opinions.

The students' relations with the faculty members have been declined due to the events that followed the January 25th Revolution of 2011. The relationship after the revolution was characterized by vitality and friendship. The ideas of professors on students have changed and there seems an atmosphere of affection between them. However, the relationship began to decline after the political events at Fayoum University such as the student demonstrations and the siege of the deans. Many faculty members view student demonstrations and strikes at the university as a messy. Moreover, professors believe that these students are directed by political groups and parties that want to reap political gains at the expense of the university and its mission. The Independent students stated about the relationship between students and professors:

What I see in my college is that the relationship between students and professors is getting worse. There are only two or three professors whom understand students and have a good conversation with them. Some professors give a lecture and take his bag from the desk and go out swiftly. Other professors are intellectually different with the rest of students, but they do not try to impose their ideas on students. However, the relationship between students and faculty members is still weak. After the events of the 30th June 2013, it is just a lecture relationship between professors and students and no more (Participant, D 3).

All of us after the revolution as, professors and students, felt happiness and freedom. Even with the division of professors and students between pro-regime and supporters of the revolution, yet after the revolution, everyone begins to feel free. However, after

---

13 This student is at the College of Engineering and he is against the thought of some groups of the political Islam at the university, especially the Muslim Brotherhood.

the 30th June of 2013, there was a significant distinction in the relationships between students and professors (Participant, D 8).

> The typical character of a professor has entirely changed after the revolution. Some professors like to create an atmosphere of freedom and discussion with students. Other professors do not understand anything about the new Egypt. So, they still, as they were before (Participant, D 7).

Consequently, the students believe that the changes that have occurred in the professors' personality after the revolution were a result of the political events that came after the revolution with which many of them agreed or disagreed. Furthermore, the gap between students and faculty members increased after the 30th June of 2013 because the security forces thought that some professors incite students to violence. The ruling regime has issued statements that certain professors support the tensions in universities. In fact, most professors suffered from a state of fear and panic. Thus, they moved away from the students in order not to be caught under the hand of power.

As for the perceptions of students about the work of professors through lectures, there were profound differences in their description of what professors do. They confirmed that there was a real change immediately after the revolution and that change came because the spirit of revolution passed through the lives of Egyptians and their bodies. An Independent female student at the College of Arts clarified:

> The year of 2011 was the best year at the university. Professors began to commit themselves to attend all lectures and engaged in the student activities. A professor was wasting time and enters just a few lectures for the whole year before the revolution. These things changed after the revolution, but for a specified period of time. After the 30th June events of 2013, the situation returned to the worst (Participant, D 8).

However, the tendency of the Brotherhood students towards the university professor was not honorable. They give much criticism to professors. A Muslim Brotherhood student at the College of Engineering stated:

> I hope that I do not hear the word lecturer who is just teaching. I wish I hear the word professor who is explaining and discussing his students. The professor's job is not only to teach, examine students, and give grades, but he should develop the students' abilities and skills (Participant, B 5).

The students' awareness of the professors' work has highly increased after the revolution. They do not need the old style of teaching, but they need a real professor to guide them to the path of knowledge. This is due to their growing sense of self after the Egyptian youth successfully removed the unjust and coercive regime. Therefore, the need for a new kind of faculty members is essential to help them genuinely to learn and actively share in making knowledge and developing skills and abilities. This awareness of the role of a faculty member in the university reflects a considerable change that the revolution has conspicuously caused in the minds of students, their patterns of thinking, and attitudes towards science and knowledge as a basis for the advancement of Egypt.

5.2.1.4 Testing and evaluation methods.

Evaluation methods are among the basic components of the educational process and the main tool in assessing the outcomes of the educational system. The evaluation techniques are the ones that validate the efficiency of the rest of other educational elements such as curricula, methods of teaching, and activities along with the potential of the instructor. The students at Fayoum University assert that the evaluation systems are now unfair. They also believe that it is close to be a goal in itself and not as a means of evaluating students. The expressions of the Muslim Brotherhood students during the interviews were as follows:

> In our college, some students succeed and get high grades, but they do not understand the practical side of the curriculum (Participant, B 5)

> Of course, the system of education in the college makes me care about what will come in the exam not what is important for me as a teacher. I take care of the study subjects and examinations, but search for information does not exist (Participant, B 9).

Besides, students see an apparent interest of professors and university administration regarding examinations. All components of the education system revolve around the system of evaluation because it determines its validity. However, students believe that interest in success and failure has lost their opportunities to prepare them for the skills of research, survey, learning, and acquiring the needed skills for the labor market. Moreover, they also believe that the exams focus only on memorizing and recalling information. A student can pass an exam although he or she could not apply this knowledge in the practical life. He lacks some of the skills that have been overlooked because of the exaggerated interest in exams. Thus, according to Bourdieu, there is nothing to serve the regime and the upper class more than tests. These tests, which are not doubted or wrong, may claim to measure the student's ability or categorizing them to perform specific professional functions and this is precisely what the regime wants through one of its tools, namely the educational system.

Despite the university attempt to develop the evaluation and examinations methods by establishing a special center for the evaluation at the Center of Projects Management at Fayoum University, the students did not feel any change in the methods of assessment and examinations. Thus, they stated that the exams focus only on facts and are indifferent to evaluating the skills and experience gained by the students in the practical and professional aspects. This approach comes to ensure a change in the students' perceptions of the means of evaluation and examinations and their desire to develop means to measure the skills and experiences that will benefit them in their professional lives.

Additionally, the methods of evaluation are, therefore, against the idea of social justice. This is because they measure the minimum level of thinking and is interested in retrieving information. It is not characterized by objectivity and many self-evident and a large number of students who apply each semester petitions to re-correct the exam paper. The test held once, and if the student is sick, he will receive half of the overall grade in the next exam, even if he gets the highest grade. However, these results contradict the studies of Mauch (1994) and Suchlicki (1969). After Velvet Revolution, there has been a change in the curricula and programs of study as well as increasing democracy at the university. In Cuba, there was a wide spread of vocational learning as the students worked and studied at the same time to engage in productive work, but in Fayoum University, there were no notable changes in the study programs or the philosophy of curricula.

5.2.1.5 Coordination Office and the absent justice.

The Coordination Office *"Maktab Al-Tansiik"* is the organization entrusted with the distribution of all high school students according to their grades and wishes to colleges and institutes in Egypt public and private universities. The basic and only criterion for the Coordination Office is the grades of students. Some experts believe that the Coordination Office is against social justice and supports class inequality because it does not distribute students according to their wishes but according to grades gained in the secondary school. Others see the Coordination Office as the last bastion for students to have a fair educational opportunity. It is also the appropriate means for our Egyptian society. If the students are distributed according to their abilities and desires, this will open the door to the problems of patronage and mediation, which is the acute disease suffered by all the state's institutions.

The students at Fayoum University see the Coordination Office as the main reason they enter the colleges they do not want to attend. Their enrollment in these colleges came against their will and desire. The Muslim Brotherhood students' comments regarding the Coordination Office were significantly critical concerning this approach:

> When I first came to this university, I have been just like my friends. We are the students who the Coordination Office threw them forcefully here (Participant, B 2).

> I am fond of literary studies and a lover of the Arabic, Islamic studies, and everything related to the history and the linguistics since I was a child. I was in the preparatory school and we took a lesson once and this lesson was about the Japanese. The noble aim of the lesson is that the student can enter the college he wants if he has learning

abilities even if his grade is low in that field. When I was young, I dreamed to become a teacher and I will be a professor in the future as I will continue my postgraduate studies, God willing. I have talents and ability to talk to students to convey information to people who sat in front of me. Besides, I love this field, so I entered the literary section in the secondary school. I intended to enroll to Dar al-Uloom at Cairo University, but my grade was a little bit low, so I got enrolled in Dar al-Uloom at Fayoum University and Iam satisfied with the will of the God. Then, in the first term of the first year, I was ranked the third over my companion so that I will continue and complete my studies, God willing (Participant, B 10).

Consequently, the students often enrolled in colleges against their own will, which affects their willingness to study. The students are pretending to like the college and study over time. However, this is a psychological feeling that they try to resist negative feelings they have by studying and showing their satisfaction with the study at college. Students are equal at the same time, but there are no job opportunities in the governmental institutions. Therefore, they entered any college. The Independent students have the same feeling as the Brotherhood students have:

> Honestly, when I was in the second year of high school, I got 95%. Many people advised me not to be enrolled in the mathematics section and to complete in the science section in high school. However, I have completed my study in the mathematics section because I wanted to enter the College of Engineering. Now I am studying at the College of Education (Participant, D 3).

> At first, I was not interested in the college and over time and with my studies at the college I started to like it. I think now that I may apply for the graduate studies (Participant, D 4).[14]

Besides, the students' perceptions about the Coordination Office are completely negative. This expresses the extent of hatred for this mechanism that prevented many students from enrolling in the colleges they want and feel that their abilities and skills will be refined if they study at those colleges. One student said that the Coordination Office did not select colleges for students, but "threw them" and that showed a lack of concern for students' interests. Besides, the main concern is only the grades and nothing else. However, some students can enter the college they wish to pursue after they reach the minimum level of grades required for this college. However, they may be distributed to a university or a college in another governorate that they do not want to go there. This is evidenced by the student, who wished to enter Dar al-Uloom at Cairo University because he dreamed of it, but his distribution according to his grades forced him to join the Dar al-Uloom at Fayoum University. And there is a a significant difference between the first and the second regarding scientific reputation and faculty potential.

---

[14] This student is in the fourth year at the College of Social Work. He wanted to enter the College of Pharmacy or Medicine, but his grades qualified him to be enrolled in the College of Social Work.

Moreover, most students may accept the de facto status and study at a college, even though they do not want to attend. The student tries to accept the study and integrate into the university life as the student of the College of Social Work, who is thinking of completing his graduate studies in his college. The reason may be that it is the only way to get a job. The other students cannot accept the field of study has chosen by the Coordination Office, which generates hatred of the college. Therefore, his performance becomes worse and may fail several times.

Thus, the idea of the Coordination Office does not support social justice; it serves the class interests of the elite in the Egyptian society through this mechanism, which deprives students from enrolling in colleges they want. While it supports the wealthy families, who can prepare their children well through private lessons, foreign books, and private language schools. Thus, they can get the highest grades in the secondary school regardless of their mental and intellectual abilities. Hence, this mechanism maintains the status of the sons of the rich and marginalizing the poor, except in a few cases that are related to the intelligent students of the low-income families overcome difficult conditions in public schools and gets the grades accepted by the Coordination Office to enter the college they wish.

5.2.2 University administration

University administration is an essential part of a university's system. Due to its roles and responsibilities, it plays a significant role in the success of the educational system and solves all the problems facing it. University administration also exercises some authority over students and all elements of the educational system at the university. Therefore, students look at university administration with a particular view of approaching it at sometimes and fear and suspicion in its intentions at other times. The Independent students' expressions regarding the administration of Fayoum University were as follows:

> The relationship between students and the university leaders were better in the revolutionary era. I mean in the past; the Dean refused to meet students or listen to their complaints about particular issues and that was before the revolution. However, after the revolution, the situation entirely changed. There was a complaint in the College of Arts that the books were costly. Consequently, the Dean met students and spoke with them. In the past, these books were not financially supported by the university, but the Dean gathered all students and talked about the financial support for these books. Thus, he has finally achieved our demands. The Dean of the college began to support student activities and began to talk to them about theater activities and cultural activities organized by the Student Union. This was the best period (Participant, D 8).

The students are conspicuously aware that their relationship with the university administration has changed after the January25th Revolution of 2011. This is due to the spread of democracy in the university. The students illustrated that the university leaders from the Dean to the Chancellor of the university have rushed to help students. This is contrary to what was happening before the revolution as the university leaders did not even listen to the demands of the students.

> Now it becomes easier to meet the Dean, Vice-Dean or professors at any time if you have a problem. Their response to the students' demands was neither fast nor enough and also takes much time. It is easy to meet them, but not easy to achieve your demands. In the past year, the students had different opinions about the exam schedule which intensified the exam days. Frankly, when some students met the Dean, he made a surprise for all of us. He said, all of you will take the exams from the 16 May until the 5 June of this month. Thus, through this period, you can arrange the schedule as all of you would like. It was a magnificent response. Also, directly after the revolution, some students had low marks at exams, yet their marks were increased and they succeeded in this year (Participant, D 9).

Besides, Fayoum University administration allowed students to present their problems and requests and endeavored tirelessly to implement these demands. This depended on the personality of the university leaders. Some of them were intended to serve students and treat them freely and genuinely democratic. Others were afraid concerning their administrative position and were consistent with the trend regarding not involved in a clash with students. Those leaders might be members of the dissolved National Democratic Party "Al-Ḥizb Al-Waṭanī Al-Dīmūqrāṭī" and still hate the revolution in their hearts, but the tide of the revolution was strong. Therefore, they were reluctantly compelled to the students' demands. A Brotherhood student stated:

> It depends on the Dean of the college and many Deans work in the interest of students and others do not meet their students. There was more freedom after the revolution to meet the Dean of the college than before the revolution. This referred to the problem of Mr. *Zakaria*, the head of the Student Affairs Department at the College of Education, but nothing happened and the Dean did not achieve the students' demands. We offered to amend the schedule of exams and the Dean of the college agreed and welcomed, but he did not achieve anything. He set the examination dates and said that we are committed to them (Participant, B 7).[15]

Moreover, the Muslim Brotherhood students dealt officially with the administration of Fayoum University as members of the Student Union. The relations after the revolution were quite good and the administration implemented the demands and solved the students' problems. The relations with the university administration have changed to the opposite after the 30th of June 2013 events and their intransigence with the students. The students also confirmed that the administration after the events of the 30th of June 2013 have been entirely in solidarity with the regime and tried as much as possible to achieve its goals at

---

[15] This student belonged to the Muslim Brotherhood Organization at the College of Education. He was a leader for the Brotherhood students at the College of Education. He was jailed for a year in charge of organizing demonstrations.

the expense of students. A female Brotherhood student at the College of Education mentioned:

> After the revolution, the relations were fine and we were dealing as the Student Union, not as ordinary students. The relationship was quite good, even with Prof. *Khaled Hamza*, who was the supervisor of the Student Affairs activities. It was a very pleasant relationship. He tried to achieve all the students' requests and he knew all members of the Student Union by their names. However, there was some stubbornness. After the January 25th Revolution of 2011, most Deans were elected. Therefore, there is a sense of freedom because the leaders have been selected through democratic elections. But now, after the 30th of June 2013, there is no cooperation at all. I do not know that the Dean of the College of Education was changed until the last week. Do we not know when or how he came? Everything became through appointing. The student who speaks will have nothing since the Dean, or the university Rector came from a higher authority which is higher than me and you, and the university and the professors. The existing policy of the university states that there has been a change since the events of the 30th of June 2013. The obvious example is the cancelation of petitions of re-correcting the exam paper, although petitions are our right. Many students are severely harmed, though it is part of our rights. When we protested, they said that it is a decision. It is a policy of hostility. No negotiation, it is a battle of existence. Thus, it is not a competitive political battle (Participant, B 1).

Additionally, the Brotherhood students confirmed that the university administration had canceled the student's petitions, which means losing the gains of the revolution for students. The university administration has tried as much as possible to restrict freedoms by maintaining order in the university and reducing all activities because it is a part of the regime according to the perceptions of the Muslim Brotherhood students.

> I am sure that the relationship does not exist at all. If we asked for the release of our colleagues from prisons, we would be arrested. There was an intransigent of the university administration when we organized a demonstration; they call the police. They are a reason behind the interference of the security forces to the university campus. The police can not enter the university without permission from the university administration (Participant, B 4).

Besides, the Muslim Brotherhood students believe that the university administration discriminates between them and the rest of the student organizations. The students felt intransigence as a result of the university administration regularly calling for the security forces to arrest the Muslim Brotherhood students. They see that the university administration is responsible for arresting their colleagues. These results disagreed with the conclusions proposed by Mauch (1994) because Fayoum university administration showed dictatorship actions against students. The democratic practices were swiftly declined in the post-revolution era. These tension relationships between students and Fayoum University administration have developed to aggressive behaviors against the administration of Fayoum University and the security forces as well.

The issue of linking higher education to the labor market gained significant attention from various sectors of Egyptian society. Among the primary objectives of modern education systems is to prepare technical and academic staff for labor market. The students at Fayoum University believed that programs, courses, and other tools of the university's education system do not prepare them adequately for competing in the Egyptian labor market.

Moreover, what they study in the college is something different from what the labor market needs. This is one of the tools of the dominant class in keeping social and class conditions intact for its interests. This is because the profound changes in the structure of the education system and its strong link with the labor market will support the low-class populations and increase their chances of improving their social conditions in the Egyptian society. The Brotherhood students' expressions were as the following:

> I am learning something and the labor market requires something else. It seems that I laugh at myself and they laugh at the students (The ruling regime). As for me, as a student at the College of Dar al-Uloom, there are many courses in which I have benefited nothing in my career such as, English, Hebrew, Persian language, and philosophy (Participant, B 4).

The students are aware that they are in an absurd situation by enrolling in theoretical and traditional colleges that are not needed anymore in the Egyptian labor market. In addition to getting preparation through old courses that are not in keeping with the development of the modern knowledge and the requirements of the labor market. The graduates of the College of Dar al-Uloom seek to work as an Arabic language teacher, which is the same job for many graduates. For instance, graduates of the Colleges of Education, Arabic Language Department at the College of Arts, Arabic Language Department at the College of Arabic Language, and the College of Arabic and Islamic Studies at Al-Azhar University are qualifying for the same job. Thus, the competition is fierce in the labor market and needs to be prepared well. However, it is not available at the College of Dar al-Uloom, according to the perceptions of the students.

> I remember the first thing that I heard when I entered the college at the first lecture for Dr. *Māmouwn* who said a word and I found its impact in reality. He said that some students enroll in the college as a young fool and graduate as a big donkey. The problem represents at the beginning of the elemaintry school education. How does classroom include 50 students? How teachers educate them? How can I develop the thought of these students? The subject needs a significant interested from the primary stage. Actually, in Egypt, there is no interest in education. Is education getting the same fund as Art, Cinema or Football? (Participant, B 2).

Indeed, there is a severe shortage in the academic preparation of students in all colleges at Fayoum University. The Dean of the college says, "*Some people enter as a young fool and then become a big donkey"* because of the college's reliance on indoctrination and lack of preparation for the labor market. The students are extremely aware that the lack of the educational infrastructure and the large numbers of students enrolled in colleges are one of the main reasons behind the low-quality. This is in addition to the students' conviction that education is not a priority of the state, as football sector or the cinema sector. The Independent students have the same perceptions as the Brotherhood students have concerning the education system at the university.

> The labor market needs other things than things taught in the College of Education. What was taught in the college indeed benefit me, but admittedly I need an increase to my specialized subjects? Honestly, we are studying courses that we have not benefited from. We need to study courses deeply such as grammar. We do study it only one semester in four years. We need extra courses to benefit us in the labor market such as scientific and micro-teaching courses in order to be more activated from the first year. Therefore, the student will have the appropriate experience, skill, and courage to enable him to teach students (Participant, D 9).

> In the English Department, it is supposed to speak like native speakers, but many students are graduating with problems in reading and speaking skills. The style of education before the revolution is still the same after the revolution and has not changed at all (Participant, D 3).

The students believed that the education system has not changed since the revolution, and there is still a severe lack of preparation. Furthermore, the low-quality of education would never help them to catch up with the labor market. The students wondered how graduates of the English Departments misread words? How can they compete in the labor market?

> On the contrary, what I am learning is something and what is needed for the labor market is another different thing. The labor market focuses on language skills, accent, and pronunciation. In the college, we learned literature and civilization that are not needed for teaching in schools. I will not teach students literature and civilization at schools. I will teach them phonetics, grammar, and accent. I may learn these subjects, but not in depth. The university did not prepare me well for the labor market (Participant, D 2).[16]

Consequently, there is a shortage in the academic preparation for students. They believe that the college will not qualify them for the labor market. And this view will, of course, affect their desire to study and their inclination towards it and the pride of their academic specialization. It will also create a state of frustration among students. Because of the difference between what is taught and what is needed in the labor market, this has a worse impact on students. This may lead them to migrate to the Gulf countries or migrate to the Euro-

---

[16] This student is a graduate of the French Language Department at the College of Education. He has severely suffered in obtaining a job opportunity despite his distinguished academic appreciation and his excellent language. However, all language schools prefer the graduates from al-Alsun departments in order to teach students.

pean countries in an attempt to search for jobs and for a decent life. Alternatively, they may drop into the trap of extremist groups that lead them to do aggressive behaviours that threaten the stability of the society.

The pressures of the expected unemployment increase the student revolt against the authority of both university and state. This is because the students at the university look forward to their future places in the society. When they have the feelings that there are no opportunities for employment, they increasingly feel alienation and start rebel against the ruling authority. This is a result of the erroneous educational policies that often serve the objectives of the regime and increases stability without changing the social conditions. Education has become a mean of social stability, not as a mean of social mobility. What is the benefit of an education that cannot provide a job opportunity that helps its holder to gain a decent life? Thus, the educational policy at the university needs to redraw again in light of the development requirements of the Egyptian society.

All in all, these negative perceptions about the education system at Fayoum University prove the state of anger and frustration among students. They were dreaming after the revolution of a deep change in the education system at university, but the reality is totally opposite. Therefore, they criticized the low-quality of educational services at the university. Thus, the low quality of education may be considered as a primary cause for these waves of protests that practiced by students at Fayoum University.

5.3 Third Theme: The Student Elections and Political Activity at Fayoum University

Student elections and the increasing political activity are among the most significant gains of the January 25th Revolution of 2011 in Egyptian universities. Besides, students embarked on an atmosphere of democracy which they had never witnessed before. Egyptian universities have opened up for all political visions and orientations. Moreover, they allowed democratic practices such as student elections, conferences, and political debates on various issues. Universities emerged in a new form that restored their status and their vital role as a fortress of knowledge and an institution for educating and cultivating human beings.

Consequently, the students' political activities at Fayoum University varied from running student elections, political discussions on the critical events that Egypt is going through, setting a new student regulation, student participation in the Parliamentary, and Presidential elections. Furthermore, the students organized political demonstrations that supported a certain political faction which resulted in severe problems in many Egyptian universities, including Fayoum University.

5.3.1 Students and Social and Political Issues of Egypt

After the January25th Revolution of 2011, a different feeling has generated for all sectors of Egyptian society especially students. The students' awareness and participation in the issues of their society, which is in the interest of the nation, has increased. Discussions on the country undergoing events have grown and resulted in moving to active participation through organizing conferences, seminars, and political debates inside Fayoum University. After the January 25th Revolution, Fayoum University became a fertile place for discussions about the future of Egypt. In every place or corner of Fayoum University campus, discussions and exchange of views were raised on a range of issues related to democracy, social justice, the exchange of power, and the rights and duties of citizens. Students expressed this positive state and a sense of responsibility towards Egypt through expressions that highlighted these trends and reflected this situation. The most prominent issues are:

5.3.1.1 Social justice.

It represents the major issue and concern of all developed and developing societies. All human societies ought to achieve the problematic equation of social justice to remove gaps between social strata and avoid any class strife that threatens social peace and harms the cohesion of the human society. That is why the issue of social justice has represented an essential pillar of the glorious Egyptian revolution and one of its leading causes and objectives at the same time (ʿAli, 2012).

Moreover, students of Fayoum University are a part of the young generation and they have perceptions of social justice in Egypt as they are affected by the absence of social justice. The obvious example is the student *Abdul Hamid Shetla*, who threw himself in the Nile as a result of the refusal of the Ministry of Foreign Affairs to appoint him in a diplomatic job. The reason was that he is socially inappropriate for the job. Thus, the students' perceptions of social justice are unique and represent the attitudes of young people. The Independent students stated:

> After the January 25th Revolution, there were justice and freedom. Besides, it was achieved in a short period immediately after the revolution. It can be said that there were freedom, social justice, and freedom of expression. However, at the current time, everything has returned to its nature as before the revolution (Participant, D 9).

The student also emphasized that social justice, which was one of the main aims of the January Revolution of 2011, was achieved by a small percentage immediately after the revolution. The new regime and the post-revolution governments attempted to pay attention to the low-income people, expand health insurance, raise wages, and other social justice issues. However, students confirm that it was for a limited time. On campus, social justice prevailed in dealing with all student groups. Equality prevailed among all students and student groups deprived of official participation in activities of the university for years, such as the Muslim Brotherhood students, have been integrated. When the political rivalry between the political forces in Egypt began, this led to the abandonment or the marginalization of the issues of social justice.

From the students' point of view, things have returned to their pre-revolutionary era and the gains of the revolution from social justice have vanished. Now, there are high prices, a decline in support for the low-income people, and the appointments in the judicial bodies are only for the sons of judges. The obvious example for that was what the Minister of Justice Counselor *Mahfuwz Saber*, in the Government of *Mahleb*, said that the son of the dustman or garbage collector is not allowed to work in the judiciary positions.

Consequently, students see that social justice did not achieve in the way that the youth in the Tahrir Square wanted during the January 25th Revolution of 2011. Conflicts and political wrangling have damaged social justice. After the events of the 30th of June 2013, the students of the Muslim Brotherhood felt that social justice did not exist and that the university administration differentiated in dealing with students. Moreover, the wealth of the state is plundered and the regime has not changed, but it is still ruling according to the policies of the old regime.

> The university administration is directed to work for excluding the opposing factions (Participant, B 2).

> If any other students organize a strike or a demonstration, no one can touch them. No one will be terrified of them. As for us, our blood is permissible *"Halal"*. Kill them; there is no problem (Participant, B 1).

Besides, the Brotherhood students' feeling of discrimination in dealing with them because they are against the policies of the current regime is, in turn, against the concept of social justice. Students are equal in rights and duties and the law is applied to all students not only the Muslim Brotherhood. They emphasize that the current administration of Fayoum university are working to eliminate them from participating in activities and prefer other student groups because they are compatible with the aims and policies of the regime.

In short, the concept of social justice is highly characterized by confusion and ambiguity among students, especially the Brotherhood students, who restricted the concept of social justice to the discrimination behaviors with them. They did not address the concept of social justice through reforming the wage system, eliminating the excellence programs that pervaded public universities, and the need to eliminate what is known as mediation and other matters that strike social justice. It may also be attributed to the package of superficial reforms carried out by the regime to improve the image of social justice in Egypt, such as increasing the wage system and expanding the area of health insurance.

5.3.1.2 Democracy.

It is still a strange and unfamiliar concept to the Arab and Egyptian society. Although the term is purely European, it has been recently translated into Arabic (Al-Kuwari & Maḍi, 2009; Saied, 2007; Touraine, 1994). All political forces and political parties in Egypt have begun to brag about democracy in their statements and conversations to the masses and elites at the same time. However, the act of democracy is entirely absent from the Egyptian society. Democracy is normally means the rule of a majority in a society through fair elections.

However, the students believe that Egypt has accomplished some achievements on the way to democracy by launching fair Parliamentary and Presidential elections after the revolution. In addition to the ability of each citizen to stand for election and to elect a certain political faction that he sees it can achieve his objectives. In Fayoum University, fair elections were held for the Presidency of the university, the Deanship of colleges, and the General Student Union. Democratic practice appeared to be the foundation of Egyptian life during the period of the revolution.

On the contrary, winds do not blow as the vessels wish. The conflicts between political forces began and democratic practice gradually diminished. Things got worse in Egypt and dictatorship practices began to escalate among the political forces in Egypt to the degree that the elected president was removed. A Brotherhood student at the College of Engineering mentioned:

> I am sure that the period after the 30th of June 2013 is the period of reproduction the ex-regime because the regime has not been removed at all. Instead of *Ahmed Ezz*[17], who wants to enter the Parliamentary elections; seventy people who belong to him will enter the elections. Instead of *Sawiris*[18] enters the election, one thousand of his followers will enter the elections (Participant, B 5).

One thing that shocked students at the same time was *Ahmed Ezz's* intention to enter the Parliamentary elections. This is a proof of a lack of democracy. Students look at these names for example *"Ahmed Ezz"* as they have corrupted the political life and must apply the law of political isolation over them until the state heads towards a democratic life. However, the intention of the National

---

[17] *Ahmed Ezz* is the former Secretary of the Organization and a member of the Policies Committee of the National Democratic party 'Al-Ḥizb Al-Waṭanī Al-Dīmūqrāṭī ''. He was accused of the monopoly of the iron and steel industry. He has had a closed relationship with Gamal Mubarak.

[18] *Naguib Sawiris* is a Coptic businessman and the owner of Orascom Company for construction and technology. He has liberal political views. He is also the founder of the Free Egyptians Party *"Ḥizb El Maṣriyin El Aḥrār"*.

Democratic Party figures to enter the elections proved to students that democracy had been assassinated. A female Brotherhood student at the College of Education mentioned:

> Now is already a coup[19]. Thus, there is no freedom. You do not have the right to elect. Even if there are elections, it will be held by imposing opinion (Participant, B 9).

Students in general and the Muslim Brotherhood students in particular doubted about the existence of democracy after the events of the 30th of June 2013. They claimed that if any elections are held, they will be manipulated and there will be neither transparency nor democratic practices. They believed that the current regime has brutally neglected democracy. The elected President Muhammad Morsi was overthrown and the power was taken over. These authoritarian actions are far from democratic practices. In their opinion, this is a coup against the legitimacy of the election box. The political freedom has been shrunk and no longer exists in the climate of intimidation prevailing in Egypt especially after the events of the 30th of June 2013. A Brotherhood student at the College of Dar al-Uloom stated:

> Firstly, I came to the university after the revolution. After the coup, I saw a different university. Before the 30th of June 2013, there was freedom and democratic elections were held. I participated in the Student Union. I registered and then I was a candidate for the Student Union. Currently, there is no Student Union because it was canceled. After the coup, when I was in the third year, I went to the Student Affairs Department to participate in the Student Union. They said that the Student Union was appointed by the President of the university (Participant, B 4).

It is a fact that students confirm that after the January 25th Revolution of 2011, democratic practices have increased and become obviously clear at university, with fair elections and free political activities. After what they call as a coup, it is completely different, indicating a state of corruption and dictatorship in all areas. A female Muslim Brotherhood student at the College of Education clarified:

> After the coup, we were surprised that the Dean of the college was appointed. We were also surprised by appointing the Student Union. We wanted to participate in the student activities. The Student Affairs said that the Brotherhood students are forbidden from participating. They are confident that the Brotherhood students have their own achievements inside the college (Participant, B 9).

Moreover, the students also thought that the democratic practice was reduced at the university after the 30th of June 2013 as it has been impacted by the political climate prevailing in Egyptian society. The democratic practices have dimin-

---

[19] The word "coup" according to the students of the Muslim Brotherhood Organization means the events of the 30th June 2013 and the overthrow of President Muhamad Morsi from the rule. The reason for this designation is that the current regime has turned against the legitimacy represented in the character of the elected President.

ished among students and professors. The petitions for re-correcting exam papers have been canceled. The Student Union at the university was also abolished because it was deemed to be the organization of the Brotherhood students as well as suspending the work of the new student regulation. All these actions contributed to the weakening of democratic process at Fayoum University as a direct result of it at the outside community. Things became more complicated with the administration of colleges, which pursued an autocratic and dictatorial path in their relations with students.

Consequently, the authoritarian structure of the university, the confiscation of freedoms, the abolition of the elections of the university leaders, the abolition of student organization, and the separation of the elected Student Union are obviously clear signs of the decline democratic climate at Fayoum University. These results are consistent with the study of Suchlicki (1969). In both studies, democratic practices were declined in the post-revolution era. In Fayoum University, the students attempted to challenge the authoritarian regime, but in Cuba, the students surrendered to the regime which had a strong ideology. Democratic practices are a firm basis for the integration of young people into societies. These autocratic universities with less democratic practices are not desirable for students. They cannot afford to learn in this type of universities. Thus, students develop a social and political awareness to reject the restrictions imposed on them in these universities. This is a highly convincing reason for the waves of rebellion that occurred later.

5.3.1.3 Freedom.

It is deemed as a vital issue that preoccupied the thought of university students in Egypt. The students have expressed their understanding of the term freedom as a primarily political term because personal freedom is almost guaranteed. No one can force a student to wear certain clothes or to eat a specific kind of food. However, the political nature or more precisely the political freedom is what it represents for students at Fayoum University.

Besides, the students expressed the need for providing more freedom in practicing political activities. This is due to their convictions that the university is the ideal place to prepare citizens in an integrated way to become members of a society. It is, therefore, necessary to make political freedom available and not just limited to a specific group with particular orientations. The Independent students' expressions of freedom were as follows:

> Freedom increased after the revolution but within limits. Freedom was curtailed when the resolution was issued to allow the President of the university to call the security forces to end the student riots and demonstration. Small numbers of students who tend to violence interacted violently with other students and the security forces as well. They confused running lectures. As for the decision issued by the Prime Minister, the

security forces remained near to the university to end demonstrations by force. I am sure that if you peacefully express your opinions and views, the university President will not call the police (Participant, D 1).

Additionally, the first blow to democracy was when the Prime Minister issued a decision to allow the university President to summon the security forces when it is necessary. The students believed that the university leadership was over-using this right and attempted to force students to be silent. They also believed that this decision has led many students from the Brotherhood Organization to do violence because it impedes their march and prevents them from conducting any demonstrations or gatherings.

The independent students have affirmed the right of all students with different political orientations to practice their political rights and their activities and express their views freely and democratically. This is because the university is the ideal place to exercise all their rights. Therefore, the university administration must support them and do not stand in the way of their political freedom to express their attitudes and their view of the social events that they live. They also assured that the university administration restricts freedoms and does not support the student political participation. Although the administration of the university was living in isolation from what was happening on campus before the revolution, it was, following the 30th of June 2013, using its power in a counter of the students' political activity. An Independent female student stated:

> The students own the right to organize political activities within the university because if they do not practice politics inside the university, they will practice more violent and dangerous activities outside it. The university administration and the Dean of each college are supposed to be neutral with the students after any political dispute. They are supposed to keep a day devoted to political activities and each one expresses his opinion and talks without any demonstrations (Participant, D 8).

The Pro-Muslim Brotherhood students believe that freedom was guaranteed after the revolution until the events of the 30th of June 2013, which slaughtered democracy. The expressions of the students demonstrate the absence of freedom and the persecution of the security forces and the university leaders against the Muslim Brotherhood students. A Brotherhood student mentioned:

> The area of political freedom after the revolution was excellent. When the coup has occurred, everything returned as before the revolution. They do not want opponents, especially in these days. The Army controlled the state and everyone is afraid to be arrested. Thousands of students are jailed and hundreds died. No, No there is no freedom now (Participant, B 3)

Consequently, the students were demonstrating because there is no enough political freedom after the events of the 30th of June 2013. The numbers of students who were detained and injured in demonstrations are becoming substantial. Although freedom was available after the January 25th Revolution of 2011, it disappeared after the events of the 30ᵗʰ of June 2013. I disagree with the Muslim Brotherhood students because suppression of freedoms began in the era of Muhammad Morsi when the Minister of Higher Education issued a decision in the so-called "Judicial Regulation" under which the university security is entitled to arrest any suspected student. The political differences that have been imposed on the university have led to the suppression of political freedom since the era of Muhammad Morsi.

> I do not see any indication that the university provides political or personal freedom. On the contrary, when the students are demonstrating or a protesting, the security forces shoot them with tear gas. Again, I do not see that the college provides any political freedom to the students. There is no place in the university where you can demonstrate. If you want to protest, the security will take your name and then you will be jailed. Therefore, you will follow the way of demonstrations. Then, the security forces will throw tear gas and end this demonstration by force. There is no kind of political freedom at university now (Participant, B 2).

Many students confirm that freedom does not exist and that the security strongly opposes any individual expressing his or her views. If students are peacefully protesting, the security will arrest them. Where is the political freedom in the university? Therefore, the students assert the need to provide freedom to practice all forms of political activity at the university and giving an opportunity to express their opinions. Because it has a significant role in building the integrated and conscious personality that will promote the homeland. The Independent student stated:

> I prefer to allow practicing activities for all students without any intervention. As for political activity, if it serves the university through increasing political awareness and students can demand their rights and do their duties. However, I reject the subversion side, the demonstrations in the university and if possible, it can be given a limited space (Participant, D 9).

Besides, the students are surprised that the university did not contribute to the development of the students' personalities. According to their perceptions, the university did not provide sufficient political freedom, leadership training for the students, and educating young people the importance of the political work and political competition in a legitimate and legal framework. The university already has this responsibility and if it does not want to do so, at least makes it possible for students to develop and educate themselves politically.

> I see that we should grant political freedom to students but under certain rules. Before providing these practices, an awareness campaign for all students should be held. The university should teach students what politics means? What democracy means? Any How we get in a dialogue among different political orientation? The university administration should illustrate these concepts to students instead of thinking that sabotage is the absolute freedom (Participant, D 6).

> Political freedom and practicing politics are necessary because if a student does not express his view at the university. Where can he do that? If the university does not raise

student's awareness, I can express it in my way and it might be inappropriate (Participant, D 2).

Despite the demands of the Independent students and their convictions that political freedom should be provided in the society in general and in the university in particular, they asked for some rules or restrictions for this freedom to not turn into chaos or not even misunderstood in a way that threatens the society. Thus, freedom is a legitimate right for every individual in a society, and students must adhere to these rights because they will contribute to building their personalities and preparing them for the leadership role in their future. The students feel bitter when talking about political freedom and the lack of sufficient space, especially at the university. This is a proof of the existence of repression, cruelty, and rigidity in dealing with the issues of political freedom due to the exercise of power by suppression for liberties after the sabotage operations carried out by the terrorist groups in Sinai and various places of the state.

However, the question remains what is the guilt of the students in that? The students are victims of such practices. To preserve security, stability, and prevent extremist forces from destabilizing the society, the political activity of students is curbed and political freedom guaranteed by the constitution is eliminated. These visions may show a contradictory position in students' personality between their passion for their country, their concern for its safety, and their right to practice political activities and freedom of expression.

5.3.2 Participation in the Parliamentary and Presidential Elections

Parliamentary elections were a democratic race in Egypt. Although many political and religious forces have controlled the minds of masses through using phrases that tickle feelings and supplies that filled the bellies, they were fair elections that did not involve any manipulation. It contrasts with the 2010 Parliamentary elections, in which the National Democratic Party won with more than 95% of the Assembly's seats. In these elections, the Muslim Brotherhood organization and the Salafis group "al-Noor Party" had considerable participation with a limited percentage of other political parties. These elections witnessed unprecedented participation from all Egyptians believing that in the end, individual's vote had a value and that elections were not manipulated. University students participated in the Parliamentary and the Presidential elections intensively deemed it as fair and democratic elections.

5.3.2.1 The Parliamentary elections.

Discussions and political debates among students at universities increased. Students, in any grouping, addressed the Parliamentary elections and showed the willingness to support one of the political parties in these elections. The Muslim Brotherhood student organization at Fayoum University was the most active and keen to highlight the achievements of candidates and the objectives sought by the organization for the Parliamentary elections.

The majority of political parties and other political organizations also sought to move inside the university. It had a significant deal of propaganda through banners and pamphlets to attract this distinguished group at the university. Because it was a democratic experience, students have sought to participate thoughtfully to select candidates. The voting was mostly for the favor of the Salafis group and the Muslim Brotherhood. This is because of the power of religious discourse in the candidates' conversations and the presence of large numbers of the Brotherhood students at Fayoum University. At that time, I noticed that the students were enThus,iastic about the first Parliamentary elections after the revolution.

Moreover, there have been increasing discussions among students about candidates, their programs, and their ability to serve the constituency. I was once at the university campus and saw a gathering of students in front of the College of Science discussing the candidates' programs for the elections in Fayoum. Most of the students said that their votes would go to the candidates of the Islamic groups, either al-Noor Party or the Muslim Brotherhood, as the superior political group at the moment. These candidates fought against corruption that prevailed under the rule of the former President. Therefore, the students' tendency to participate in these elections was extremely high and positive. The Muslim Brotherhood students participated in the electoral campaigns of the Brotherhood candidates in various constituencies in Fayoum.

5.3.2.2 The Presidential elections.

There was a state of anticipation and anxiety during that time as a result of the political ploys between the Military Council and other political forces, especially the Muslim Brotherhood, al-Noor Party, and the Popular Movement. This period has witnessed significant clamor regarding the candidates for the presidency. Some candidates were excluded because they were charged in cases and others because of their mother's nationality. It became apparently clear that the Presidential elections may not take place because of problems that accompanied it.

This troubled climate has affected professors, students, and the university administration. They began discussions on these political games, the eligibility of each candidate, his chances to win, and his ability to rule the country. The students are divided into many groups, some of them stressed that the ruling power, represented in the Military Junta, wants a particular candidate and, therefore, do these political tricks. Others students said that the ruling regime is working in the interest of the country.

Besides, it was agreed to hold the elections and nominated *Muhammad Morsi, Ahmed Shafiq, Amr Mussa, Hamdeen Sabahy, Muhammad Silim al-ʿAwa*, and *Abdel Moneim Abu-Al-ftuwh*. Electoral propaganda began intensively. *Muhammad Morsi* held his electoral conference at Fayoum Stadium with a massive attendance of the Brotherhood students. On the other hand, *Abdel-Moneim Abu-Al-ftuwh* and *Muhammad Selim al-ʿAwa* came to Fayoum University and met students. Each candidate attempted to co-opt that bloc of youth at the university.

Discussions, seminars, and political conferences that took place in the main hall of Fayoum University have been increased. Students participated in the election propaganda of particular candidates. The students of the Brotherhood also supported *Muhammad Morsi* and the students of Miṣr Al-Qawia supported *Abdel Moneim Abu-Al-ftuwh,* and many other students were distributing some papers concerning the candidate *Amr Mussa*. It is noted that most students were not likely to elect *Ahmed Shafiq* as he was a symbol of the former regime. Thus, voting for him means the return of the former regime and its re-production

Figure 1. The presidential candidate Abdel-Moneim Abu-Al-ftuwh during a meeting with the students at Fayoum University in the presence of the President of the University.

once again. Students participated heavily in the Presidential elections. Despite their division in this round on candidates, all students were agreed not to elect *Ahmed Shafiq* and, therefore, elect *Muhammad Morsi*.

The political participation of students following the January 25th Revolution of 2011 has increased significantly. The students' involvement in politics, participation in elections, and support the presidential candidates have increased. The significant participation rate indicates a fundamental change in the culture of students after the revolution. Therefore, students seem to be more positive and tend to participate in all national and local events whether social or political. Therefore, students became active members of their society.

5.3.3 Student Regulation

The student regulation prepared by students in 2012 is deemed as a bright sign in the history of the student movement at Egyptian universities. The Student Union of the Egyptian Universities issued a regulation of activities and student affairs after a long time of meetings, workshops, and gathering proposals for each college and university. After a while, the Egyptian General Student Union

Figure 2. The presidential candidate Hazim Abu Isma'il with the President of the University during a meeting with the students at Fayoum University.

stated the executive regulations. They expressed their happiness in accomplishing this work, which is represented in the interest of the student community at Egyptian universities. Many students were quoted as saying that the regulation has a deficiency, but the total praised this regulation, whether students of the Muslim Brotherhood or other student organizations. A Brotherhood Student said:

> We prepared the student regulation and stayed for two weeks at Helwan University. Students came from all universities and discussed the student regulation and agreed on it (Participant, B 1).

It is noted that the Brotherhood students are the ones who prepared the student regulation, simply because they are the ones who won the majority of the student union elections at all Egyptian universities. Through the tone of the female student's speech, *"We prepared the student regulation"*, it is obviously clear that she meant that the Brotherhood students who made the regulation. She was supposed to say that students in general who made the regulation because the regulation belonged to all students and any student group have not the right to dominate the work of this regulation. Another Brotherhood student mentioned:

> As I was a member of the Student Union at the College of Dar al-Uloom, the student regulation is a significant achievement for students. This regulation was suitable for achieving the students' aims (Participant, B 2).

It is highly important to mention that the students confirmed that this regulation was a hope for students and one of the most important gains that students got after the January 25th Revolution of 2011. This regulation frames student activities that they wish to do. The rest of students confirmed their happiness with this regulation, although some students were not aware of this regulation claiming that they were not members of the Student Union. The Independent students clarified:

> The students said that we would prepare a student regulation, but I did not feel that. Because the President of the university used the old regulation and what he wanted to do, it would be done. However, after the revolution, they said that students are the ones who change and modify many things in the interest of students. Therefore, the Student Union elections were competitive in which all of them want to participate in the amendment of the student regulation (Participant, D 9).

> I do not have any background about it. I have heard that the regulation has renovations that benefit students (Participant, D 5).

It is obviously clear that the Brotherhood students did not involve other student factions in writing the student regulation at Fayoum University. They presented the proposals of the regulations to the members of the Student Union of each college to write their vision about it. They did not publicly present the suggested regulation to the masses of students to know if the regulation reflects what students want or not. Thus, the Brotherhood students frankly showed a degree of authoritarianism and dictatorship in decision-making. This regulation should have been submitted to the student referendum and not to take a sample of opinions of the Student Union.

Moreover, these actions of the Brotherhood students are closed to what the Office for Consolidation of Unity performed after the Islamic Revolution in Iran. This student group showed authoritarian behaviors against other student fictions at Tehran University (Mashyekhi, 2001). It noted that the religious background of the two organizations (the Office for Consolidation of Unity and the Brotherhood students) was prevalent. This puts us in front of a question, why most religious student organizations act in a toleration manner with other student groups in post-revolutions?

5.3.3.1 The Regulation of freedoms.

Many problems are plaguing the regulation such as the split of the student community on it and the reluctance of some student factions to participate in the preparation of that regulation, whether exclusively or voluntarily. However, the regulation included many items, which from the students' point of view, whether belonging to the Brotherhood or the opponents, has many advantages. The Brotherhood students stated:

> The student regulation included much freedom. Items such as the student, who failed or has low grades in the exam will not be a candidate for the student elections, was deleted (Participant, B 7).

> Some items have been abolished from the old regulation. For example, if you are sick and wants to visit a doctor at a university hospital, you should have a student identification card after paying the study fees. If the student does not have this card, he will not get any cure. The new regulation deleted this item because you will not graduate until you pay all the study fees. Therefore, why the old regulation tries to prevent students from getting treatment? The Egyptian Student Union is the one that worked for students' benefit and it was excellent (Participant, B 7).

Additionally, the students see that modifying many items in the old regulation is one of the positives of the new regulation and a component of student freedom. In the past, the students who failed in the study and were not transferred to the next year were prevented from being candidates for the Student Union elections. These students found this as an obstacle to their candidacy and were amended in the new regulation. The possibility of nominating students who have not paid the tuition fees was also a positive thing. Previously, students were not allowed to nominate for the Student Union elections until paying the tuition fees.

However, the abolition of this item is a positive thing that supports freedom for all students and reserves their right to run for the election of the Student Union. Thus, students have hardly tried to remove the obstacles in front of them through the student regulation. Therefore, the growing awareness among students of their rights, which led them to take the democratic and legal path, is an apparent change in the culture of students after the January Revolution.

5.3.3.2 The Student Affairs Circles and the Regulation.

The student regulation encountered many objections not only from some student groups but also from the Student Affairs Circles at Fayoum University. The Student Affairs Circles were previously responsible for organizing activities, holding elections, trips, and competitions and determining the financial allocations for each student activity. However, students in the new regulation have amended many items related to the financial aspects that prevent Student Affairs Circles from supervising financial matters. Allocating financial for activities are only paid after the signature of the President of the Student Union. A Brotherhood student leader at the College of Education stated:

> The story of the checks, signed by the President of the Student Union to control the financial expenses, was beneficial. There was more freedom in this regulation than the old one. The Student Affairs Circles fight this regulation (Participant, B 7).

Besides, the signature of the President of the Student Union on the payment checks restored the balance to the expenditure on student activities and reduced the chances of stealing these funds according to students' perceptions. For these reasons, the regulation suffered a fierce war from the Student Affairs Circles, which have been working according to the old regulation and extremely excluded the new regulation. This is in addition to the difference between the university leadership, on the one hand, and students, on the other hand, on some items, which the university adminstration asked to correct. A Brotherhood student leader at the College of Dar al-Uloom stated:

> The regulation had some disadvantages, such as the Student Affairs Circles were only represented by a member who dealt with the Student Union and the rest of the staff were not allowed. This was a mistake. The disagreement was on a few items and it was easy to modify and agree, but this did not happen. Despite this, the regulation was passed and was supposed to be implemented, in some Student Affairs Departments; they have not worked according to the new regulation. They worked according to the old regulation. They preferred to use the title of the secretary of the Student Union instead of the President of the Student Union. The distinction between both titles is that the title of President of Student Union has more powers than the title of the secretary of the Student Union. One of the objections is, how can the student sign a check for activities of the union? What is the authority of students to do that? Before the revolution, we heard about thefts in the Student Affairs Circles. They made fraudulent activi-

ties on paper. It was a practical solution that the secretary of the union could sign checks. All praise is to Allah; There is no stealing now (Participant, B 2).

Moreover, the students confirmed that the new regulation helped to control the way of spending money and preventing any attempts to steal the funds of the Student Union by the Student Affairs Officials. Most of the activities, as the Brotherhood students believe, were implemented on paper. Before the issuance of this regulation, spending on student activities did not represent 25% of the money allocated to student activities and the rest is spent as incentives and compensations for the Student Affairs employees. This is a deliberate waste of the student rights and a waste of the public money as well.

However, after the events of the 30ᵗʰ of June 2013, the Muslim Brotherhood students began a process of self-criticism. They believe that the Student Affairs Circles were not represented in a suitable way in the new regulation. There only one member of the Student Affairs is allowed to communicate with the President of the Student Union. This has contributed significantly to increasing the discontent of the Student Affairs Circles in all colleges against the student regulation. The university administration also ran against the student regulation. This was because the Brotherhood students treated with the university administration from a position of power. This did not satisfy the university President or Vice- President at that time. Therefore, they began to raise obstacles and problems aginst the Student Union.

> Before the revolution, each college was allocated a fixed amount of money for the Student Union to spend on activities. After the revolution, the process of allocating money was changed according to the new regulation. At the beginning of the year before the new regulation, a female member of the Student Union of the College of Education inquired about the amount of money allocated for the College of Education. The Student Affairs Official said that the budget of the previous year still existed and this will be allocated for the next year. We knew that the amount of 22,000 Egyptian pound for the College of Education activities for the union and all other activities. If the Student Affairs Circle, at the College of Education, allocates 5,000 Egyptian pounds for the Student Union activities, you would implement trips, exhibitions, and activities throughout the year. At the end of the whole year, at the closing ceremony of the student activities, we asked the Student Affairs Department for 20 Egyptian pounds to buy a banner for announcing the end of activities. They said that the budget was finished. Of course, because you do not know the items of the old regulation, you will not be able to argue him. He will tell you that the budget was 5000 pound and it finished. However, how can you know that? You cannot prove that. In the new regulation, the students were the ones who signed checks for the expenses of the Student Union activities. The idea is that you know how much money the Student Affair Department has? And how much money you spend? The new regulation states that the Student Union is the only responsible for expense money for the students' activities. If the college endowed 20,000 Egyptian pounds and, 5,000 of them for the Student Union will not pay without the signature of the President of Student Union. This is beneficial for students but for the thief is a terrible thing. This affected the Student Affairs Officials (Participant, B 7).

This new regulation bothered the Student Affairs Officials and they fiercely fight it. They found that the powers of the students are increasing significantly and that their role has been marginalized. The responsible of the Student Affairs Department at the College of Education expressed concern about the new regulation and the amount of power granted to the Student Union. Besides, I have tried hard to explain to him the utility of this power in building a broad base of young leaders who will take responsibility for leading the country in the future, but he insisted on his situation and his upset from this regulation.

I have also noted the intransigence of this Student Affairs Officer for not giving me any papers or copies of the new student regulation. I have been intensively seeking for a copy of the new regulation at the Student Affairs Circle both at colleges and at the university, but I did not find it. Because of their rejection of this regulation, which is contrary to their interests in controlling the money of the Student Union by their perceptions and instructions received by them? They hid the new regulation and worked according to some items in the old regulation. This is an internal feeling of rejection and resistance to this regulation in different ways.

This is normal in the post-revolution era. Given the state of conflict that the Egyptian state has experienced in this transitional period, especially the internal conflicts in the state's institutions, some of these circles are of a conservative nature that fighting all procedures and laws aimed to development and freedom. These institutions have become resistant to change that harm their interests. They have, therefore, lost sight of the distinction between their institutional interests and the public interest of the state. This result was consistent with what happened at the Czech Universities after the Velvet Revolution. Mauch (1994) showed that there are some departments and circles at the university were anti-change.

5.3.3.3 The Regulation and the Constitution.

Many students have stated that the new student regulation has confronted many objections from the students on one hand and from the administration and the Student Affairs Circles on the other hand. This is similar to what happened to the new constitution prepared by the Muslim Brotherhood who has received intense criticism and opposition because the Muslim Brotherhood is the ones who have legislated it. They considered it the Brotherhood's Constitution. A Brotherhood student mentioned:

> I explained the regulation on a general level. I came to the university after the revolution. The elections occurred in the country and I chose the President and everything was finished. Ok, if we have a deep understanding and awareness that I agree with the new president or I disagree with him, he has four years as a president and afterward, the presidential election can be held. The university administration claimed that there

some phrases in the new regulation that are insulting them. The Student Affairs Departments fought the regulation because some members were part of the former regime and others are opponents to the new regime (the Brotherhood regime). They fought because the student faction that took control over the elections and then ruling are opposed to them. Whether the regulation has some accomplishments or not they will fight it. In my opinion, I applied what happened to the regulation on what the Constitution confronted. The Constitution has been fought as the student regulation has been fought (Participant, B 2).

The students rationally and logically connect between what happened to both the student regulation and the Egyptian Constitution prepared by the Muslim Brotherhood when they were in power. As the Constitution has all this opposition from the other political forces such as the Delegation Party, the dignity party, leftists, liberals that constitute the political map in Egypt. At the university, the student forces such as the Salafis, leftists, and Miṣr Al-Qawia opposed the new regulation because the Muslim Brotherhood's monopoly on preparing the regulation. This ideological conflict remained until the fall of the Brotherhood's regime and, thus, the constitution and the student regulation was suspended.

Consequently, students had lost a student regulation containing various clauses of freedoms and powers for the Student Union. The reason for this was the exclusion policy used by the organization of the Muslim Brotherhood students, as well as the policy of intimidation of the other student forces inside Fayoum University. These forces believe that the Brotherhood students are trying to put the regulation according to their policies whatever students agree with them or not because what they want is what they will do. Thus, the student regulation has failed in the second democratic test for the students after the Student Union elections. It proved its failure, or in other words, it was thwarted until the students fall prey to the demagogy and administrative bureaucracy prevailing in the minds of the university leaders in Egypt.

5.3.4 Student Union Elections

It is significant to assert that the Student Union elections are one of the most prominent manifestations of the student political activity at Fayoum University after the revolution. Fayoum University has allowed the establishment of fair elections in a framework of freedom and democracy and under the full supervision of the faculty members. The first Student Union elections were immediately after the revolution in 2011 and the second Student Union election was in 2012. These elections reflected a change in the situation of the Egyptian society and the inception of a new era of democracy and active participation of all student groups at the university.

Additionally, the Student Union elections at Fayoum University represented an example of real democracy, openness, and freedom of expression. The stu-

Figure 3. The students are voting in the Student Union elections at the College of Science.

dents from different intellectual and political orientations have participated in the elections and the university allowed electoral propaganda and other administrative procedures that contributed to the success of these elections. The participants described their views towards these elections as the following:

> I was happy that the elections were held because it is evident that there is a change (Participant, D 2).

> The election period was quite nice through which I felt that the college had a spirit. Every candidate wanted to reach to students and get the votes. I remember in the elections; we were from 8, 00 A.M., until the end of sorting out the votes in the night (Participant, D 6).

> It was the first time that I know what elections mean in front of my eyes. It was allowed to attend the sorting process even if you are not a candidate (Participant, D 7).

> The elections after the revolution were good in everything. If we speak about freedom, we can highlight every positive thing such as the student activities. The elections were transparent and fair (Participant, D 10).

The elections were fair and transparent based on my field observations and the expressions of the participants. The participants stressed that it was a fantastic and positive period that gave them a sense of hope and optimism to the extent that one of the students regarded it as the first fair elections he has witnessed. Indeed, these elections have witnessed unrivaled participation from students. This pleasant experience was engraved in the minds of the students.

Fayoum University has adequately provided all the available resources to get the elections. As for the students of the Muslim Brotherhood, their perceptions and attitudes towards the Student Union elections were positive. They agreed with the rest of the Independent students. This is due to the integrity and the transparency of these elections. Moreover, the Muslim Brotherhood's won most of the Student Union elections, which made their attitudes positive towards the student elections.

The Student Union elections were honestly conducted in all colleges. The students took their right because some students were prevented from running for the Student Union elections. They began to enter the student union and participated in providing activities (Participant, B 1).

Before the revolution, the Student Union elections were for the students who were supported by the university administration and were known for the security forces. They usually succeed in the elections. The first-time fair election took place in the university was after the January 25th Revolution of 2011. The majority was the Brotherhood students because they are more organized and experienced in the political work (Participant, B 6).

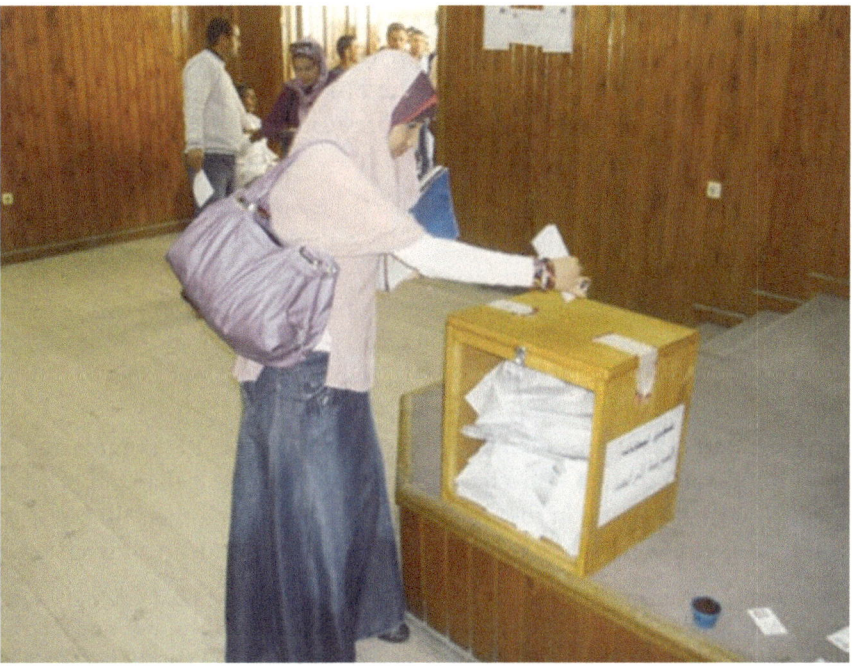

Figure 4. A female student is voting in the Student Union elections at the College of Education.

In a nutshell, the government at this time has given the Student Union elections a special importance. It sought a great deal towards the adoption of the democratic practices in that period in Egypt. Besides, the Student Union elections were the living experience, a principal, and an honest indicator of the electoral process in the Egyptian state that will be held in the next stage.

5.3.4.1 The participants in the elections.

The percentage of participation in the Student Union elections at Fayoum University was significantly high. The turnout was historic in voting. The elections were held directly in the post-revolution era, while the students were thrilled to win over the old regime. All student groups were also allowed for the first time to participate in the Student Union elections. Factual data showed the multiplicity of the student factions participating in these elections. The student factions included the Muslim Brotherhood, the Salafis movement, Miṣr Al-Qawia, Leftist students, and the Independent students who participated heavily in these elections.

Moreover, they were the majority of the student factions that submitted to the Student Union elections in the 2011as well as in 2012. Thus, the students of the religious organizations as the Muslim Brotherhood and the Salafis movement managed to win the majority of the Student Union election. They obtained more than 90% of the votes. The expressions of the Brotherhood participants illustrated this proposition:

> The Salafis and the Brotherhood students in the College of Dar al-Uloom were contestants. Therefore, they wanted to take over all the seats, even if the candidates have no skills (Participant, B 10).

> We have been running the elections twice in the last of 2011 and 2012 when I was a new student in the first year and the second year. The atmosphere after the revolution was open. All colleges allowed students to express their views and demands freely (Participant, B 4).

Despite the participation of many students in this democratic event at the university, some students are still characterized by negative behaviors. They abstained from participating in the student elections claiming their illness or travel or the difficulty of satisfaction of all parties. An Independent student stated:

> I did not participate in the election within the university because I did not find a suitable candidate in the Student Union elections inside the university. I was sure that all the candidates would not achieve anything for the students. They wanted only to take control of the student union and gain a social prestige in the university (Participant, D 9).

> I did not participate in these elections because I was late to come to the college. I did not want any candidates to ask why you did not vote for me (Participant, D 5).

154

However, many students refused to participate in the Student Union elections because the majority of candidates were the Muslim Brotherhood, the Salafis, and Miṣr Al-Qawia students. According to what they said, they believed that the Independent students or the students of religious organizations would not achieve their goals and demands. Therefore, they insisted on not voting in these elections, due to the lack of confidence in any of the candidates and the entire electoral process and because of their previous negative experience in the election process, where the success of students depends on the security assistance.

5.3.4.2 *The mechanisms of advertising and propaganda in the Student Union elections.*

The students of Fayoum University successfully organized impressive campaigns for the Student Union elections. The students showed an intellectual maturity in addition to enormous creative energy in creating new methods for publicizing the elections. Also, they used many tools of advertising including the establishment of electoral conferences, banners, and pamphlets. Additionally, the students used social media (Facebook, Twitter, and YouTube) and prepared electoral programs and presented them to students on the Facebook pages and after lectures.

1. organizing electoral conferences. The students held a massive electoral conference and who took the lead in preparing this conference was the Muslim Brotherhood students. They set up a large theater in the middle of the university campus and invited all candidates; of course, belonging to the Muslim Brotherhood, independent candidates, and some other student groups to present their electoral programs. This is in addition to conducting discussions and debates between the candidates on their electoral programs and the activities that they attempt to achieve through the Student Union. A female Muslim Brotherhood student at the College of Education stated:

> One day, we organized a conference in the middle of the university and we have all the candidates in the elections lists. We presented our programs and our point of view. The other students also attended the conference. It was a reasonably successful conference. We had a feeling of happiness because the Student Union elections were real and effective elections as the assembly elections. The students did not witness a democratic and fair election for thirty years. This was achieved in this year after the January 25th Revolution of 2011 (Participant, B 1).

Additionally, the students invested the space of freedom guaranteed at the university after the revolution in creating electoral methods to help them in the election rally. The preparation of these conferences, the permits, and the approvals from the university administration and the substantial cost of these conferences may represent challenges for the students. However, these difficulties did not affect the students' desire to succeed the Student Union elections. The students equated those elections with the elections of the Assembly and the Consultative Council. The revolution made the students feel optimism and this has increased the degree of their belonging to their country. A brotherhood student leader mentioned:

> There was a student conference at the university and we participated in it. In the beginning, it represented a particular student faction. The participation among students was very high. There were ethical values prevalent among students at that time. We wanted the administration to help us to keep these values on the university campus (Participant, B 2).

However, the Muslim Brotherhood students were the ones who prepared and established this student conference. Although the invitation was directed to other student groups to participate in the electoral conference, the candidates of the Brotherhood students were the only group who presented their electoral programs. This indicated the degree of competition and lack of cooperation between student bodies in post-revolution.

2. banners and posters. Other students used banners and posters to display their pictures in order that the students could know them. The students also presented a brief description of their curriculum vitae and the details of the electoral program for each candidate in small pamphlet or brochure to give it to the students on campus and in lectures. The students aimed at mobilizing a big number of students to vote for them. A female Brotherhood student stated that:

> We have made banners with the students' names, a biography of each candidate, and the electoral program for every candidate (Participant, B 1).

> The most prominent were banners for the candidates. The candidate gives students pamphlet for the activities that he wants to do in the future (Participant, B 4).

> The students used banners which were better than what it was used in the Assembly elections. In each studying hall, a small piece of paper was printed with some influential words on it (Participant, B 5).

Moreover, the Independent students have relevant views about the tools of advertising in their colleges. Their views are compatible with the Brotherhood students. They have stated that:

> As for the students of the College of Social Work, they made all banners by themselves. Every candidate made his banners. Many posters were stuck on the college's walls (Participant, D 4).

> The students made banners, electoral programs, invitation cards, and goals for the electoral campaign (Participant, D 2).

Consequently, these methods had considerable value in mobilizing students for the electoral process despite the low of its cost and the simplicity of its idea. The students used the entrances of the colleges to hang paper on them. The administration of the colleges did not allocate specific places for students to paste paintings and means of election propaganda. The students were also supposed to consider the aesthetically of the colleges and not to hang elections' posters and banners on the walls of the college. It is noted that there are some banners, which did not show the photos of some students, especially girls.

This method is basically related to the Salafis students, whose members refuse to show the photos of female students. According to them, this is a religious obligation and cannot be waived in any way. In addition, some of the students who are candidates on the Brotherhood elections list are afraid to be combined with the Brotherhood because they are not organizationally affiliated to the Brotherhood. The phrases of the Brotherhood students are indicative of this:

> Some student candidates in our electoral list are not Brotherhood students, but they wanted to participate with us. When we asked them to put their photos on the banners, they said no. However, there was a picture of girls on our banners. We do not have any problems that a girl appears with her face (Participant, B 1).

> Some female students did not agree to put their photos on the banners. Her name is known among students. A certain faction "Salafis" meant that the girls were Salafis (Participant, B 2).

Figure 5. Blocking the female students' photos on the election banners.

It is worth noted that the ideology of the religious groups has not changed after the revolution. They consider displaying females' photos on the electoral banners as immoral and should be rejected. These ideas and customs did not change even after the dawn of freedom and democracy in the sky of Egypt, but they did not realize it. Additionally, some students were afraid of linking with the Muslim Brotherhood and to be known by the security and are constantly subjected to harassment later. This is compatible with the study of Mashyekhi (2001). The Male students at the Iranian universities showed increasing conservative views towards equality with the female students. The religious background may also be the reason for this conservative outlook and practices.

Alternatively, the pattern of rising children and discrimination between male and female in these conservative societies is still a factor for these practices. Students also believe that displaying photo of the girl on the electoral lists is socially unacceptable especially since the place where the students came from is a rural center, interspersed with customs and traditions that diminish the value of women and make them as junk in themselves. These are the areas where religious groups are widely spread and conservative ideas are existed.

3. advertising via Facebook. The students used modern means of communication, especially social networks, in the Student Uunion elections for the first time in 2012. The candidates posted their electoral programs on the Facebook pages. All student candidates from different student groups published their photos, election list, and electoral programs. Social media such as the Facebook was used widely in the Student Union elections at Fayoum University because of being free and most students have accounts on the Facebook. Therefore, the candidate ensures that many students will know about his electoral program.

Moreover, these technological devices are highly speeding in sending messages and comments and the possibility of responding in a few seconds with freedom. Facebook is also the suitable way for female students who do not want to talk to male students and invite them to vote in the elections. Talking through the Facebook's comments will be suitable for her beliefs and ideas than talking to students face to face on campus. I browsed many Facebook pages for the Brotherhood and the Salafis students. The students received a vast amount of comments regarding their electoral programs. I was surprised by this intensive interaction between candidates and the voters.

4. speaking to students orally. In addition to using social media in the election propaganda, the candidates did not neglect to talk with students face to face on campus or after lectures in order to encourage students to vote for them. This tool also has a significant influence on students. A female Brotherhood student mentioned:

> We worked on an individual and collective side. For the personal side, we wanted to raise the student awareness by talking with them (Participant, B 1).

Moreover, the Brotherhood students adopting methods of dialogue and persuasion has had a significant impact on changing the attitudes and convictions of students regarding the Student Union election. Additionally, the exploitation of student groups for lectures and presenting electoral programs for candidates to familiarize students with candidates and their programs. Besides, they answered any questions regarding their programs or services that students seek to provide. Therefore, the answer is quick and persuasion is easy. A Brotherhood student Leader at the College of Dar al-Uloom clarified:

> We orally talked to students and gave them our brochures and electoral lists. We aimed that the students know our names, departments, and programs. We displayed our programs and invited students to elect us as a complete list. It was a fierce competition (Participant, B 2).

Additionally, the Independent candidates who entered the elections have followed the same approach in individual and collective propaganda. They used the same means of election propaganda and this was due to the lack of their experience in the electoral process. They also have perceptions that the Muslim Brotherhood students are the most organized and experienced group in managing electoral process. In fact, they had to do the same work as the Brotherhood candidates do to ensure students' votes.

> I usually enter the studying hall after a professor ends his lecture. I speak to students, I am a candidate for the Student Union elections and who see me a suitable candidate, supports me and gives me his vote. Other candidates hand out pamphlets about their electoral program, including activities and trips. The students of the Salafis group applied the same method to the Individual student propaganda along with mass propaganda. The students of the Salafis group imagined that candidate must have scientific excellence and good morals to win the confidence and voice of the students (Participant, B 10).

> I introduced my electoral program with the whole election list. We usually come ten minutes before the beginning of a lecture and display our electoral program to students at the studying hall speedily and fluently. We gathered all on the podium ten minutes before a lecture. The students had chosen us on that basis (Participant, B 10).

It is apparently clear that the student organizations that competed in the student union elections, at Fayoum University, used the same methods of the election propaganda. And there is no distinction between them except by the strength of the Brotherhood student organization, who had a stable organizational structure at Fayoum University and considerable experience in the election process. However, the primary question remains how these student organizations provide money to spend on the election propaganda? We can assume that these groups such as the Muslim Brotherhood, Miṣr Al-Qawia, and the Salafis movement provided financial resources from their parties outside the university.

> The Independent candidates were mostly providing money by themselves. In entities such as the Salafis group and the Brotherhood, it is possible to finance them from their parties outside the university. The Salafis have their party and they give them money as well as the Brotherhood group does (Participant, B 2).

This is because the cost of advertising for student entities is higher than the cost for individuals. Students can outsource funding from the parent organization "Brotherhood and Salafis". Thus, they can reap a more significant number of votes and control the Students Union. The victory of Students Union is the ultimate gain for the Salafis and the Brotherhood organizations because it ensures a legitimate power within the decision-making centers of Fayoum University. It also helps them to provide services to students intensively and influencing the student community.

5.3.4.3 Candidate and the selection criteria (list vs. individual).

The student elections were mainly characterized by transparency, fairness, and high turnout in the voting process. The electoral list, of course, helped one or more student factions to control the student union. Besides, it may also contain some individuals who are not eligible for the elections, but they may succeed because they belong to specific student groups such as the Brotherhood or the Salafis. Each student faction has drawn up its list of candidates for the Student Union elections.

The list included students outside the group. Moreover, most of the students were in the first and second years in colleges. This is a remarkable change in the mentality of students. They are becoming more positive and willing to participate efficiently in the state's issues. However, many students have criticized the electoral list system even the Brotherhood students:

> Unfortunately, the two student groups were not open to the students. All the students who believe in the Salafis thought are gathered in one electoral list. The Brotherhood has the same way (Participant, B 10).

> Some candidates were nominated as independent and others were nominated for lists.

> Some of the students who were included in our electoral list were not Muslim Brotherhood. We had them because they wanted to participate with us (Participant, B 9).

In fact, the students were aware of the disadvantages of the lists system which separated students from each other and increased intolerance among them. This is because they will elect the ideas of a particular student faction regardless the students who represent this trend. There has also been an intellectual closure as a result of raising the ideas of the organization followed by the students and not to include any students who are not believers in the ideas of the organization.

It is obviously clear that the political leadership at that time had given the Student Union elections particular importance because it deemed it as an experiment of the lists system, which have been used at a later stage in the elections of the Parliament Assembly and the Consultative Council. It also resulted in the superiority of one or two factions in the total number of seats in the Parliament election. The decision makers should have carefully studied the student elections so that they could understand the results of their selection of the electoral system during the electoral process.

5.3.4.4 Criteria for selecting candidates.

Despite students' happiness of holding the first elections in a fair and a democratic manner, the process of selecting candidates had many shortcomings that left adverse effects on the overall picture of the elections. The selection criteria for students, either on the lists or the individual system, are based on personal knowledge of candidates. This is in addition to the intellectual and organizational affiliation of the student group expressed by the candidate in the list. The Independent students mentioned:

> There were compliments in choosing candidates at these elections. I have chosen my companions because I know them. No one had a clear electoral program and even if it exists, it will not be implemented (Participant, D 9).

Additionally, friendship and personal relations are among the most common criteria which the students deemed them as a basis for their choice of candidates because of the absence of reliable electoral programs. The students believe that in the case of strong electoral programs, they will not be implemented. Frustration still dominates some students. They imagine that students will not have the opportunity to carry out their electoral promises by providing services and activities to students. Another Independent student at the College of Education stated:

> The criteria I choose were by two things as a friend or a robust electoral program. If my friend in the college asks to vote for him in the election, I will do because he is my friend. There were high expectations among candidates for having votes based on the relationships with their colleagues. This has affected the student elections negatively (Participant, D 3).

The pro-Muslim Brotherhood students expressed the criteria that they adopted for selecting a candidate. They stated that the electoral program, the services, and activities he will provide and the ability to implement the program are the main criteria. They mentioned:

> The situation that each family or student faction has nominated one candidate or one election list. Some students choose from many electoral lists and others chose just one electoral list. I elected by the individual and the ability to achieve the objectives of the

electoral program. We were the only college among all colleges that were carefully selected and elected candidates. We see religious groups were not perfect in everything. The other groups which include the socialist with the Secular and Independent were not also perfect (Participant, B 5).

Some students are not belonging to the Brotherhood and were nominated in our election list. We see that she is successful in her study and well known among her colleagues. She also has acceptance among students. Therefore, we choose her to join us on our election list (Participant, B 1).

The courtesies were one of the standers upon which the candidates have been chosen. The personal knowledge of candidates has overcome the objective choice based on the candidate's abilities or an electoral program that he seeks to achieve. This proves that the tribal system still prevails and governs the electoral system in general, whether it is Parliamentary elections or the Student Union elections. Thus, this system will produce inactive members who implement the ideas and directions of the faction that helped them to succeed in the elections.

The Student Union elections witnessed a considerable polarization of ineffective student elements, but they are characterized by academic excellence and an academic status among students. Because, the Muslim Brotherhood students have attracted students, who characterized by scientific excellence and acceptance among their colleagues, they added them to their electoral lists and, thus, achieved gains to the Muslim Brotherhood students. Additionally, with this policy, the Muslim Brotherhood students attempted to enhance their image at Fayoum University and push the negative image mixed with extremism and the desire to control the Student Union. They also aimed to hide the idea of intolerance to the thoughts of the Brotherhood organization and people who carry their thought. Involving students who are not Brotherhood will help to obtain a large number of votes as a result of the nomination of the outstanding students who are characterized by their ethics. Besides, these students represent a significant attraction for the rest of students to elect them as a result of their academic excellence. Thus, the list earns many electoral votes to win the election.

5.3.5 Demonstrations and Student Violence.

The wave of demonstrations that swept Egypt after the fall of Mubarak's regime in February 2011 called for reconstructing the state through activating freedom, social justice, and respect human dignity. The youth of the Tahrir Square and the revolutionary forces continued in holding demonstrations to complete the aims of the revolution. Demands for democracy, a civil state, the return of smuggled money, and trial of Mubarak's regime were the main aims of the demonstrations. As a result of this general feeling of hope and optimism, students organized massive demonstrations at all Egyptian universities demanding educational reforms and students' political and social rights. In Fayoum University, the students of the College of Engineering supported faculty members in their strike to dismiss the Dean of the college or, more precisely, urged him to resign to start elections of the college's deanship. At that time, the elections of the deanship were held at Fayoum University. A Brotherhood student at the College of Engineering stated:

> Dr. *Hazim 'Attiah*, who taught us the meaning of the word elections, said to us that we want to remove the Dean of the college and afterward running an election for selecting another Dean (Participant, B 5).

The students participated in the faculty members' strike to hold the elections of the college deanship. This was a definite indicator of change in student culture. It also proves that the students are an active component of the university community and that their marches are always in support of justice and freedom. This illustrates how the concept of demonstration transmitted to the students through what the faculty members did. They are considering demonstration as a legitimate tool to restore their rights. The students used demonstrations to press on the university administration to release their fellow detainees or to demand improvements in educational services. In another context, there were protest vigils of students from different colleges such as the College of Science, the College of Arts, and the College of Education to reduce the prices of text books.

The students have sought to reduce the prices of the textbooks and to increase the university fund for printing textbooks. Students often stand in front of the adminstration building of the College for protest. Moreover, students have taken many steps to recognize their rights in attending the process of recorrections exam paper and attending a personal session with the examiner during reviwing and recorrecting answer sheet. Another group of students at the College of Education held a protest in front of the Dean's office. The students wanted to urge the Dean not to transfer the director of the Student Affairs Department Mr. *Zakaria 'Antar* whom many students trust and respect him because he is close to the students and provides help to all students. This is because the College's Vic-Dean at that time, Dr. *Murad ṣaleh* insisted on transferring Mr. *Zakaria* from the College of Education. The reason was an administrative mistake in the score sheet for a female student at the third year in the Department of Arabic Language. The college administration and the Student Affairs Department have participated in this mistake. A Brotherhood student leader at the College of Education clarified:

> Mr. *Zakaria* is a respected and a cooperative man. He advised all students. He was close to all students. Mr. *Zakaria* had charity activities for all students and even for Christian students. The students presented an appeal to the Dean to keep Mr. *Zakaria* in the College as a director of the Student Affairs Department. Mr. *Zakaria* is working now at the College of Arts and his first year, the students deemed him as a brother. The problem

was an administrative mistake that was committed by the test committee for a female student. They were wrong and Mr. *Zakria* was the victim to hide this problem (Participant, B 7).

However, the laws are still reversed and some rules at the university need to be modified. In the course of that, the students gathered and wrote a petition signed by more than twenty students from various academic departments at the College of Education and the Dean promised not to transfer Mr. *Zakaria*, but he did not implement his promise. Mr. *Zakaria* has been moved to the same job at the College of Arts and many students of the College of Education in different academic departments are always in contact with Mr. *Zakaria ʿAntar*. They go to meet him at his office in the College of Arts at Fayoum University.

5.3.5.1 Demonstrations.

A) The nature of the demonstrations. The students' perceptions of the demonstrations and their awareness of their constitutional right to demonstrate, will determine the way in which students use this tool in expressing their legitmate rights. After the January 25th Revolution of 2011, the space of political freedom and democracy has increased. The students of Fayoum University demanded more democracy and freedom. They expressed their views about protest and demonstrations consciously and courageously despite their differentiation in their political affiliation and religious background. The students who are not belonging to any intellectual or political group have expressed their perceptions objectively about the demonstrations as follow:

> It is not a problem that they are organizing demonstrations. The most important thing is that they express their opinions. I reject a specific thing or action in the political system; I suppose to express my views through demonstration in the place that I work or study in. Is there any evidence that the demonstration was not peaceful? Did the students destroy any infrastructure at the university or outside? If the answer is no. Why you attack them? I express my ideas that may peacefully reject the policies of the regime. Therefore, why the university deals in a non-peaceful way with the students? (Participant, D 8).

Additionally, the students are aware of their rights to hold demonstrations in order to express their views whether by rejecting policies or by supporting the regime in its ongoing policies. The important part is not to destroy buildings, harm people or to use tools that threaten the lives of students. The best place for demonstrations from the students' point of view is the university because it is a citadel for freedom and a platform for sound democratic practice. It is also the place that trains them and teaches them the freedom of expression.

> I believe that the peaceful and legal methods are the best and most suitable to achieve the students' demands. The demonstrations did not achieve the goals of the students because the security forces broke it up. However, when my colleagues and I sit with

the university officials and ask for our demands, they should understand the students' situation and demands. If they refuse our demands, we should ask about the reasons. Sometimes they may convince by our speech and sometimes not. In this case, you must follow the system at the university (Participant, D 9).

Emphasis on the peaceful nature of demonstration is the prevailing opinion among the masses of the students whatever their political and ideological affiliations. Due to the hard intervention of the security forces in the student demonstrations, most Independent students do not find it useful to carry out these demonstrations because of the brutally of the security. They see the need to start a peaceful process by meeting the officials and the university leadership to presenting their demands for them to solve. In case of rejection, the university leadership must explain the reasons for that. The students find demonstrations as the only outlet to express their frustration over fascist policies of the regime against opponents. They understand that peaceful protest is guaranteed to all, as long as it does not damage lives and property.

> The students have the energy of anger and they want to discharge it. They are acting in a wrong way. It supposed to organize a peaceful demonstration not to sabotage or disrupt the study. However, the students are not acting in the same way. Therefore, demonstrations turned from peaceful to violence because the students have faced violence from the security forces. The security forces are now inside the university. It is not normal that the police wear the formal clothes. It is possible to wear informal clothes and he is a military officer (Participant, D 2).

Many students tend to violence and riot and this is a result of certain pattern of education for some groups in Egyptian society, which tend to use force in the face of its political opponents. Some religious groups, such as *"Al-Jihad"*, the Islamic group, and the Muslim Brotherhood are an obviously clear example of this type which follows the views of *"Sayyid Qutb"* in his famous book*"Mᶜallem Ala Al-Tarik"* which means landmarks on the road. Many researchers on the religious movements stated that this book is the constitution on which all religious movements adopt its ideas. The violent handling by the security forces, the excessive use of force, arrests, and raids against students forced them to take a violent course in dealing with their opponents.

Therefore, the relationship in the political sphere at the university takes the form of conflict (power/resistance). The ruling regime with the university administration imposes his vision, purposes, and terminology about the events that followed the events of the 30th of June 2013. They tried to justify some events and to show some student groups in a non-national manifestation. On the contrary, the Muslim Brotherhood students are trying to present a different view of the issues and events that followed the revolution. A female Brotherhood student at the College of Education stated:

> The civil security reported our colleagues to the police. There are reasons why we committed violence? Ok, you call it violence, but what about rape and murder of students? An enemy is fighting us violently, so what can we do? The people who were beaten and

their office were burned reported the students who are arrested without any fault. The security forces arrested students in the midnight from the student dormitories. We wanted to punish them and to tell them, 'You will never break us. This is just a sign of punishment, but if we do violence, it will be more than that. We can force them to stay at home and not to go out (Participant, B 1).

The students participating in the demonstrations see the security forces as the cause of the violence waves at Fayoum University. From their point of view, the police pushed them to act violently by repeated arrests of students, shooting tear gases, and rubber bullets on demonstrations and the attempt to break demonstration up by force. The Muslim Brotherhood students link between actions of rape, arrest, shoots students, and their violent behaviors.

You will not lose the right if you are continually demanding it. This is just a reaction, not real violence. We did not begin violence yet. We react to the violence (shooting or gas bombs from the security forces) by just throwing a stone or fireworks. Moreover, this is a small thing compared to what the security forces do. This is just a reaction (Participant, B 1).

The Brotherhood students believe that demonstrations are their legitimate right and they are insisting on the return of their stolen rights. Namely, the return of the legitimate regime, the release of the Muslim Brotherhood students, and the trial of murderers who killed thousands in *Rab'ah and Al-Nahdah* were the crucial demands. The students affirm that what they are doing is nothing but a reaction to violence. This is a definite proof of the hardness of these student organizations and their ability to surprise the security forces through massive violent actions. The response to the aggression of the security forces by throwing stones may be a start for using more potent tools if the security forces continue to deal in this way.

Demonstrations are not the primary objective. The major aim is to increase the student's awareness and to fight injustice. If I walk down in the street and someone stole my handbag. If I stay silent, the thief will escape with my bag. However, if I scream a thief stole my handbag, the people who walk in the street will punish him. In this case, my handbag will be returned (Participant, B 9).

We want people outside the university to know that the university students reject the current regime. It is our right to reject anything at the university, such as certain curricula, university book, and our right to protest (Participant, B 8).

The Brotherhood students see demonstrations as the only way to respond to the aggression of the security forces and to demand the stolen rights. They also wanted to inform the outside community that the university students reject what is happening in the society. All revolutionary forces must rally around the student to overthrow this brutal regime. We can assert that the students from different political backgrounds believe that the demonstrations are a legitimate right. The difference between them is that the Muslim Brotherhood students do not mind responding to the aggression by the security forces, while the rest of the students reject violent practices. This is because it threatens the lives of the students and leads to disruption of the educational process and chaos in the university.

B) The causes of the student demonstrations. There are many reasons for the student demonstrations at Fayoum University, some demonstrations related to the political aspects and others related to the student's rights, educational demands, and society issues. Among the prominent reasons for the student demonstrations at Fayoum University are:

1. the Constitutional Amendments. The beginning of the political demonstrations was since the adoption of the Constitutional Amendments. The referendum was held on a set of articles in the Egyptian Constitution that are related to the period and criteria of a presidential candidate, judicial supervision of the elections, appointing a deputy for the President, and setting a committee to draft a new Constitution after the Parliamentary elections. These Amendments have been followed by wide discussions and conflicts among the political forces on its validity. The radical forces supported those amendments to the extent that one of the leaders of these organizations described that those who voted for these amendments, they chose the religion and who voted against them are the Secularists.

Therefore, the students of Fayoum University have been divided into two major groups regarding these Constitutional Amendments. Demonstrations and rallies for supporting these amendments began by the Muslim Brotherhood, the Salafis, and Miṣr Al-Qawia students who believed in the correctness of these Amendments. On the other hand, there have been some marches aiming to raise awareness of students to reject these amendments because they do not have many benefits and will be in the interest of the firm organization such as the Brotherhood and Salafis. The opponents of these amendments believed that we need a new Constitution that reflects all visions and orientations of Egyptians. This was the beginning of the rift in the student community at Fayoum University.

2. overthrowing the Muslim Brotherhood regime. Egyptian society witnessed a state of tension due to the Parliamentary and Presidential elections and the efforts of the revolutionary forces to attract most of the voters to enter the Parliament. Therefore, the wave of criticism to the Muslim Brotherhood has increased regarding its inability to fulfill the electoral promises and the President's failure to manage the country. The Brotherhood regime was unable to solve the problems that existed in Egypt or were raised by the Counter-Revolution.

Additionally, this political scene, at that time, impacted the university regarding dividing students into two opposing blocks. The first group has opposed the stay of the president in the rule because he is not able to lead a central state in the region like Egypt. The other group supported the President and stressed the existence of obstacles that prevented him from carrying out his full duties. Additionally, the former regime's figures made many crises to force people to overthrow the elected President. The situation did not last long. Therefore, the divisions increased among students and they came out to organize demonstrations for demanding the departure of Muhammad Morsi and other demonstrations for supporting him. An Independent female student mentioned:

> Demonstrations, of course, started again at the University under the rule of Muhammad Morsi. After 7 or 8 months, people began to demonstrate because of the presence of rebellion movement *"Harakit Tamarrud"*. People wanted to overthrow Muhammad Morsi. Demonstrations began at the university calling for the impeachment of Muhammad Morsi. On the contrary, the demonstrations supporting the Brotherhood President began by the Brotherhood students and other religious movements. The demonstrations in that period, especially before the events of the 30th of June, were not violent. There were peaceful demonstrations. There was only a limited amount of insults. The security forces did not exist at the university at that time. Therefore, there was no danger (Participant, D 8).

The state of discontent from the Brotherhood regime has been increased by the criticism of opponents, especially through the media. They launched a sharp criticism which aroused the resentment of people from the ruling regime. The rebel movement*"Tamarrud"*has also contributed significantly to raise voices called for the ousting of Muhammad Morsi. There were also demonstrations in support of Muhammad Morsi. This conflict between the student groups has exacerbated the rift in the student community. Moreover, it increased the tensions and quarrels between different student organizations regarding the future of the Brotherhood regime in that period. One of the students who witnessed the revolution and the events before and after the revolution at university said that the demonstrations before the January 25th Revolution have rarely occurred.

> There were a few demonstrations before the revolution. From time to time, the Brotherhood students organized marches on the issues of *Al-Masjid Al-Aqsay*, the case of Palestine and the support for the *Intifada*. They clashed with the security forces only by speech. After the revolution, the demonstrations increased dramatically due to the political situation. After the revolution, marches started after the Constitutional Amendments. At the time of Muhammad Morsi, there were demonstrations against his rule. The Brotherhood supported Muhammad Morsi with marches and demonstrations (Participant, D 2).

The students of the Muslim Brotherhood before the revolution had experience in organizing demonstrations, which criticized the regime for not supporting Palestine. The students of the Brotherhood organization also held demonstrations to support the regime of *Muhammad Morsi* during the rule of the Brotherhood in response to the demonstrations against the anti-*Muhammad Morsi*, which demanded to drop him. As a consequence of the toppling of the elected

President, the Brotherhood students rushed to hold mass demonstrations to press the regime to bring back the elected President. The students were disappointed by the toppling of the President. The Muslim Brotherhood students accused the Army and the security forces of overthrowing the President. Correspondingly, the overthrow of the elected President was the spark that moved the massive student demonstrations at the university.

3. break down *Rabʿah and Al-Nahdah*. After the overthrown of the Muslim Brotherhood regime from the rule, thousands of the Muslim Brotherhood and pro-Muslim Brotherhood sit-in *Rabʿah Al-ʿdawiyah* and *Al-Nahdah* Square. The sit-in lasted nearly two months and it was broken up with hundreds of victims and injuries from both sides (the police and the protesters). No official statistics are showing the exact numbers of the deaths from both sides. These events contributed to enlarging demonstrations at Fayoum University. The students' perceptions of the reasons for these demonstrations are shaped by their political affiliations and their religious background. Some students who support the ideas of the Brotherhood thought that these demonstrations have political objectives related to what happened in *Rabʿah*. A female Brotherhood student at the College of Education stated:

> Demonstrations at the university have many aims. The first aim is blood. We started demonstrations here in the university after the massacre of *Rabʿah*. There are many students were killed in *Rabʿah and Al-Nahdah* (Participant, B 1).

Those who belong to this political ideology believe that demonstrations are basically directed against the current regime, which has destroyed democracy and political life. They are insisting on taking revenge for the martyrs who fell in the *Rabʿah and al-Nahdah*. The term "blood" stands out the idea of revenge in the minds of the Brotherhood students. They see the inevitability of getting the rights of those who died. The term "blood" in Egyptian traditions is related to the incidents of revenge in Upper Egypt where there is always in the minds of Egyptian people in general and Upper Egypt, particularly, the belief that blood will not remove except with blood. This is an obviously clear indication of opening the door to the use of violent means to recover the lost rights.

Besides, many students died in *Rabʿah and Al-Nahdah*. The students of the Brotherhood wanted to punish those who killed the protesters in *Rabʿah Al-ʿdawiya*h. Moreover, they are willing to push themselves to death to return the rights of the martyrs who were killed by the security forces in *Rabʿah* and *Al-Nahdah*. An Independent student clarified:

> Most of the participants in demonstrations are belonging to the organization of the Muslim Brotherhood. They took *Rabʿah* as a high believed issue because many of their colleagues have died (Participant, D 3).

Moreover, the events that the Brotherhood organization witnessed have increased the intensity of demonstrations at Fayoum University. The case took the ideological form to restore the rights of victims. This is a real reason for the students who do not belong to any political groups but participate in the demonstration. This is because of the degree of friendship that binds the students together, but for The Muslim Brotherhood is not the only reason. The main reason for the Muslim Brotherhood students is to regain the throne and authority that they have lost or have been forced to leave. Therefore, they believe that they have the right to take over the affairs of the Egyptian state. They also insisted on confronting the new regime until it collapses. These are noble and lofty goals from their point of view.

4. the arbitrary policy of the security forces. The security system in Egypt needs re-evaluate and re-correct its path because of the harassment in dealing with citizens in general and students in particular. There is an old heritage of hate between students and security forces because of the excesses of the security forces in the right of the students since the student resistance against the British colonial occupation of Egypt till now. The security forces deemed students as a dangerous element that their activity and effectiveness should be limited. These tactics have led to an obviously clear hostility between students and security forces.

In the time after *Rabʿah and Al-Nahdah* events, the security forces intensified the circle of suspicion of students because of their participation in various political events. The arrest of students has increased and there have been serious injuries. The security guards and its spies have been deployed among students to monitor their movements. This is in addition to the security constraints towards students. One student, who does not belong to any political or religious organization, said that the brutality of the police was one of the reasons for these violent actions at the university:

> The arbitrary policy and the extending of the suspicion circle of students lead to this crisis. If the security arrested me, my brothers and my friends would not be satisfied with that. They will protest until release me. Demonstrations are a reaction to the arbitrary policy of the security forces. Many students protest because of the events of *Rabʿah*. They deemed it as an ideological case. And this is true. Some students protest in support of their arrested colleagues and other students participate to see girls. Primarily, the Brotherhood students participate against the regime. They use the current crises to inflame the feelings of students who are not affiliated with the Brotherhood against the regime (Participant, D 2).

Additionally, dealing with students as criminals or outlaws will lead to excessive violence between the two sides and increase demonstrations against the security forces and the regime as well. The student emphasizes the solidarity of students with their colleagues who were arrested or who were killed in *Rabʿah* and *Al-Nahdah*. The regime should be more aware and try to absorb the students' anger because it is in the interest of the state. However, insisting on the violent confrontations with students will increase the degree of congestion of the student community towards the regime and its tools. A Brotherhood female student at the College of Education mentioned:

> In the midst of arrests and violations, there was nothing in our hearts and minds except blood which people have seen it in everywhere. We are not against the President of the University or the Dean of the college. We are protesting in support of our died colleagues. The university administration was not on our minds. They began to confront us by calling the police and make investigations for students. They tried to threaten of dismissing us from the university. Ok, I did not do anything wrong. I am in solidarity with people who were died. That is my point of view. Why do you try to prevent me from my right? The security forces began to hit and arrest students. They started to follow the students at the student dormitories and spy on their activities (Participant, B 9).

The aim of the demonstrations is the fundamental criterion. The student indicates that neither the performance of the university President nor the availability of educational services was important for the students. However, taking the revenge for the dead colleagues in *Rab'ah* and *Al-Nahdah* was the nominal goal for them. The students are aware of the policy of the security forces towards them. They are convinced that the regime is trying to dissuade them from demanding the return of the elected President and preventing them from their right to express their opinions freely and democratically. The arrest of students and their anger and threats of dismissal because of their participation in demonstrations led to a state of discontent among students. A student who does not belong to any political organization mentioned that there are real reasons for demonstrations and those students seek their rights through this mechanism:

> Demonstrations are not certainly raised from nothing. The students protest for supporting their detained colleagues and parents. This is also a logical reason for the demonstrations (Participant, D 7).

Thus, many reasons led to the student demonstrations which have a political nature, although there were many demonstrations, which was for educational rights. Due to a large number of demonstrations at specified times following specific events, such as the judicial rulings of the symbols of the ex-regime, these demonstrations represented a real obstacle to the stability of Egyptian universities because of the repetition of almost its daily occurrence and the hardness of the security forces in facing it.

(C) **Organizing demonstrations.** Organizing demonstrations at Fayoum University is a complicated process because of many reasons. First, the state of tension between the students, administrative security, and the security forces are increasing. Second, the political and economic situation in Egypt is getting worse day after day. The third reason is the engagement of the students, "the Muslim Brotherhood students", in the conflict as a significant actor in the equation of the Egyptian politics. Finally, the students were used as pressure tool by religious groups especially the Brotherhood in fueling the conflict and brought it to the university.

Therefore, the student demonstrations at the university are now political. The process of of preparing demonstration goes through several stages, starting with with establishing a program for the demonstration and setting a date for the demonstration, as well as preparing a list of slogans and chants that will be echoed by the participants, and the tactics to protect the demonstration in case of a clash with the security forces or with other student groups.

1. setting a date for the demonstrations. Setting up a date for the demonstrations is essential for the Muslim Brotherhood students. Time is a crucial factor in the success of a demonstration. There are days when the students gathering at the university in large numbers and the number of lectures is abundant, which gives the Brotherhood students a chance to see many students as possible. A member of the Muslim Brotherhood organization expressed his willingness to set a date for the demonstration.

> The students plan to organize a demonstration by meeting and agreeing on a particular place where they gather to express their opinions. The aims may be a student who was arrested or a student who was killed. They start the demonstration and go to all colleges on campus. I would have been against them if they destroyed infrastructure or disabled the study. However, the administration called the security forces to put an end to the strike. Many students were injured and others died. Then, the student starts to react to the security forces and this is normal (Participant, B 2).

Therefore, there is an agreement among the organizers of the demonstration on determining a specific date and track for the demonstration. This comes within the framework of consultation between the student leaders responsible for the demonstration. When I asked a student, who is not affiliated with any political or religious groups about the dates of the demonstrations, he said:

> The Brotherhood students often make demonstrations and marches on Sunday, Monday, and Wednesday afternoon (Participant, D 5).

Sunday, Monday, and Wednesday are the days filled with lectures for all students in all disciplines at all Colleges. They are days in which massive gathering of students and an increase in student activity at Fayoum University. The Brotherhood students choose the time of 12, 00 P.M., because of the time when the increasing influx of students to the university, which gives a more significant opportunity for demonstrations to be seen by large numbers of students.

In brief, the Muslim Brotherhood students, especially after the events of the 30th of June 2013, began to set a timetable for the demonstrations that was determined flexibly. Most of these demonstrations start on Sunday, Monday, and Wednesday and in a change for days so as not to know by the security forces or informants who are inside the university. The demonstration usually starts at 11, 00 A.M. and the students start to gather at a certain point. The gathering point exists in the colleges that have an active organization for the Muslim

Figure 6. The method of organizing student demonstrations.

Brotherhood students and often the College of Education and starts walking from this point to the other colleges in order to collect large numbers of students.

Additionally, the students walk in parallel rows in the middle of the campus in an organized way. Often some students are responsible for organizing the march and determining the roles of individuals according to their potentials. When I asked one of the Muslim Brotherhood student leaders about the organization's mechanisms, he laughed, that we are not in a war. He is trying not to answer this question because it is an organizational matter that should not be known by anyone outside the organization. However, I have listed some details for the members of the Muslim Brotherhood in their demonstrations, which I observed during my participation as a participant observer. The student stated.

> We are not in a war to keep the safety of the demonstration. At most times, the demonstrations go automatically, although there is a leader who guided it. If there were clashes between the students and the security, there are no special students to protect and clash with the security. When there are clashes with other students, the leader of the demonstration says go ahead and not to confront these students. However, sometimes students may be enThus,iastic and clash with the opponents (Participant, B 2).

On this basis, organizing demonstrations is a vast of ticktacks and mental effort. The demonstration achieves its goals and shows the students in an organizational manner that attracts everyone who sees it.

The picture shows that male students are at the front and female students are at the back of the demonstration. Through the organization of the demonstration, we can conclude that the idea of a man's guardianship over a woman is still common and prevalent in the student organizations that have a religious reference. The female students are still at the tail of the demonstration and their roles are almost limited to chanting slogans and raising banners only. Moreover, there are grouping in the demonstration, each group of students has friendship relations or fellowship walking next to each other and that spread among many students.

2. the path of the demonstration. The student demonstrations often take their paths, starting and ending in a specific place. The course of the demonstration depends on the target which the organizers want. If the goal is to communicate their views to the university administration, the path of the demonstration will be towards the administration building of the university where the offices of the university President and his three Vice-Presidents are located. If the goal is to gather students' support and provoke anger against the policies of the current regime, the path of the demonstration will be to all colleges in an organized march. This is the right way to achieve its goals.

Figure 7. Male students at the forefront of the demonstration and female students at the back.

The demonstrations often start from one of the major colleges, which include large numbers of cadres of the Muslim Brotherhood students, including the College of Education, College of Dar Al-Uloom, and College of Arts. These colleges are characterized by the existence of large numbers of students who represent nucleus of the large-scale demonstrations. The demonstration usually begins at the College of Education at 11 A.M. and continues for about an hour after which the participants of demonstration go to pray. After Noon prayer "ṣalāt al-ẓuhr", the demonstration intensively begins gathering at the College of Education. The demonstration goes to the rest colleges from the College of Education via the bridge, which links the campus of the College of Education to the main campus of the university, where the other colleges are located. The demonstration begins immediately after the bridge to move towards the College of Agriculture in parallel rows. Male students are in the front and females are in the back and they chanted slogans condemning the injustice inflicted on students.

Moreover, the demonstration also passes on the College of Science and then the College of Tourism and Hotels and through the College of Engineering and College of Arts and finally the College of Social work. The place in which the demonstration stops is mostly in front of the main door of the university. At other times, the demonstration is trying to go out of the university to bring the street's support and to show that the university students are rejecting what is happening in the country. An Independent student said that there are precise routes for the demonstrations.

> They go with a map of specific colleges which include a large number of supporters to communicate their message and gather massive numbers of the students. They understood what they were going to do and when they go towards colleges, some students come to join them. Many students from each college participate. The students try to attract other students to gather the most substantial number as they can because if they stand in their place, the students will go and will not stay for half an hour at most (Participant, D 3).

It is important to mention that the demonstration aimed to mobilize large numbers of students to participate with the Brotherhood students in their protest and to instigate anger among students for the detention and injustice carried out by the current regime. The demonstration completed after passing through colleges. The Independent students see that if they are protesting in a specific place, the pro-Muslim Brotherhood students will feel boring and will not wait more than a quarter or half an hour at most. If this happened, the demonstration seems to be failed. The movement gives an atmosphere of activity and vitality among students. It also avoids security surveillance in one of the ambushes next to the campus or in the center of the university, especially with the presence of cameras that reports the movements of the students.

Figure 8. The path of the demonstration in front of the College of Agriculture on its way to the rest of the Colleges.

There is a specific tactic reflects an organizational awareness of the demonstration's leaders. The strategy of standing in a particular place will weaken the demonstration and will not be attractive for other students to join the demonstration. Walking around various colleges encourages students to join the demonstration and break the fear barrier for, where many students see their colleagues are joining the demonstration. A brotherhood students' leader stated:

> Once we decided to organize a demonstration and go outside the university, male students usually secure the demonstration from any Armed cars or the security forces. They tell us if anything will threaten the demonstration (Participant, B 7).

Moreover, when the demonstration goes outside the university, it is easy for the students to be subjected for the security harassment and sometimes the students are arrested because during that period the Demonstration Law was applied. Thus, the tracks followed by the demonstrations in the university are to go out to the surrounding community to bring support to the students.

> We are still saying that the student is the solution. I need to express my opinion to people outside the university. The university is my home and the place where I express my opinion (Participant, B 8).

> The goal is to convey protest to the surrounding areas of the university. The students try to say that the university is opposed to what is happening in the country. Then, they wanted to tell people outside the university, do not be afraid to demand their rights, we are demanding for our rights (Participant, B 9).

Figure 9. Student demonstration goes out from the behind gate of the university.

The Brotherhood students believed at this time that the student is the main power for change and that the students also played an important role in enlighten people about the defeat of 1968 and their role now is to display the oppression of the political regime. The solution is the students protest to break the barrier of fear and dread among the masses of people for supporting the demands of students to end injustice and brutality in dealing with the political opponents.

> If anyone walks in front of the university and sees the demonstration, he will be surprised. He will ask, what is going on at the university? A university is a place for education. When something happens and we demonstrate against this, people will say is there anything happening and we do not know? (Participant, B 9).

It is noted that the students are forced to go out into streets to get support. Further, they are trying to break the barrier of fear among the masses to move and restore the rights that were robbed. The Muslim Brotherhood students organization emphasize that a university is primarily a place for education and if the demonstrations were carried out and the security forces surrounded the university, this will attract attention of the passers-by to ask about what is happening inside the university? Why all this number of security forces in front of the university? Why do students pretend?

All these questions will lead the masses and the residents of neighborhoods adjacent to the university to understand what the students are doing against the regime. One student said that the middle and high school students were watching the student demonstrations when they go out from the university's door at the College of Engineering. However, this perceptions of the Brotherhood stu-

Figure 10. Student demonstration goes out from the main gate of the university.

dents indicate the pragmatic goals of the students. According to their words, *"A university is a place for education"* reflects their conservative orientation regarding political work at university. Although their demands are related to democracy, freedom, and the country's issues, they are demonstrating to support the Brotherhood political goals. This reduces the motivation and enThus,iasm of the other students to participate with them.

Therefore, the demonstration goes outside the university is an evident development in the students' strategy to escalate the situation by trying to attract the attention of the surrounding streets. This shows that the students have become rebels against the rampant injustice in the country. One of the reasons for that is their attempt to drag the security forces into a clash with them to show that the security is attacking the rights of students to demonstrate and express their opinion. However, this is doubtful because the security forces are trying to spoil the student schemes by dispersing the demonstrations and the ongoing arresting students and spy to monitor the movements of students and their activity.

On the other side, the students who do not belong to any political orientation see the exit of the Muslim Brotherhood students outside the university is to convey a message that the university is not silent. It also has rebelled to break its shackles and confront the harshness of the regime through its students. An Independent student clarified:

> The Brotherhood students feel suppression. If they protested inside the university, no one would know about that. Every day there are demonstrations in the university, so it became normal. They want to come out and show people that they are protesting. The Brotherhood students are trying to provoke the security forces to clash with them to be

the victim. We are students in the fourth year and we see demonstrations every day. When I was talking on the phone and one of my friends say what that voice is? I said a demonstration (Participant, D 3).

Consequently, a reasonable explanation for that is the sense of neglect, lack of listening to them, and ignore responding to their expectations will drag them to get out from the university to get support from the street. The university administration dealt with the student demonstrations in a careless way. This led to a predicament situation and the exit of the students to the street and the fall of many injuries, arrest others, and injuring the police.

> They want to go outside the university to clash with the security forces. The students threw stones at the security. In counter, the police shoot tear gases on them. The people's everyday activities outside the university will stop. In this way, they make crises for the regime and many students will sympathize with them. Last year in front of the student dormitories, the security forces entered to prevent students from protesting during a meeting between the university President and the Governor. The Brotherhood made a massive demonstration in front of the rector's office (Participant, D 9).

Moreover, some students, especially from the political opponents of the Muslim Brotherhood, may see that the students are trying to clash with the security forces in order to push them to to make mistakes and beat the students. As a result of this, they tried to force the security apparatus to show its ugly face. According to his explanation, the more victims are in the interest of the Brotherhood organization because this increases the sympathy for their cause and increases the widespread anger against the policies of the regime. Although this opinion is valid in some cases, the Brotherhood organization will not benefit if the security sticks crush the students. This may lead to the opposite result, apprehension the rest of students from participation in the demonstrations, and may instill fear in the hearts of parents and prevent their sons from going to the university.

D) Participants in demonstrations. Although the demonstrations after the January 25th Revolution was attended by all student groups for noble objectives such as social justice at the university and the access of students to their educational, political, and social rights, the demonstrations that took place after the 30th of June 2013 in Egyptian universities differed according to the participants. Most of the participants in these dmostrations are students of the Muslim Brotherhood who feel oppressed and injustice to what happened to the Brotherhood regime. The Independent students stated:

> Most of the students who engaged in the demonstrations are from the Muslim Brotherhood (Participant, D 6).

> Most of the demonstrators are from the students of the Muslim Brotherhood. More than 90% of students are Muslim Brotherhood students (Participant, D 5).

Most of the participants are the students of the Muslim Brotherhood and some students are sympathetic to the idea of the Brotherhood and some other student organizations such as the Revolutionary Socialists. However, in a few cases when there is a major event in the state such as the unfair verdicts or the discovery of corruption or other issues, the students of these organizations join the Muslim Brotherhood students. This is precisely what occurred at the university after the acquittal of Hosni Mubarak and his assistants in the case of killing the protesters. The Independent students reported that the students of the Brotherhood were the organizers and participants in these demonstrations.

> The demonstrations after the 30th of June 2013 were in one direction which is the direction of the Muslim Brotherhood students (Participant, D 2).

> The demonstrations that are now taking place in the university are for a specific student faction which is the Muslim Brotherhood students (Participant, D 1).

Through the involvement of the researcher in these demonstrations as a participant observer, he noted that most of the demonstrators follow the Muslim Brotherhood students. The students participating in the demonstrations are from different scientific discipline in all colleges. The demonstrations include male and female students. The number of students at the demonstration usually ranges between 100 to 150 students under the usual circumstances, but it may reach up to 1000 students if other student organizations participate in demonstrations.

E) Chants and slogans of the demonstrations. Chants and slogans are among the most prominent manifestations of the January 25th Revolution of 2011, which lasted from the beginning till even with the revolutionary waves and subsequent protest movements. Mughiyth (2014) defines chants as the loud voice aiming to announce or refers to an event which the speaker wants to reveal or achieve. Slogans and chants are a social phenomenon that has a long and deep history since the beginning of the Egyptian civilization until modern times. Because the chants aim to communicate and to integrate individuals and their strong mobilization against the tyrannical regimes. For this reason, chants have a significant power to mobilize individuals and are characterized by their ease and rapid spread of demands among society members.

The chants were evident in the corridors of Egyptian universities after the January 25th Revolution and until the fall of the Muslim Brotherhood on the 30th of June 2013. The student demonstrations at Fayoum University forced students to launch a series of loud chants and slogans against all elements of the ruling authority, from the head of the regime to the university President. The students fired these slogans and chants to undermine the ruling regime and to honor the martyrs who fell in their sit-in. The most prominent part of the chants was against security forces because of its harsh actions against students.

During my walk in the College of Education square in front of the main building and the intermediate location between the buildings of the College of Education at 11,30 A.M., on 25/3/2015, the students held a protest and had

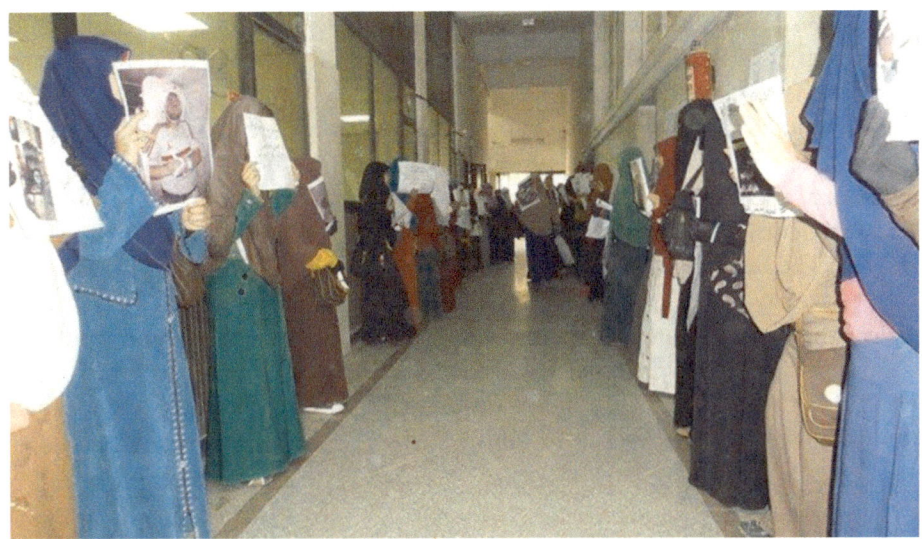

Figure 11. The Brotherhood female student is holding slogans at the College of Education.

more than 25 students. The activities of this strike were for the students of the Muslim Brotherhood, who stood to hold signs in parallel rows opposite each other. Moreover, students carrying balloons and chanting slogans against what the regime did to the students and other leaders of the group. Among the most critical slogans which were echoed by students:

– *Mish hatnsuwna al-qaḍiah –Yaskut , yaskut hukm al-ʿAskar* (You will not force us forget the case-overthrow the Military rule).
– *Basm Allāh al-malik al-haq jina naquwl lill ẓalim lā* (In the name of the God, the owner the right, we came to say no to the unjust).
– *Qālwo ṣuwt al-maraʾh ʿauwrah, qataluw al-maraʾh we sarquw al-thaūrt* (They said the woman's voice is loins. They killed the woman and stole the revolution).
– *Al-anqalab hū al-arhab* (The Coup is the terrorism).
– *Lina zamayil juwah al-sajn nafas al-ʿumir wa nafas al-shakil* (We have friends at the prison with the same age and the same shape).
– *ʿAlī wa ʿali al-ṣuwt, ilī biahtaf mish haymūt* (raise, and raise your voice. Who protest will not die).
– *Haya al-ṭalābah ītqatalat lih, yamkin hatafat ḍid al-ʿAskar, ṭayib yaskut , Yaskut hukm Al-ʿAskar* (Why the students are arrested. They may shout against the military rule. OK down falls the rule of the Generals).
– *Amn al-dawlah kalaab al-dawlah, fiin al-amn wa fiin al-dawlah* (The Security Forces is the State's dogs. Where is the Security and where is the State?).

- *Mahmaa tamsah haktib akatar, yaskut , yaskut hukm al-ʿAskar* (Whatever you erase my writings, I will write more and more. Down falls, down falls the military rule).
- *Kul ma aquwl ana habqaī fi haly ṣuwart Rabʿah tiyjī fi baly* (Every time I decided not to engage in politics, the picture of Rabʿah come into my mind).

Moreover, these slogans express many issues that are essential to the Brotherhood students. The *Rabʿah and Al-Nahdah* massacre is central to the students' slogans. The case of political liberty for students is also important. The violence of the security forces is also mentioned in the students' slogans. These slogans reflect the students' anger and they are symbolic in many situations and sarcasm in others. I asked one of the students belonging to the Muslim Brotherhood that the content of these slogans and chants is significantly undermined the ruling regime. She responded to me:

> They are rigid and severe slogans, but these slogans came from our reality. These slogans are nothing as compared to the destroying of houses and arresting students by the security forces (Participant, B 1).

> These slogans are nothing as compared to killing and arrested students and parents. This is the least duty we do towards our detained colleagues. There are Ministers in European countries has faced criticism. Moreover, Mr. *El-Sayed Al-Badawī* was hit on his scruff. We have many other means (Participant, B 9).

It is important to mention that the students believe that slogans are nothing compared to what the security forces do such as; killing, arresting students, and burning the property of the Brotherhood leaders. These messages are the reality of students' lives and reflect their struggles and tragedies. The female student points out that those European countries follow the style of irony and ridicule in criticizing the Ministers' policies. This is quite natural according to their view.

These slogans are a tool for relieving the repression and frustration suffered by the Muslim Brotherhood students. Their use of these slogans raises feelings and increases the sympathy of other students with them. The content of these slogans is also strongly linked to the contradictory policies of the ruling regime. Through analyzing the chants and slogans echoed by students during their demonstrations, it is noted that they address many important issues that students want such as freedom, justice, and legitimacy.

F) Securing the demonstration and methods of protection. There is a development in the strategies of the Brotherhood students to devise methods to secure the demonstrations against the interference of the security forces or the opponents. The students have devised a variety of techniques to help them confront dangers in and outside the university. Through my participation in the student demonstrations, they are extremely cautious and organized in everything such as the distribution of roles and responsibilities. There is a leader, who chants and determines where the demonstration begins and where it ends and where it goes.

There are also many students who protect the demonstration and prevent anyone from taking photos. If any person attempts to photograph the demonstration, these students take the camera from him by force. Other students play the role of mentor or observer who informs the leader of the demonstration of any external threat either from the security or the opponent students. These students walk before the march, on the right side, from the left side, and at the back for protection. An Independent student mentioned:

> After the revolution, all students were expressing their views. There were many professors participated in marches and demonstrations such as pro-Syrian demonstrations and others. All people had one aim, but now there was a need to protect the demonstration. The students should be sure that all the participating students are safe. Moreover, the female students participate in the demonstration need more protection. Usually, the opponent students tried to confront the demonstration. In this case, the student protects all who participate with them (Participant, D 2).

The students belonging to the Muslim Brotherhood organization see the need to secure demonstration because many students are participating in it, As well as fear of the objection of other organizations. In the voice tone of the interviewee, it was obviously clear that the issue of securing the demonstrations is a necessary action for repelling any aggression against them. A Brotherhood student stated:

> We know when and from which street the police come. Therefore, we increase our reserves and re-plan the demonstration's paths (Participant, B 4).

The Muslim Brotherhood students are aware that the security forces will immediately break up demonstrations by force. The students secured demonstrations through the "observer" who informs the protesters with the arrival of the security forces. This will help the students or the demonstration leader to avoid any confrontation with the security forces and return to the university. Not only that but also there are individuals who are responsible for securing the demonstration. They know any strange individual from the demonstrators and forces him to leave the demonstration. Sometimes they beat him to leave the demonstration. A Brotherhood student leader at the College of Dar al-Uloom stated:

> If any student is spying, we know him because we know each other. We know who is participating in the demonstrations and who is not. If someone strange join us in the demonstration, we will ask, who is this student? If he is a friend to our colleagues, therefore, it is Ok. If he is not, he can be hit because it is possible to hurt the students in the march (Participant, B 2).

In one of the demonstrations in which I took part, I found that the students who are responsible for securing the demonstration preventing someone from taking photos for the demonstration. They took him away from the demonstration by force. They took him to the student dormitory. The Brotherhood students know the students who belong to the organization and they can identify any person who tries to hide among the demonstrators.

> One of the students said that the armored vehicles began moving from Fayoum Directorate in the direction of the university. We rushed quickly and wanted to go back to enter the female students quickly to the university. Male students can escape but female students cannot (Participant, B 7).

Consequently, this proves the secure system for protecting the demonstration and the massive database and intelligence at the high level of accuracy that enables students to know the movements of the security forces. The distribution of roles to individuals responsible for securing the demonstrations guarantees protection from the police's attacks on them. In other circumstances, the female students secure themselves when the male students are not available to protect the demonstration. This occurs in colleges that have large numbers of the Brotherhood female members. A female Brotherhood student stated:

> It is not necessary that the Brotherhood male students protect us. Most of us are girls and there are no many Brotherhood male students here at the College of Education. We, as female students, have a presence here more than the male students. We organize our strike without any help or protection from the male students. Of course, we are focusing on a place in which all the students can see us. The strike itself is not the goal. The goal is that the students see us and know about our grievances (Participant, B 1).

It is important to mention that in many cases, the students wear masks on their faces so that the security forces or the administrative security cannot identify them. These masks also prevent the arrival of gas-fired bombs shooting by the security forces from reaching the students' respiratory system and then injuring them. This is in addition to their use of vinegar bottles, which reduce the injury of students' suffocation and caused red eyes as a result of inhaling the smoke generated by these bombs. This is one of the defensive strategies developed by students to protect themselves and to reduce the injuries.

5.3.5.2 Political Violence inside the University

Violence is a social phenomenon which accompanied the evolution of human societies since ancient times (Lal, 2007, p.7). The action of violence has developed according to the changing and evolution of means of aggression (Arendt, 1970). It prevails in all societies when peaceful ways are closed in the face of individuals to express their opinions, attitudes, and beliefs in a democratic and free manner. Most social and political studies deem violence as a human behavior which denies and excludes the other from social life by subjugation and negation (Graham and Gurr, 1970; Morgan, 2004; Tilly, 2003). Therefore, violence is "the use of physical force to harm someone or to damage property" (Webster dictionary, 2016). According to this concept, violence is a group of working actions to create a condition of fear, anxiety, and instability in a society. For that reasons, the events of destruction are the main feature of violence.

Moreover, political violence is a prominent form of violence, which is linked to political issues (Mars, 1975; Zimmermann, 2011). It can be defined as "all collective attacks within a political community against the political regime, its actors including competing political groups as well as incumbents or its policies "(Gurr, 2016, pp. 3- 4). It is not only a behavior against the state but also, the state can apply violence towards civilians and political groups as Nieburg stated. He defined political violence as:

"is act of disruption, injury of whose purpose, choice of the targets, or victims, surrounding circumstance, implementation and/or effects have political significance that is tend to modify the behaviour of others in a bargaining situation that has consequences for the social system" (Nieburg, 1969, p13).

The political aim is the motivating key factor in the political violence cycle at the university as well as, the desire to modify a profound change in the political system. Therefore, *"Political violence depends basically on the use of physical power to cause affliction for a political adversary"* (Della Porta, 1995, p. 2). Thus, political violence is entirely different from political protests (Zimmermann, 2011). Political protests inside universities are commonly concerned with political cases such as social justice, fair wealth distribution, democratic elections, and fighting corruption which are vital and important for all society members. Students tried to call these cases by peaceful protests instead of violence towards university's facilities, professors, and their colleagues.

Political violence within Egyptian universities cannot be seen in isolation from the outer perimeter walls of those universities. Some of it comes as a reflection of what is happening in Egyptian society. Although there should be a reflection and positive impact of universities as centers of spreading educational, cultural, and intellectual facing the outside community, the opposite usually happens. Therefore, the aggressive behavior is a serious problem facing Fayoum University in post-revolution. In sum, political violence usually occurs when the crisis arises and the process of democracy decline in societies. Besides, the political regime, especially in the third world countries tries to control the whole political process and prevent any political opposition to express their critique or efficiently participating in the society.

A) The causes of violence. Many reasons led students to demonstrate and resort to violence in their dealings with the authority and its representatives both inside and outside Fayoum University. The political crises were the first causes that pushed the students to excessive violence in the university. Among the most important reasons are:

1. the toppling of the elected President Muhammad Morsi and the exclusion of the Muslim Brotherhood from the rule. The Brotherhood has begun to pursue useless policies at the local level, such as appointing members of the Brotherhood in the leadership positions, as well as violating the announced political promises. On the external level, relations with Shiite Iran have been restored and the president visited Iran despite the doctrinal and ideological differences between the two countries since Sadat sheltered the Shah after the Islamic Revolution in Iran.

All these reasons decreased the popularity of the Brotherhood regime in Egypt in addition to a growing public discontent from their policies. Consequently, large crowds of people protested on the 30th of June 2013 for overthrowing President Muhammad Morsi from the rule and setting a map for the future through appointing the President of the Constitutional High Court as interim president of the country until the presidential elections. Besides, disrupting the Egyptian Constitution of 2012, which was legislated in the era of the Muslim Brotherhood and working on setting a new constitution guaranteeing freedoms led to limiting the power of the President, appointing of a national consensus government to run the transitional phase until the presidential elections and forming a supreme committee for national reconciliation among all national forces in Egypt. A female Brotherhood student stated:

> We do not recognize this regime, laws, the government, or anything. As for the people who witnessed the murders in *Rab'ah*, they will not be afraid of bullets, fire or anything. Also, we have our relatives in prisons and others who were dead. Therefore, we are not afraid at all. Our parents educated us that we do not be afraid of anyone as long as we have the right. We know that the one who supports justice is exposed to that. So, we are convinced of it (Participant, B 1).

The students see their approach to violence and escalation because of the regime's disregard for their demands, which is the nominal goal and the only demand: the return of the Brotherhood regime to power once again. The overthrow of the elected President by the political forces led to a state of agitation to the Muslim students in universities for the return of the Brotherhood President. The students of the Muslim Brotherhood do not recognize the current regime or the laws that have been issued during his rule. Because of their affiliation to the Brotherhood regime, they are demanding of returning the Brotherhood regime to the rule and insisting on taking the rights of the martyrs who were killed by this illegal regime from their point of view.

The violent practices of the regime against students have made them engage in counter-violence to survive and continue to defend the stolen rights. It is noted that the authority is often planning for violence and repression to silence the angry students and exclude them from the public scene. The policy of violence has been initiated by the security forces to prevent students from demonstrating and expressing their views.

2. the security restrictions and violence of the Police practices. The student demonstrations have become a source of concern for the current regime. The security forces followed the student demonstrations inside and outside the university. Because of the frequent egress of the demonstrations to the surrounding streets after taking many rounds through colleges within the university, this led to an intense security intervention and hardness on students and arrested and beaten with tear gas. This has resulted in escalating the spirit of challenging the students to encounter this security glut that deprives them of the gains of the glorious Egyptian revolution. A Brotherhood student stated:

> The civil security takes the names of the students and gives them to the security forces. They detained students in the civil security's office and then hand them over to the police. This is the point of disagreement between them and us (Participant, B 7).

The security forces tried to impose their control over the university to prevent demonstrations from going out to the surrounding streets. They ordered the civil security to follow the protesters and identify their names and, thus, arrest them on charges of vandalism and stirring up riots at the university. On one occasion, the members of the civil security detained some students of the Muslim Brotherhood organization in the civic security's room at the College of Education to hand them over to the police. This made the students angry from those aggressive measures by the security.

> Now the informants and concealed security men to catch students represent a threat in the university. The security Chief at the College of Education was beaten because he informed the security forces about two students who participated in the demonstrations. Therefore, the students gave him a lesson which he will not forget (Participant, B 1).

> The administration was wrong in the latest events (The clashes with the civil security at the College of Arts and College of Education) why the administration allowed informants to be at the university? The student comes to learn and expresses his opinion. Leave them to express their view if there is freedom at the university. The administration called the police to catch the students who protest. Further, it also dismisses the protesters from the study and prevents them from having a room in the students' dormitories and other more arbitrary actions against the protester students who express their opinion (Participant, B 5).

Therefore, the students accused the political regime and the university administration of causing violence. If the university administration has the vision to endeavor to avoid the ongoing incidents of violence by meeting the protesters and listening to know their demands and try to achieve them according to the law of universities, the violence would not have occurred. The view of both male and female students is similar regarding the causes of violence at Fayoum University. A female student asserted her right to react to the violence and aggression of the security forces.

Many reasons pushed us to commit violence. We did not start violence until the security forces violently dealt with us. Ok, what about violence, rape, and murder against students? I am obviously clear with you; an enemy is fighting us violently, what should we do now? (Participant, B 1).

For the violence that occurred in our college because male students in the march have beaten a security officer. This year, we are acting peacefully, but the security forces are very hard in dealing with us (Participant, B 9).

Consequently, the causes of violence from the students' point of view revolve to the intervention of the security forces based on a call from the university President as well as breaking up the demonstrations by force. Additionally, the students did not start violence only after the security forces using gas against students. The students did not find any objection to the police. They also showed that beating the security forces with stones and fireworks is not comparable to what the security forces are committing everyday against the students.

3. The Law of Demonstration. Restricting liberties through the Law of Demonstration which has had a multiplier impact in exacerbating unrest and violence within Egyptian society in general and in universities in particular. In this law, the students found a restriction of freedoms, which is one of the gains of the revolution, especially for young people. Therefore, the 6th April Movement took the lead in protesting against this law in front of the People's Assembly. The Police attacked them and arrested their leaders *Ahmed Maher* and *Ahmed Duwma* for violating the Law of Demonstration. The students expressed their rejection of this law as the following:

Sure, that you suppress the freedom of expression that existed after the January 25th Revolution with this law and this will lead to multiplying demonstrations. How can I get permission for a demonstration which is basically will be against the non-expression of opinion? How can I get permission from one of the regime's institutions which the demonstration will be against it? Surely, demonstrations should be carried out without any permission and I do violence without any limitation (Participant, B 5).

Moreover, the students are still rejecting this law, which has restricted their freedom and accused the acquisition of the revolution that has been achieved. The students complain about the intentions of the state to give them permits to organize a demonstration. Therefore, how can they be the judge and the opponent at the same time? The students' rejection of this law reflects an increase in the collective awareness of students whether Independent or affiliated to the religious and political organizations. A Brotherhood student stated:

You said (the regime) students can make peaceful demonstrations and then the security forces shoot them with gases and rubber bullets. It is ridiculous that you say (the regime) if you want to protest, just come and I will give you permission for that. He can permit you to demonstrate in a desert or at a far place. Thus, the university administration is politically directed (Participant, B 2).

The students find the idea of law as futile and useless. How does the regime agree to hold a demonstration that will criticize its policies? If the demonstration is approved, it is possible to change the location of demonstrations to remote areas on the pretext of securing them. The students do not trust the regime and do not believe in its promises. The students may come out in a demonstration and the security forces will attack them with gunshots, fire, and gas. The lack of trust between the ruling authority and the students has produced this excessive violence from both sides.

Therefore, the state legislated many laws that are in line with its interests and objectives. The state applied these laws to react any attempt to undermine their hegemony and damage their interests by any social group in the society. Thus, laws are a form of control exercised by the state over students. Some groups within the student community believe that the enactment of such laws would protect them from any dangers, even though these laws are the primary tool of the ruling authority to restrict their freedom. Thus, the awareness of the students arose after the January 25th Revolution and the events that followed, which increased their ability to understand the political shortcomings of the ruling regime.

Therefore, the regime did not stand static towards the events that prevailed in the universities. It tried to falsify the awareness of students, especially whom not affiliated to any political parties or have any political orientations, for its interests and purposes. As for the students who always criticize the regime and whom the regime has failed to include them in the political game, he did not stand idly in the face of those students or the events that took place on campus and which often threaten its domination. Therefore, he has taken many tricks to block or falsify this group or promote a counter-culture against this culture. This what the current regime did against the Brotherhood students at Egyptian universities.

C) **Forms of students' violence at Fayoum University.** There were numerous incidents of violence from the security forces and the Brotherhood students, which posed an obvious threat to the university life and the educational process as well. The students' insistence on demonstrations to go out of the university and the insistence of the security forces on breaking up the demonstrations by force represent the essence of the problem. All these factors have led to increased violence. The incidents of violence varied within the university, especially after the 30th of June 2013. It included protests, gatherings, and disabling the study to clash with the security, throwing stones in a flagrant challenge to the security forces. Thus, the forms of violence practiced by the Brotherhood students and the security forces in Fayoum University were represented in:

1. **protests in front of the offices of the Deans and the university President.** Since the beginning of the January25th Revolution, the students' protests were increasing to restore the students' freedom and rights. They protested to enhance the educational services and to prevent the interference of the security forces in the university life. However, the situation quickly changed after the

events of the 30th of June 2013 as result of the increase of protests of the Brotherhood students. This has become a manifestation of everyday life within Fayoum University.

It is important to mention that most of these protests were for returning the deposed President Muhammad Morsi to the rule again, in addition to condemning what they called the Military Coup on the legitimacy and asking the university President to release the students detained by the security forces. Most of these protests expressed on the political demands, especially the condemnations of what the Egyptian Army did to exclude President Muhammad Morsi from the rule. They also focused on what the security forces did in *Rab'ah and Al-Nahdah* which has caused hundreds of victims and thousands of detained. Therefore, these protests incited students not to attend lectures or examinations, which made matters worse.

The Muslim Brotherhood students protested at every place of Fayoum University such as inside colleges, inside studying halls, at campus, and in front of the office of the university President. They wore masks on their faces so as not to be recognized by the security forces or the civil security. They used to knock drums, chants, and condemnations condemning what happened in the dismantling of the *Rab'ah and Al-Nahdah*. A Brotherhood student at the College of Dar-Uloom mentioned:

Figure 12. The students sit in front of the Dean's office of the College of Engineering[20].

---

[20] -Pictures number (12, 14, 16) was taken with a permission of the Brotherhood students at Fayoum University.

190

> The students adopt the pressure style. If we do want something, we offer it to the university administration. If they agreed, it would be okay. If they do not agree, we make a strike at the center of the campus with slogans. Of course, if no one comes to negotiate with us, we transmit the strike to the front of the Dean's office. This achieves good results. For example, the problem of exam times, we protested and we spoke finally to the Vice Dean and the Dean. Therefore, the problem was solved (Participant, B 4).

The students used the method of pressure on the university administration to restore the rights which were stolen. Therefore, they believe that their demands are a legitimate right for them and the university President should help them to achieve these requests. The students' insistence on the sit-in in front of the university President's office and the offices of the Deans may be due to the belief that the university President has the power to release the students from prisons because there is an obvious coordination between the university President and the security forces.

Through the previous picture, it is clear that many students gathered in a sit-in outside the Dean's office at the College of Engineering to release their colleagues who had been arrested by the police. It is noted that the corridor is full of students to prevent the Dean of the college or any professor from entering or exiting the office. This disrupts the university life, but the fault lies on the university and its inability to manage the crisis and to start an open dialogue with the students to discuss their demands and solve their problems. This will be better than ignoring their demands. This ignorance will push the students to escalate and resort to violence to achieve their demands. One of the Muslim Brotherhood students said that the way the university administration handled students' demands differed after the events of the 30th of June 2013.

> We can say after the 30th of June 2013 is differed from before it. The situation differed with the university President. If the students have any demands, we gathered or sit in front of the dome (the university presidency building). The President of the university before the 30 of June 2013 responded to our demands via strikes. He is now after the 30th of June neglected our demands and refused even to meet us in his office, although he can meet a delegation from us to tell him about our demands like what he does with the students who support the current regime (Participant, B 3).

The students also wore signs for *Rabʿah* as a symbolic slogan used by the leaders of the Brotherhood to express and perpetuate the memory of *Rabʿah and Al-Nahdah*, which witnessed the bloodletting of the protesters. They also made banners condemning what Army did in Rabaa like *"Rabʿah in the heart"* as well as *"the coup is terrorism."* And other slogans condemning the military rule and demand the release of leaders of the Muslim Brotherhood and the detained students. This result is compatible with the study of Petras (1965). The American students at Berkeley University sit-in at the administration building to force the university administration to achieve their demands. It seems that students all over the world have a bassline of behaviors and hopes that they share regarding place, time, and language.

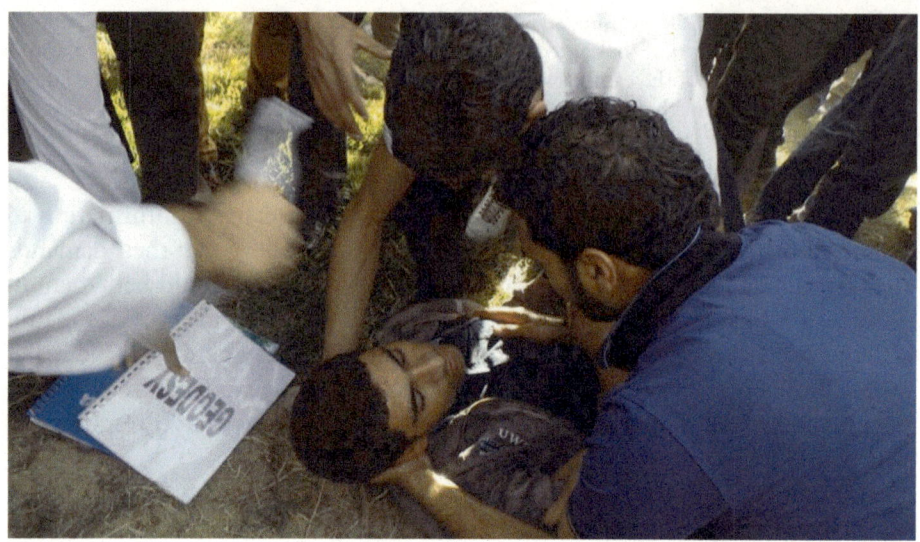

Figure 13. The suffocation of students as a result of inhaling tear gas.

2. clashes with the security. The student protests have intensified to the extent that the security forces stormed the university to curb the student rallies by force. The main reason for this is the insistence of the students on going out to the street after their demonstrations at the university to get widespread support for their demonstrations and to give some legitimacy to them. This led to the security intervention to prevent them from going to the streets around the university, which led to clash with the students and the security launched tear gas to force students to return to the university. This scene led to many students being suffocated by inhaling this tear gas.

It is obviously clear from the picture that the student has inhaled gas bombs and the other students tried to provide medical assistance to him. This scene has been repeated daily to the degree that it became a manifestation of the daily life at Fayoum University. The students did not stand idly, but they used fireworks and threw stones at the security forces.

> There is a physical law state for every action; always there is an equal action and oppo-
> site reaction to it. If you were attacked, you would react with the possible means (Par-
> ticipant, B 5).

The students' doctrine is to defend themselves by all the available tools and ways to respond to the aggression of the security forces. The students use the term "a physical law" to demonstrate that the response to aggression is a law of nature which we must believe and act according to it. Consequently, the students have the intention of acting violently. They consider violence something natural and legitimate in the face of internal aggression. A Brotherhood student at the College of Engineering states:

The students could not raise their heads due to shooting of gases and rubber bullets. The door of the Department of Civil Engineering is still broken and no one said that the security forces destroyed it. Further, the accident of the Black Monday when the security sweep the university and a solider with a tank run behind Dr. Muhammad Essa who escaped to the building of the university President (Participant, B 5).

The harassment of the security forces in dealing with the protesters and faculty members led to a state of tension at Fayoum University. The security forces have acted to prevent demonstrations and riots by entering campus, chasing students, and shooting gas bombs on students.

Figure 14. The Armored vehicles storm the main campus of Fayoum University.

Through the picture, the Armored vehicles entered the university campus to break up the demonstrations. Additionally, the security forces have turned the campus into a battlefield rather than a place for education. The students were stunned by the entry of Armored vehicles into the campus. The students expressed disappointment and shock from the behavior of the university leadership to allow the security forces to storm the campus. A Muslim Brotherhood student at the College of Engineering stated:

Um … Moreover, I ask you, why the demonstrations are not peaceful? The security forces confronted the students' demonstrations with violence and shot gases on them. There are many videos prove my speech that the security forces dealt harshly with the students and it was the first who start violence. I do not think that the students can bring Molotov to the university. The students come to the university for study not to fight. We did not begin violence against the security forces. For example, the security shot a gas bomb on my colleague in the front of the Institute of Nile Basin Studies because he tried to record a video via his mobile. He could not breathe because of the bomb gases and smoke. We carried him to the university hospital. The following picture shows the entrance of Armored vehicles and gas and smoke bombs from the center of the campus of Fayoum University (Participant, B 5).

Figure 15. The Armored vehicles are launching gas and smoke bombs on students.

The Muslim Brotherhood students at Fayoum University pose a controversial question about the comparison of damage caused by beatings with rubber bullets, tear gas or throwing stones. This is an anarchic question because both have a significant damaging effect. Both rubber bullets and stones can kill innocent people. On the background of re-aggression, some students wearing masks attacked the Chief of the civil security at the College of Arts. The security officer was injured in his neck and his kidney. He was transferred to the intensive care at the university hospital. The students also injured the security officer at the College of Education with injuries in his forehead and his arms. I visited the security officer at the university hospital and he had stabbed in different parts of the body. In his account of what happened, he said during his resistance to the students; he found them older than the age of students at the university.

Consequently, this may lead us to ask a puzzling question, is the Brotherhood organization has pushed some of its men to catch up with the administrative security to ease the burden on the Brotherhood students? In addition to terrifying the civil security officials so as not to repeat what they did. The Muslim

Brotherhood students have singled out the reason for the violence against the civil security due primarily to the actions of the civil security towards the students.

> The members of the civil security were beaten because they kept (detain) some students in the security's room to hand them over to the police. They also informed about the names of six students to the police. Therefore, the security forces arrested them at the university's dormitories in the night. There was coordination between the civil security and the security forces (Participant, B 7).

The students feel that the security forces are monitoring them. Because of the permanent cases of detention and that the members of civil security reported the students, the students tried to give them a lesson so that they would not recur these actions again. The students aimed to send a message to the security officials that whoever informs about the students will cast the fate of the administrative security officers in the Colleges of Arts and Education. This is a terrible development in the methods of students to respond to the aggression through violent response.

Moreover, the students' strategies have changed to confront aggression. They committed physical abuse against administrative security that proved a profound change in the policy of confrontation. The students are trying to control the political space at the university at the same time the regime struggling with them to access, dominate, and impose its perceptions of events in the university. Therefore, clash is inevitable and losses are massive between the two sides.

> One of the students hit a member of the civil security and he runs away. Some of the security men at the gate of the College of Agriculture came to the accident place to help their colleague. They came holding knives and want to clash with the students. One of the students tried to take the knife from the hand of the security member, but he got injured. Other security member tried to hit the students with a piece of iron which results in the injury to our friend (Participant, B 7).

It is noteworthy that the administrative security received orders to close the gates in front of the demonstrations and this led to a conflict between the administrative security and students. Closing doors in front of the students will expose them to beatings and be arrested by the security forces. Therefore, the hatred between the security and students remained because of these acts, which developed into insults until they reached the clash between them. The civil security mostly consists of young men at the age of 25 years with a low level of education. Therefore, low-educated people are full of a street's ethics, which may endanger students from collisions with these people. The mere occurrence of a quarrel that sharp knives have been used for hitting students. They considered themselves on the street, not at the campus.

The state of security chaos that followed the events of the 30th of June 2013 and the events of *Rab'ah* led to a security alert may reach the level of obsession because of the acts of some terrorist groups from the destruction of government facilities and bombings. This has cast a shadow over the university where the security sticks have intensified and the cruelty and intensity of dealing with students have emerged. These actions are partly related to the violent events that happened at universities during the sixths in Italy, USA, and Japan (Levine, 1979; Michiya Shimbori et al., 1980; Statera, 1979). The students' violent actions developed to the making of armed groups as the Red Brigades in Italy. In Fayoum University, violence was directed to the security forces that begun violence towards students.

3. throwing stones. Due to the security intervention and the excessive use of force in dealing with the student demonstrations and protests, the students throw stones at the security outside the university. It has evolved to burn the cars and tried to cut the streets outside the university to press on the security to leave the university.

> • Shooting gas and smoke by the security forces make us feel tired. If any student has fireworks, he will throw it at them. The fireworks do not cause any harm to them, but it is a kind of self-defense. Sometimes the security forces shoot rubber bullets into air while students throw stones at them (Participant, B 5).

Figure 16. Students are igniting fireworks in front of the College of Engineering.

It is clear from this picture that the students used fireworks in their demonstrations. The critical question is how did these fireworks enter the university? And how did the civil security did not inspect for those things? In fact, the entry of these tools comes in two ways: the first way with the bags of girls who are wearing veiled or perhaps under their clothes. Because of the lack of inspection devices, these materials can pass into the university. As for the safe way of putting these fireworks in a bag and throwing it from the top of the university wall and a student is waiting inside the campus will take it and, thus, the civic security cannot reach them. Consequently, the violence and political disorder that has occurred in Fayoum University after the events of the 30th of June 2013 give us some crucial indicators about the situation at the university.

– The political polarization has increased in the university among students. The polarization of a group is a social phenomenon that helps in creating an atmosphere of extremism and violence in a society that has this group. This has occurred with the Brotherhood group and resulted in increasing the level of polarization. The individuals who have similar ideas take another situation after consultations. The conditions of social and political isolation are imposed by the regime on the brotherhood group through creating a feeling of suspicion in this group or belonging to it. Therefore, the degree of polarization, violence, and extremism increased. The group practiced a self-isolation as well. Thus, it is logical not to believe any information or opinions from those who are from other groups. As a result of this, the political polarization increased and created different political belongings in the student community as the Brotherhood, Salafis, and Liberal students at Fayoum University.

– In the climate of repression of freedom and dictatorship, the unwilling of university administration to react to students' demands and the security grip on the university, the students feeling frustration, alienation, and injustice led the students to violence and rejected any source of authority in the university. The students are usually looking forward to a role and identity in the society. Therefore, they reacted to the political recession and authoritarian regimes by rebellion and riots. This has occurred to the students after the breakdown of the democratic practices in post-revolution.

– The non-constitutional legislative restriction is considered one of the regime's tools to dominate on the student protests. This method proved its failure and had pushed the university to a dangerous situation. The unconstitutional legislative restriction is one of the tools of the regime to control the protesting students. This method has proved its failure and has dragged the university to a dangerous juncture of confrontations between students and the regime. The issuance of resolutions that banned political action and restrict liberties is one of the main reasons for the clash between the state and students. It has also contributed significantly to the intensification of conflict and the emergence of violent currents among students.

– The absence of laws that regulates political work within the university. This is left to the discretion of the university President or the Deans of the colleges. Therefore, the political practice is characterized by ambiguity in the university. Moreover, the weakness of some universities administration and their instability under the revolution was one of the reasons that contributed to the waves of the student violence.

- The internal rule of universities is characterized by dictatorship and following the willing of the ruling regime. It is against any political movements within the university for democracy. These results prove that the administrations of Egyptian universities loss of vision. The universities' independence does not exist and the security is still controlling universities. Moreover, the absence of political spaces within the university to contain the movements of students for democracy.
- Universities have become victims of the confusion of concepts within society. This led to the decline of the rule of law and its position for the students. Moreover, the dependence of students to bullying groups outside the campus, where their movement has become attached to its organizational bases and intellectual orientations.
- The weakness and the decline of the educational process at the university. The curricula rely heavily on the overloading of information without attention to the development of critical dialogue and the spirit of criticism among students. Furthermore, the vast numbers of students in the classrooms, which prevents any dialogue between professors and their students. All this led to the demise of dialogue skills and accepted other opinions.
- Political violence within universities demonstrates the futility of policies designed to deal with young people. The slogans of empowering young people and qualifying them for leadership and responsibility in society are empty slogans. What is happening at Fayoum University is the best proof of that.
- The dysfunction of the security profession within the university. Administrative security lacks communication skills with students. The old idea of students is still engraved in the minds of the security forces. Administrative security also monitors student movements rather than maintaining security at universities. Therefore, this threatens the students' identity, affected the concept of belonging, and makes them feel insecure. This leads to the involvement of students in extremist and violent activities in and outside the university.

5.4 Fourth Theme: Forms of Social Interaction among Students at Fayoum University

Social interaction is a fundamental dimension of human practice within a social organization. It is a dynamic process of mutual influence among all individuals within a social milieu which result in various relationships and patterns of behavior forming a significant part of a culture of this social category. These social relationships and patterns of behavior arise from group members' meeting, exchanging feelings, their contact with each other, and their interaction in a so-ciety (Byrd, 2014; Chang, et al., 2006). Moreover, social relationships that arise between individuals in a society as a consequence of their interaction with one another are among necessities of life. Nobody or an institution can be envi-sioned to be successfully pursued unless it strives to regulate its social relations. Among them, there are forms of social interactions that reflect a cultural style prevailing within a group and contribute to its formation as well.

Within the student community at Fayoum University, there are many types of social interaction between students as individuals and as social groups. The prominent types of these relationships are solidarity, competition, and conflict, which play a social role in cohesion, integration or collapse of a student com-munity. In addition to the structure of power within a student community, which highlights means and forms of power distribution among them.

4.5.1 Relations of Solidarity, Competition, and Conflict.

4.5.1.1 Solidarity relations.

Solidarity relationships in a student community are represented in a set of so-cial processes that have an effective influence on the behavior of a social group and its members. Besides, social solidarity among students ensures integration of a group and leads to the formation of common intellectual and emotional symbols among members of this group. Solidarity relations include coopera-tion and mutual assistance as well as participation in all cheerful and painful situations among members of a student community. Thus, the relations of soli-darity are increasingly intensifying between student organizations with similar ideas such as the Salafis, the Brotherhood, the Independent, and Miṣr Al-Qawia students. Although students are different in their political and intellectual ori-entations, they are friends and classmates at the end.

One situation highlights solidarity of students who are ideologically different from each other, as there is an emotional solidarity with their colleagues. Dur-ing my conversation with a student in the third year at the College of Engineer-ing, Department of Civil Engineering about the current situation at the univer-sity and the clash between the students and the security forces. He expressed his view that some students had closed their eyes and followed some extreme ideas that linked to violence and revenge. This resulted in many violent events such as the attack on the security officials at the College of Education and College of Arts.

I expected a different answer from that student because he differs ideological-ly from the Muslim Brotherhood students who have committed these violent behaviors. However, I was surprised by his persuasive response to me that these students had fallen as victims to some destructive ideas. Then, they were treated harshly by the security forces. Because of their sense of surveillance, injustice, and suppression of their freedoms, they have been terrified and afraid of the cruelty and violence of the regime, which prompted them to act in such a violent manner. The Independent students mentioned:

> I sympathize with the students because I find there is violence acted by the security forces. The students express their opinion by drawing a caricature and by acting as a protest. Surely these things do not require hitting a gas bomb or rubber bullets. This generates solidarity with those students. I am a student if I see a person carries a paper and a pen, and another person carries a gas bomb and a weapon. I will sympathize with the ones who carry paper and pen (participant, D 1).

> The students, at first, were peaceful protesters. They did not start violence unless the security forces began violence. The students were injured, dismissed from the university, and arrested. Because of these practices, the students turned to violence (participant, D 4).

These attitudes highlight the degree of sympathy and solidarity with the Brotherhood students despite the rejection of some of their actions. The student finds the Brotherhood students as victims of the extremist ideas and the harassment of the security forces. This does not reflect schizophrenia in the students' personalities who feel solidarity with the Muslim Brotherhood students, but it reflects a degree of unity with them against the oppressive state machine "police", which enjoys hatred much among the masses of Egyptian people, especially the students. The solidarity among students was not only emotional, but also students took practical steps for their colleagues who had been dismissed from the college or arrested by the security forces. They were trying to meet the Dean of the college to mediate for not dismiss those students or to demand releasing the detainees. A Brotherhood student stated:

> We met the Dean to speak about the examinations. Another time, we met him for our colleagues who were arrested. Some students were dismissed from the college. We were as intermediaries for them (participant, B 4).

These meetings were not always helpful with the Dean of the college. The students organized many sit-ins in front of the office of the Dean and the university President to demand releasing their colleagues who had been arrested. An example of that was the strike of students at the College of Engineering to urge the university administration or, more precisely, to force it to mediate for releasing those students. From the students' perspective, the students were arrested indiscriminately without any guilt or crime. The university administration must acts quickly to release them from the prison.

> The past two days, we had a strike in the college because six students were dismissed. Ok, you dismissed them on which basis? One of these students was absent the whole week before the strike. He was not in the college at all! The reason for the dismissal is that the students participated in the demonstrations. Because of this, the students

made a strike not to attend lectures, while a small number who does not care about anything except success attended lectures [21](participant, B 5).

> The President of the university has the authority to release students. We knew that in the last strike at the College of Engineering. The President of the university and the Deans intervened and spoke to the security forces and the students were released. They can do that (participant, B 10).

The students deplore the arrest of their colleagues and believe that the reasons for the arrest are unclear and vague. They also suppose that the dismissal of students is random. Furthermore, their conviction that the President of the university can release the detained students by providing a certificate of proper conduct for students and they can be released. This may be an unrealistic sense of the Rector's power in his intervention with the security forces. However, the students have high expectations for the political position of the President of the university and his ability to release the students from the grip of the police.

> The university President can release the detained students. This was obvious through what happened to those students. We organized a sit-in and no one attended lectures until releasing our colleagues. The President of the university made a phone call to release these students. If the Chief of the university's security issued a certificate of good behavior for students and it is signed by the Dean of the college and the university President, the detained students will be released. This is because they declared their proper conduct and behavior before turning the police report into a criminal case (participant, B 3).

The students suspended the study at the College of Engineering and entered in an open sit-in to release their colleagues who had been arrested at the college. All students of the college joined the strike and refused to enter the studying halls until their colleagues were released. The students who were arrested did not involve in the demonstrations or any political activity, but the security forces came and randomly arrested them.

> Our strike at the College of Engineering was a result of the arrest of twenty students. Eighteen of them were released and this was a good result. I can not confront the state and we are a group of students. Fifty-One Institute of Engineering supported us during the strike. They said if the situation is getting worse, we are possible to participate with the engineering students at Fayoum ... We voted on the strike and we decided that if 51% of students agreed on the decision of the strike, the other 49% of the students must participate with us. The results of the vote were 99% of the students agreed to make the strike. The students who refused were the first students came to the strike. We continued the strike for fifteen days, but as students, we cannot resist more than that. This is because the security forces will come to us with heavy weapons and behave in a brutal way (participant, B 5).

---

[21] In fact, the students were in solidarity with the dismissed students and did not attend lectures or any scientific activity within the college. Many students, who do not have any political or ideological affiliations, joined them. I watched this strike, which lasted almost a week. Indeed, the university administration responded and addressed the security until the detained students are finally released.

The students also carry out a form of financial solidarity by collecting money to pay fines for the detained students, whose families cannot pay to release them from the prison. The public prosecution has imposed fines on students who are politically active and who have been arrested by the security forces. These fines are often higher than the family's financial income. The students' contributions through money facilitate releasing the detained students. Despite the small amount of the collected money, it contributes to some extent in reliving the financial crises of the detained students and their families. The students do not work and they still receiving money from their parents. When a student gives money of his or her daily or monthly pocket money to help the detainees, this reflects a high degree of solidarity with the students regardless of their political orientation.

> The security forces arrest students and those students will be released after paying fines. The amount of fines is between 10,000 and 50,000 Egyptian pounds. Some families cannot pay the fines. We collect an Egyptian pound from every student at the studying hall (Participant, B 2).

Moreover, one of the prominent methods of solidarity that students often do is to write on the walls of colleges for the students who have been arrested or dismissed. This offers a simple example of assistance to those students who have been oppressed according to the student's view. The students' writings are spread intensively on the outer walls of colleges and the doors of bathrooms. This highlights the state of repression and the weakness of freedom of expression at the university, which prompts students to write in these places and in this way.

> When I write freedom to someone, he may be my colleague, but I do not know him. When he or she read his name, she or he should say, He is a detainee. In this way, I let her or him know. It is, of course, not something beautiful to write on the walls of the college but this is the only way (participant, B 1).

> No, of course, for all students. For example, a student called Abdul Rahman has been judged for three years in prison and he has no relationship with the Brotherhood (participant, B 8)[22].

---

[22] Although the Muslim Brotherhood students are trying to show that the detained students have no political activity at all and this is partly true, most of the detained students are following the organization of the Brotherhood and they have an explicit political activity. They have prepared student cadres in the organization of the Muslim Brotherhood. However, some students may suddenly pass next to the demonstration or the march at the moment of the security entries to the university. In this way, they are arrested with the rest of the members of the organization. This reflects the lack of professionalism of the Police. The students of the Muslim Brotherhood take the seeds that there are students who are not affiliated with the Muslim Brotherhood. This is a kind of negative propaganda that highly strengthens students' solidarity with the Muslim Brotherhood and rapidly increases anger towards the security force.

Although this is a way of solidarity, it is also a way of making students aware of the arrested and dismissed students to mobilize anger against the state. The students usually publish news about students, both dismissed and detainees, whether they are members of the Muslim Brotherhood or not. They take advantage of arresting students to distort the image of the ruling regime as it restricts freedom and practices dictatorship in its ugliest forms. The picture shows some students' writing on the walls of College of Education.

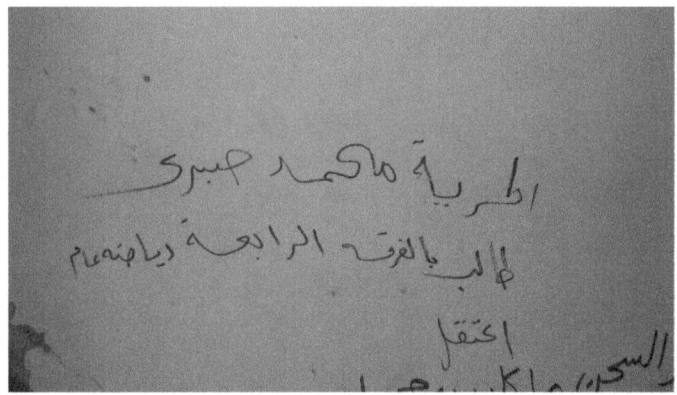

Figure 17. The students' writing on the walls of the College of Education demanding the release of a student detained by the security forces.

It presents the students' demand for releasing the arrested students by the security forces. Besides, the writing is obviously clear on the wall of all buildings at the College of Education. The writings are usually in the area that the students can see it clearly. The students also made graffiti pictures of the students who were arrested and who died because of their political activity both in the university and in the events of *Rabʿah Al-ʿdawiyah*. This mechanism is also designed to prevent the administrative security or the cleaning workers in the college from removing the drawings and writings of the Brotherhood students. It is also a kind of innovation in the mobilization of students' anger against the practices of the regime.

However, on the educational level, the solidarity relationships are highlighted by assisting their colleagues who have been unfairly failed in exams. The students can help and assist other students by providing notes or trying to explain and summarizing lectures so that they can succeed in these subjects.

> For example, the exam result in this year is quite bad. The students who failed entirely in the exam were about 30 students from 238 students. More than 100 students failed partly in one or two courses. This is a high percentage of failing in the exam. Thus, we are in solidarity with those students. I am one of the students who succeeded in the exam and my general grade is good. I have no problem, but I was in support of the requests of the students to re-correct the exam papers (participant, B 5).

Figure 18. The students' graffiti on the walls of the College of Engineering.

The students support their colleagues who have experienced difficulties from professors. They attempt to find ways to help them overcome this impasse. The succeeded students assist other students who failed in the exam by explaining the course's subjects and summarizing papers to them. Moreover, the solidarity relations are manifested in the emotional and practical participation of the students with their fellows in the social events, whether pleasant or sad. This reflects a significant deal of cohesion among student.

> The students support their colleagues in pleasent times. For example, in the wedding of my sister, I invited my colleagues. All of them came to the wedding (Participant, B 8).

The solidarity relationships are also noticeable in cases of the death of any member of astudent's family. The students support their colleague in these difficult circumstances. This shows cohesion of the student community at the university and the degree of awareness among students, despite the problems left by the political events that followed the January 25th Revolution of 2011 and the events of the 30th of June 2013.

> When my father died, I was in my first year in the College of Engineering. I was new and just knew a few colleagues. Most of the students who know me or not came to my home. The students who could not come, they took my phone number and called to solace me. I saw students for the first time at my father's home. Before that, we had no connections between each other (participant, B 5).

> One of our friends named Muhammad Adel his father died last year. We said; let us go to the funeral. Thus, we went and attended the burial and consolation. We were able to solace Muhammad in the death of his father (participant, D 3).

These solidarity relations enhance cohesion of the student community. The students are moving quickly to help their colleagues in times of adversity or distress. It demonstrates the authenticity and uniqueness of Egyptian personality and the unity and adhesion of the student community regardless of political and ideological orientation.

4.5.1.2 Competitive relations.

Competition is a fundamental feature of social interaction in human societies. It involves interaction and struggle to achieve specific goals set by a social group. Although this interaction does not involve hostile tendencies between individuals and competing social groups, after the January 25th Revolution of 2011, competition between student organizations intensified to control the student community. The freedom zone at Fayoum University after the revolution increased competition between the masses of students of different attitudes.

Each team attempted to show its ideas, visions, and provide services and activities to students. The competition on the Student Union elections has emerged clearly. In this context, some questions arise about the nature of competition among student groups. Why are they competing? And with those who allow this kind of relationship to emerge? What are the main areas of competition?

> Elections were conducted transparently and impartially. However, the spirit of rivalry was a loathsome one (participant, B 3).

Moreover, the student union elections have been run, every student factions attempted to present itself correctly and not to harm the competing parties. The students invented tools and methods to use in the elections and to compete other candidates. For example, they prepared electoral programs, conferences, and meetings to present their vision and provide services to students.

> When I nominated for the Student Union elections, I was in the second year at the college. There were candidates from the fourth year in the college. I noticed that conflict was fierce among students. I found it as a strong completion, not a real conflict and this is acceptable. However, the situation getting worse because the students of the Brotherhood won the Student Union and the other students did not want to cooperate with them. I am a candidate for the Student Union elections; if I win, it is ok. If I lose, I will participate in the student activities (participant, B 2).

It is noted that the Brotherhood students believe that competition was for serving students. Moreover, they considered it useful for all students. The relationship between the Salafis students and the Brotherhood students has many problems that may be back to ideological differences between the two groups. Further, the Salafis students are the real student group that can compete the Brotherhood students at Fayoum University. The Salafis students sought strongly to win the Student Union elections. Indeed, they won the first student elections after the revolution at Fayoum University in 2011/2012. The Independent students' responses were closed to the Brotherhood. They mention:

> There was freedom in practicing activities after the January 25th Revolution of 2011. All students were open-mindedness. Professors wanted to help students. All students were competing for providing activities including making abstracts for courses and summarizing lectures (participant, D 2).

> After the revolution, there were many problems between students; no one can deny that. However, it was problems for competition. All student factions want to win and want to take the majority of the Student Union. It was honest competition. It has a meaning that I want to serve other students. The competition was all about serving students. It is not because that I want just to win. It was a very fierce competition (Participant, B 4).

> The students participated in the Student Union elections with an enormous desire because there were real freedom and democracy after the revolution. We thought that it is a real and honest competition. The student who wins will provide services and who did not win, will participate in the student activities (participant, D 3).

> There was a variance between students in some events because it is not normal to agree on everything all the time. The beginning of splits was before the Presidential election in 2012. There were some verbal clashes between students during the Student Union elections. However, it was a real competitive election among students (participant, D 9).

After the January 25th Revolution of 2011, the student community at Fayoum University was characterized by freedom and democracy. The spirit of positive participation and honest competition among students were spread. There was nothing in the students' minds except working hard to develop the country through the provision of services to students to establish a better university life. However, the events that followed the 30th of June 2013 have deeply impacted and caused divisions and rivalry between various student factions at Fayoum University.

4.5.1.3 Conflict relations.

Conflict is a pattern of social interaction that arises from opposing interests. Competitors realize that there is no solution to reconcile their interests and this moves competition to a conflict that each party tries to destroy the interests of his rival. The competition relationships between student organizations have evolved to take a more serious form which is the relationship of conflict. This began when the Constitutional Amendments were adopted and then followed by the Presidential elections.

The student community has divided and the discord between student organizations has increased. Conflict became apparent in the students' actions and behavior. In the Student Union elections, the Muslim Brotherhood students described students who did not want to work with them as they are having personal desires and did not want to work in a team or follow orders from a leader.

> Those students do not want to provide activities for other students. They do not want to work under the name of the Muslim Brotherhood. They want to make personal activities, or he wants to be a commander and not a soldier under the Muslim Brotherhood flag (participant, B 1)[23].

It is noted that the Muslim Brotherhood students, after winning the Student Union elections, have sought to work under the title of the Brotherhood, which led to hatred of the other students to work under this name. Because what the students do, it will not belong to the student organization as a whole, but it will be attributed to the organization of the Muslim Brotherhood students. As a result, the students of the Brotherhood felt that other students refuse to work with them and the rest of student factions oppresses them. This may be unrealistic feeling as students who follow other political organizations, or the Independent students have a genuine desire for political and voluntary work at the university. However, the bureaucracy of the Brotherhood students, their passion for control and leadership, and their desire to be always at the center of command and decision-making have alienated students and make them refuse to participate with them in activities.

> We expected that it is a real and honest competition. However, we found it a battle. You or me. When we won the Student Union elections, they said; how the students elect them? How can they win? It was a survival battle for the strongest or a battle for existence (participant, B 1).

> Some students refused to join us in activities. They said we would not participate with you under any circumstances, regardless of any reasons (participant, B 9).

The Muslim Brotherhood students insisted on their position, which caused problems with other students. The recognition that the students are the actors and that they will carry out all activities as a team does not satisfy the Brotherhood students. They want all student groups to work on their orders and under the name of the Muslim Brotherhood students.

> After the events of the 30th of June 2013, the competition turned into a battle of existence. Your blood is cheap and valueless. Even they wish death to you. Some students

---

23 This female student is one of the active leaders of the Muslim Brotherhood students at the College of Education. She has several explicit participation and leadership roles in the process of preparing for the Student Union elections and supporting candidates in the university in general and in the College of Education in particular.

said to us that you deserve kill and slaughter. Those students are our colleagues at the university. Their view is this. They also insulted us. You are sons of a bitch and you are a terrorist. I change the concept from competition to lose of conscience (participant, B 1).

The Muslim Brotherhood students imagine that the rest of students, especially the Independent students and the liberal students have hatred and wish harm and troubles for them. This is due to the actions of the Muslim Brotherhood students to disable the study and endanger the lives of students because of the ongoing security raids on the university. We conclude from this, the ability of the regime through its media machine, to mobilize the public opinion against the actions of the Brotherhood students and provide a space for the students of the Muslim Brotherhood to act foolishly, increasing the hatred of the society to them.

One day, I think on Wednesday, 12/11/2014, I observed a group of students in front of the College of Engineering holding in their hands many batons and broken bottles. They tried to prevent the demonstration of the Brotherhood students from passing in front of the College of Engineering. I noticed that the Muslim Brotherhood students drop back and they decided to change the demonstration's route. Besides, I noticed many students of the Muslim Brotherhood insisted that the march must go in front of the College of Engineering whatever happens. Through this horrific situation, some students from the Muslim Brotherhood and some students who reject the Brotherhood demonstrations made short-term negotiations. As a result, the Brotherhood students return from where they came and not to go in front of the College of Engineering. The students of the College of Engineering, especially the students of the third year, prevent the demonstration from going in front of the College of Engineering. This is because a student of the third year at the Civil Engineering Department was hit in his legs during a fight with a student of the Muslim Brotherhood while hiding in the building of electric engineering.

Consequently, the third-year students of the Civil Engineering Department made a meeting to confront the Muslim Brotherhood students who hurt their colleague. The student has been moved to the university hospital to get treatment and medication for his hand and leg. The third-year students thought that this was intended action towards their colleague and they decided to prevent the Muslim students from passing in front of the College of Engineering. The students were aiming to send a particular message to the Muslim Brotherhood students that you will not be able to go from here and we can prevent all of you if we want that. If you have large numbers of the Brotherhood students, we also have enormous numbers and we can prevent you and clash with you if you want. We can stop you and take the right of our injured colleague.

During the demonstration and the ongoing clashes, I asked a Brotherhood student why the students of the College of Engineering try to prevent the demonstration from passing in front of the college? He said that there is a conflict between the supporters and the opponents of the regime's policies in Egypt. There is an allusion to the presence of non-student element entered by the security forces to create chaos and clashes with the Muslim Brotherhood students. Therefore, the conspiracy theory is still a reasonable explanation for the Brotherhood students that the security forces do all the procedures to create chaos in universities. Due to this, they could mobilize the public opinion to what students especially the Muslim Brotherhood students from the actions of the cracker, vandalism, and assaulting the other students at the university.

Moreover, the atmosphere was repleted with suspicion between the Muslims Brotherhood students and the students of the third year of the Civil Engineering Department. The situation has been possible to develop for severe clashes between the masses of students and this could lead to many violent events between them. However, the negotiations have ended this dilemma. This gives us an indicator that the students still have a basis for the open discussion with others who have different perspectives.

The violence practiced by the students of the Civil Engineering Department reflects the degree of anger from the Brotherhood students' actions towards their colleague. There were also feelings of discontent of some of the Muslim Brotherhood students from preventing them from passing in front of the College of Engineering. A Muslim Brotherhood student said, "*Mish Hansibhuwm Yirkabuwna*" this slang meaning expresses not to allow the students of the College of Engineering to implement their willings and decisions and that will make them dare to the Brotherhood students at the university. Those students were extremely nervous and if there was no leader for the demonstration and some individuals who tried to calm things down the situation might be exploded and become difficult to control. This reflects intolerance between student groups which contributed significantly to the existence of tension between the masses of students on campus.

It is noted that the Muslim Brotherhood students within the university follow the protracted policy and their organization within the university is strong and stable. This organization involves large numbers of students within the university. Moreover, the overriding goal of the demonstrations is to mobilize the public opinion and bring out more of discontent against the Military rule of the country. It is also noted that the state of fear, panic, and concern among the protesters because the security continues detention of students, in addition to the presence of many surveillance cameras deployed inside the campus and colleges. This result is comparable with the results of many studies (Petras, 1 969; Levine, 1979; Michiya Shimbori et al., 1980; Statera, 1979).

4.5.2 The Structure of Power in the Student Community at Fayoum University.

Power is among the central concepts in politics and sociology. Many scientists were studying the concept since ancient times, from Plato to Foucault and Botomore (Al-Hadiniy, 1999). It is a sociopolitical phenomenon that exists in any social or human groupings, whether small or large. It is an instrument of one of the parties of social interaction in imposing its control and will on the other party through oppression and domination. Thus, power is a social relation in which one party accepts to be subject to the other and then the other exercises control, coercion, and violence.

Moreover, the concept of power is linked to several other concepts, such as control, through which the mechanisms of power are exercised by the regime over people through violence, maneuvering, negotiation, and lying. The concept of dominance refers to the temptation of the other to submission and keeps away from the opposition (ṣiyam, 2009). There are many power relations between student groups themselves and between them and university administration. In this context, some questions arise about the nature of the power relations that exist in the student community? Their forms and determinants? And the methods of authority in dominating the student organizations at Fayoum University?

4.5.2.1 Forms and distribution of power in the student community.

Power is distributed in the student community at Fayoum University across two levels: horizontal and vertical. The first level represents practice power among student groups on campus where the force is disproportionately distributed among student groups. The group that possesses and practice power has multiple sources of power, which includes large numbers of members, its organizational power, and its attachment to the decision-making circles of the university. The physical power and verbal ability govern interaction between student organizations. A good example is what happened between the students of the Muslim Brotherhood and the Independent students at the College of Engineering and the College of Social Work.

> The students at the university divided into two sects one with the regime and the other against the regime ... If the Brotherhood students are organizing a march, it is highly possible that the other students confront it. I saw here at the College of Social Work that the students in the demonstration stand in front of the university's main gate which is in front of the College of the Social Work. The students of the College of Social Work do not want demonstrations in front of their College because they want to enjoy their time. Each student sits with his girlfriend. Sometimes, these students beat the pro-Brotherhood students with wood and bricks. I swear to God that many stu-

210

dents beat their colleague because of the difference of views or because he does not want any student to pretend (participant, D 4).

Students fight each other with knives, baton and broken bottles. This has not existed before (participle, D 3).

I am with the protest if it is peaceful without insulting opponents. The insults sometimes were terrible words that are not suitable for the university life (participant, D 1).

Their students said to us that we deserve slaughtering and death (participant, B 1).

Although there are large numbers of the Muslim Brotherhood students in various colleges of the university and the strength of their organization, they were not strong after the events of the 30th June of 2013. This is because many students have dared and challenge them as a result of the political events and the state's hostility to them. However, before that, they had the upper hand in the student community. They practiced a social control over individual students or groups. They used religion as an important weapon in deterring any dissent and spreading the discipline within student groups. This happened when some students at the College of Arts wanted to organize cultural activities such as poetry, acting, and writing stories. The answer of the President of the Student Union, *"You are contrary to Sunnah and the Shari'ah"* (participant, D 8).

There were also things that gave the Brotherhood students a plenty of power than the rest of the other student organizations. Namely, their ability to resolve differences and influence on other student groups or their influence on the university administration, as the sole representative of authority in this educational space, is a source of power. This is because the Muslim Brotherhood students have a long history of political practice and their access to the position of president of the Student Union has contributed significantly to making them closer to the university administration.

The students of the Brotherhood also have an official responsible in the organization of the Muslim Brotherhood outside the university, which provides them with solutions to their problems and proposals to increase their activity and influence among other student groups. The following picture shows the ceremony of inauguration for the Student Union in the era of the Muslim Brotherhood and the presence of the university President and his three Vice-Presidents. This result is consistent with the results of (Mashyekhi, 2001). As after the Islamic Revolution in Iran, the Islamists student groups were closer to the university administration as they had the same ideology of the regime. This represented in the Office for Consolidation of Unity who dominated over student groups at the university.

Figure 19. The university President is attending the celebration of the inauguration of the new Student Union at Fayoum University[24].

The Brotherhood students were closely associated with the university administration after the revolution, especially during the reign of President Morsi. They increased their adhesion to the university administration and seemed to have a significant impact on the university administration regarding consultation with them on the problems and demands of students. The university administration celebrated the investiture of the Student Union. The access to the university president's office and meeting him became easy for the Muslim Brotherhood students. In the following picture, strong relations between the members of the Student Union and the university administration where the students sit at a table in exchange for the university President to discuss how to develop student activities within the university and to overcome all the obstacles that are facing students.

---

[24] Pictures number (19, 20) was taken with a permission of the Fayoum University website, www.fayoum.edu.eg.

Figure 20. The university President and the Vice-Presidents had a meeting with the Student Union to figure out the students' problems at Fayoum University.

The leader of the student group can resolve any clashes and conflicts that arise among members of the same group or between the student group and other groups. He leads the process of negotiations with other student groups to resolve conflict between them. Sometimes, when a member rejects the commands of the leader, or he declines in the tasks that are given to him, the leader rebuke him. There are set of rules for interaction that are predefined and must be respected.

If a member of this group exceeds those rules, he is exposed to reprimand, or he may be deprived of practicing activities of the group. This was clear during my presence in one of the student marches, in which a student who supports the regime came to the march and wanted to clash with the Brotherhood students. The leader of the march rebuked the other students and ordered them to retreat immediately. The students quickly retreated as soon as they heard the commander's instructions. This reflects a substantial control within the ranks of the group during the implementation of demonstrations and marches. However, on the second level of power, the vertical level is between the students and the university administration. Power practice at this level takes three forms, including visible power relations, invisible power relations, and hidden power relations. For the first type, which represents the visible power relations, the administration of the university governs through formal legislations and administrative decisions that block or allow areas of student activity within the university.

Fayoum University issued many decisions to prevent demonstrations, especially after the events of the 30th of June 2013, recalling many students to investigation and dismissed many students from the university. Furthermore, the university administration prevents students from using the studying halls to deliver political speeches at the university. All these decisions are for preventing the Brotherhood students from practicing their political activities which often run counter to the interests of the university administration and the ruling regime.

> They take the decision firstly. If the decision is in our favor, of course, it is okay. If it is not in our favor, we will refuse and make a complaint. We talk to the administration and sometimes they answer and sometimes not (participant, D 3).

> The administration has a specific direction. It takes the decisions that in favor of it but decisions in favor of the students no (Participant, B 2).

> The university administration called students for investigation. They said to students; we will dismiss you from the university. Do not do that and I will do other things for you (participant, B 1).

> We want to participate in the student activities, but they said, you are the Muslim Brotherhood student, you are forbidden from participation (participant, B 9).

Moreover, these decisions have given students a sense of persecution and that the university administration is intransigent in dealing with them. These decisions prevented them from expressing their views and demanding their rights, which they dreamed of obtaining them in the atmosphere of democracy and freedom that prevailed after the revolution. The invisible power relations were exemplified by the role of the university administration in showing students' political activity as violence against the state's institutions and other students. Moreover, the university administration has bonding charges of espionage and betrayal and portraying them in the role of criminals who attack their colleagues and threaten their educational future.

> They named us as thugs. And I said how you knew that these students are thugs? Did you ever discuss those thugs? Did you know how they think? (Participant, B 5).

> Falcon Company inspected students and even self-inspection. They forced students to pass through digital gates as criminals (Participant, D 9).

The university administration represented the relations of hidden power in blocking students' voices and preventing them from expressing their grievances and their demands for democracy. Other student groups were used to create the public domain of the university for the ideology of the regime. The university administration adopted specific student groups to confront the opposition of the student organizations (the Brotherhood students) or present the general atmosphere of the university as the regime sees it. Those students group called "patriotic students." This term has been widespread among university administrations after the events of the 30th of June 2013. The Brotherhood students stated:

> The number of student families began to decline because of the security. The student family remained a monopoly on a particular student group. It was forbidden for the Brotherhood to establish an official student family. Groups and activities are allowed to the students who are supporting the current regime or who have no political orientation (participant, B 2).

> The university administration and the Student Affairs Circles see that we have no right to exercise any activities (participant, B 7).

> The situation became worse; the university administration remained intransigent in tightening control on us (participant, B 1).

> The Vice Dean wanted to impose his opinion and ideas on how to organize student activities. He wanted us to make activities that he wants (participant, B 2).

4.5.2.2 methods of reward and punishment.

The methods of reward and punishment are used by the power holders to control and dominate other parties that are less powerful or have no power at all. In the student community, the university administration or the student group that hold power use various forms of punishment. As for the administration of the university, methods of punishment are represented in recalling students to investigation or dismiss of students entirely or partly from the university. It is also exemplified in calling the security forces to end the student demonstrations on campus, in addition to preventing the opposition students from practicing their activities within the university. As for students, they use several methods, including charges against students who oppose them. The Independent students have attributed many accusations to the Muslim Brotherhood students and deemed them as terrorists in addition to annoying them with obscene words. It has evolved into a clash with them by removing their paintings and banners hanging or written on the walls of colleges.

> The students are hanging posters about the events in Libya, Syria, and the Brotherhood suffering. The administrative security quickly removed the posters, which belong to the Brotherhood. However, the posters of Libya and Syria still existed (participant, D 5).

> In the marches, the students insulted us and called us as terrorists (participant, B 6).

> There are some students refused to talk with me, because I joined to the Brotherhood students in the college, but when the coup took place, they welcomed to talk to me again (participant, B 8).

> Some students blocked their friends on the Facebook (participant, D 1).

> Our slogan has been the Islam is the solution. Some students said you want to monopoly Islam on you (participant, B 1).

The Brotherhood students also use many methods of punishment within the university or between the Brotherhood group and other groups. They use the same methods as the Independent students used regarding bonding charges to other students. For example, they are the followers of the regime and they follow *Al-Sisi*. The Brotherhood students also mocked other students and sometimes clash and quarrel with them.

> The Muslim Brotherhood students are proud of their views and anyone who disagrees with them, they treat him savagely and violently (participant, D 3).

> The students of the Brotherhood despised the other students (participant, D 8).

As for the rewards, the university administration provides some incentives for the student groups who follow its orders and visions. The administration has opened the university's public domain for those student groups to carry out their activities. Furthermore, it provided them with financial and incorporeal support by issuing approvals quickly while this is far from reachable for different student groups with them in orientations.

> In order not to be a liar, the administration responds the students' requests that agree with its interests, but not all the requests (participant, D 3).

> We witnessed a situation from the university President that made us laugh. There was an event called the university Got Talent and it was a beautiful event. The university President came and attended, but he refused to sit with the students who have urgent problems. That is a shame (participant, B 5).

In this way, the university administration attempts to control the student community through methods of punishment and practice of soft or coarse power with students or by rewarding some student groups to impose its vision on students. It strives in various ways to push students toward acceptance of the dominant regime by establishing ideological control and domination. This result intersects with the studies of Suchlicki (1969), Lane (1973), and Sakurai (2004). Most regimes after revolutions try to attract and dominate the student movement at universities through granting more privileges to the regime-related students. In Iran, an entrance examination to the university according to the loyalty to the Islamic Revolution was implemented. In Russia, the job opportunities and academic positions were subject to the loyalty to the communist ideology. In Cuba, the scholarship system was based on the loyalty to the new regime.

5.5 Fifth Theme: Voluntary and Charity Activities

Voluntary and charity work is conspicuously a key pillar in supporting social cohesion in societies. It motivates students to engage in community issues and raise the level of their awareness and responsibility along with the exploitation of their energies in meeting the needs of a society and solve its problems. Moreover, it helps students to open up to their communities and creates an indispensable role for them to feel their ability to change and influence people around them. It is a tool and a means to develop students' personalities and abilities as well as imparting important skills and positive values such as solidarity, tolerance, fraternity, compassion, cooperation, and responsibility (Cnaan et al., 2010; McCabe et al., 2007).

Voluntary and charity action is the contribution of individuals to the work of welfare and social development, whether by opinion, effort or finance. It is a characteristic of volunteerism that it is based on the cooperation of individuals with each other to provide the needs of their community. This leads to a fundamental point that volunteering comes from an understanding of a society's needs. Voluntary is the effort that an individual makes deliberately and freely to provide service to the community without expecting a reward for this effort.

The students at Fayoum University have enormous interest and increasing participation in charity and voluntary activities inside and outside the university. There were many different student organizations which aimed to provide services for students within the university. In addition, the community surrounding the university became a scene of practicing many voluntary and charity activities. In the midst of the revolution, change began to affect all the pillars of Fayoum University and then the area of charity and voluntary activities began to increase in the university.

All student groups were able to enter and to practice activities on campus, which was previously out of reach. The new student organizations that were established after the revolution such as *Fiqrah Group*, *Snaᶜ Al-Hayah*, and *Miṣr Al-Qawia* group have engaged in the student activities. Consequently, the state of democracy and freedom formed at the university after the January 25th Revolution of 2011, has already contributed significantly to flourishing volunteer activities of the student factions in Fayoum University. The Islamist student factions, which have had a long history of voluntary and charity action, had a heavy agenda of political activity in the post-revolution era. The political activities have dominated their efforts which contributed to giving the new student organizations an opportunity to impose themselves on the scene of activities on campus. Everyone rushed to serve the community and to solve its problems hoping for the desired change. The university was ready for the student activities, charity, and voluntary.

All student groups from different ideological orientations have started organizing medical convoys and exhibitions for books and clothes which increased significantly from the era before the revolution. There has been a change in the content of these activities and in the target groups especially after the events of the 30th of June 2013. This is due to the tendency of students to work in more voluntary activities because they are safer than political activities that turned into riots and violence between the Brotherhood students and the security forces.

The charity and voluntary actions are an important component of the student activities at the university. The students' reasons to join in the voluntary action at Fayoum University are due to their desire for change, which was a dominant feature of the society after the January 25th Revolution of 2011. In addition to the desire to provide services that contribute to the development of the local community in Fayoum Governorate. The incentive to do well and the desire to participate was the main reason which led large numbers of students to join the charity work. The members of the *Enactus* team and *Giil Waʿiy* Family expressed their aims for joining voluntary work as the following:

> The idea that you will change the world or makes a difference will feel it while working in Enactus (A member of Enactus Fayoum)[25].

> The university students have energies, potential, and want to work and change the society.

> At first, it is a personal attitude and desire of student that he wants to help when he sees another student offers help. Thus, he wants to do like him (The President of Giil Waʿiy Family)[26].

The aims and targets of voluntary and charity activities are varied among students. Serving society, solving its crises, and participating actively in its development are considered substantial goals for the students. Also, helping critical cases in the community, who need much support such as the poor, the homeless, the orphans, the elderly, and the widows are among their aims. This is represented a vital issue for students to direct their activities towards the disadvantaged and marginalized groups that are suffering from the harshness of life. The aims of voluntary activities have also expanded to provide an educational care for the orphaned children in shelters which are neglected by the state, as well as providing educational services for the illiterate workers at Fayoum University and to the children of the low-income families in slums at Fayoum.

> Each one has a mission in his life such as you help others; you see a smile on the face of your colleague or the workers at the college. Any charity activity aims to serve the other and sow in your life that you do an honorable thing (A member of the Giil Waʿiy Family)[27].

---

[25] This female student is in the second year at the Department of English Language, College of Arts.

[26] This female student is in the third year at the Department of Chemistry, College of Education. She has a highly rich religious background.

[27] This female student is in the third year at the Department of Biology, College of Education.

There is a project in which we are working on it now called *Baṣirah* and aims to help the blind people (The President of Enactus Fayoum)[28].

Our goal, along with social care, was to provide educational services. Why do these children not enroll in the high school education then university? (The President of Giil Waʿiy Family).

5.5.1 Volunteerism as a Human Situation

Voluntary and charity activities carried out by students have varied inside and outside Fayoum University. Many student organizations have provided activities within the university because they do not have the organizational capacity or the financial resources to provide activities outside the university. One of the major activities that were offered within the university is the Blood Donation Campaigns led by the Giil Waʿiy and Resalah Family. They provided blood bags to the governmental hospitals which are in a constant need of it in Fayoum. Most patients in those hospitals are poor and needy. Consequently, these activities are also steered indirectly to this category.

> In the Blood Donation Campaigns, students agreed with the university's hospital doctors to participate in the campaign and then give the blood bags to the hospitals (A member of the Giil Waʿiy Family)[29].

Welcoming the new students and providing assistance, at the beginning of the study year, helped them to adapt quickly to the university atmosphere. These also help them to conduct a medical examination, submission of their documents to the staff of the Student Affairs, pay tuition, and choose academic sections, especially in the College of Education and College of Arts. Giil Waʿiy Family sought to provide these services in most colleges at Fayoum University, where the students stood to organize rows for applicants and provide them with water and food (dates).

> As for my experience with the team here in the College of Education, we have noticed that the new students do not find water to drink and the place in front of the office of the Student Affairs is extremely crowded. Most of the new students have lost and did not know how to apply or go to the medical examination. This was the first start of our family. We talked to each other, let's help these new students. This was successful work. In the second year, many students interacted with us from other families to help in this task (The President of Giil Waʿiy Family).

---

[28] This student is in the third year at the Department of Electrical Power, College of Engineering. He is very active and has significant leadership potentials. He also has good relationships with the university administration.

[29] This female student is in the second year at the Department of History, College of Education.

Figure 21. A book fair at the College of Education organized by Giil Waʿiy Family.

The exhibitions of clothes and study stationery, offered by many student organizations to the poor and needy students at a subsidized or low price, are one of the main student activities with a human nature. The aim is to help the poor students to afford the burden of study and its costs, because of the high prices of clothing, study tools and textbooks imposed in a compulsory way to students by professors. These exhibitions help to alleviate students' suffering and are often offered merchandise at the actual cost.

> They were making sorting clothes for the clothing exhibitions for the needy students. Each student in the family has a role in preparing for that exhibition such as washing sorting or reorganizing that clothes (A member of Giil Waʿiy Family)[30].

> With experience, we spoke to each other that we are doing charity activities and we should organize low priced exhibitions. We should not get any profit because the students need it (The President of Giil Waʿiy Family).

Some of the clothes exhibitions are not for the new clothes, but they were for the second- hand clothes. Members of the student family are cleaning, arranging, and displaying clothing in an attractive way for the students at these exhibi-

---

[30] This female student is in the second year at the Department of History, College of Education.

tions. The student families also invited some commercial institutions to offer their goods to the students with a minimum profit. This, in turn, is a kind of social solidarity among students. One of the crucial issues, in which the revolution had a significant impact, was the expansion of the student activity into the community outside the university.

Conditions were not appropriate for student activities within the university, especially after the events of the 30th of June 2013, and the passion of students to demonstrate their ability to bring about the required change as a mechanism to solve the problems of Egyptian society. One of the essential activities provided by a student organization called Enactus. This student organization presents voluntary and charity activities based on the idea of entrepreneurship. The students established a project for vegetable marketing to help the poor and needy people. The project began with a woman who was begging in the mosques in "Al-Sufi" area at Fayoum city.

> It means that when a poor man in need for 100 Egyptian pounds and I gave it to him, he is still poor and in need of 100 Egyptian pounds. By these 100 Egyptian pounds, I have started a small project for him and I can apply all the principles of entrepreneurship that I have learned at Enactus such as Business Model - Business Shorter - Business Plan (The President of Enactus Fayoum).

The woman changed from the begging life to a stable social life. She has a role and an influence in the society in where she lives. All the social problems of this woman have been solved and this project has contributed to providing a steady income for this family. Although the idea and cost of the project are simple, the method of implementing and following-up is surprise and excitement. The fact that the students follow the scientific method in studying, planning, and implementing projects is an indicator of the changes in the pattern of thinking and addressing the issues of the society.

> I started to consult with the team about the appropriate projects that save her time and to be close to her children and her sick husband. The suggested project was the vegetable marketing. This is because there was no one selling vegetables on this street or the adjacent streets. Any inhabitant wants to buy vegetables; he walks long to the main street. We agreed on the vegetable project is the basis, but it was necessary to consider three factors which are the economic factor, social factor, and environmental factor. The economic factor is to provide a source of income for that family. The social factor is to raise the living standard of this family. As for the environmental factor, I make a project which does not harm the environment. Therefore, we put the vegetables in a proper plastic envelope. We brought the vegetables from the big market "Al-Shadir" and prepared a place in her house to sell these vegetables. Day after day, we were monitoring the project and we were in contact with her to solve any problems that she faces. Besides, she was trying to rely basically on herself and the phone calls between us did not exceed that she was trying to thank us. She started a project with 100 pounds began to supply potatoes and tomatoes to the neighbors and reached to the whole area. The sense of pride that you established a project like this with a short budget. I turned

my knowledge in business to real action. How do you take care of your product? How do you keep this simple project running? (The President of Enactus Fayoum).

Finally, the importance of these projects stems from supporting the poor and marginalized and providing a chance for students to apply what they have learned from entrepreneurship in Enactus. The *Baṣirah* project is a vision of voluntary projects to help the blind people to integrate them into the society and become productive members. This contributes significantly to break their isolation in the society and increase confidence in their potentials.

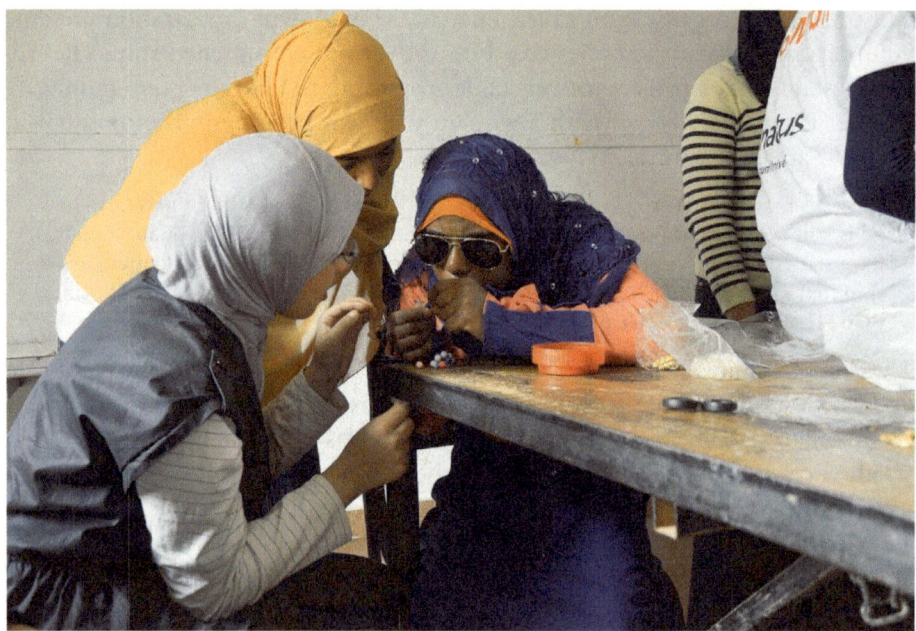

Figure 22. The Enactus students support the blind people in their training on craft works.

The students provided the necessary training for the blind people to master the craft work and tried to market products to ensure the continuity of the production process. Paying attention to these people has significance regarding trying to achieve social justice. The human and societal nature of these projects and the insistence on success are indicative of changes in the culture of voluntary and humanistic work for the students.

There is a project in which we are working on now called *Baṣirah*. The project aims to help the blind people to use the loom to produce craft works. We have a man who trains them on the loom and other activities. He is blind like them, but he is skillful in such things. We made an agreement with the art shops to add aesthetic recipes to the handwork of the blind people. We went to many boutiques to sell the blind's products with the actual cost. In this stage, we did not aim to get a profit from that; we need the work to be continued. We started with five people and other five will be trained in the next weeks (The President of Enactus Fayoum).

The students also carried out educational activities for the orphaned children in shelters. Giil Waʿiy family provided an educational service for these children to help them succeeding in schools. The orphan children do not receive any educational care in shelters which causing dropping out from schools. Many of these children cannot read or write even though they are in different stages of education in primary and middle school. Moreover, the students have condensed social welfare and educational attention for these children to encouraging the Social Welfare Institutions to pay attention to them in an integrated way. The students found the intransigence of the Director of ʿAisha Hassanein Institution for orphans in Fayoum city. The students tried to overcome the bureaucracy of these institutions, but they found that the Director and all the staff of ʿAisha Hassanein Institution for Orphans had negative thoughts about the abilities of orphaned children, which could destroy any attempts to rescue these children.

> One of the most significant activities we have started is that my team was taking care of the orphanage of ʿAisha Hassanein Institute. Our goal, alongside with social welfare, was to provide an educational care for the children. Why do children not enroll in the high school or university? This came to our minds form a long time when we went to the orphanage and met the responsible and talked to the children. We found the children educational level is quite low and the responsible for the children said that these children could not go to high school. The words remained in our minds; the children cannot get into a high school and a university. We talked to the Director of the institute that we will care about the children and teach them reading and writing. There was a student in the preparatory school; we said that we would care about him and I gave a promise to the head of the institute that this child will go to the high school. Frankly, I felt that the educational problems came from the institute and did not relate to the children abilities (The President of Giil Waʿiy Family).

It is important to point out that the activities of the student family have extended to the children of the poor and deprived areas, the slums and popular neighborhoods in Fayoum and also in some of the poor villages. The students established an educational center to help children to be interested in education and construct good educational values such as accepting school, rejecting cheating, and mastering the skills of reading and writing. Many-if not-most of the children in those areas are suffering from poor reading and writing skills, school antipathy, and the entire educational process.

Figure 23. A female student of Giil Waʿiy Family with the orphan children.

Under the circumstances that Egypt is witnessing from the economic crises and the low income families which are not enough for anyone. Teachers get 25 Egyptian pounds for every student in a private lesson for one hour... We were interested that the students like education and teachers even under the culture of beatings cruelly... For example, we met a child whose parent was divorced and he has many psychological problems. Therefore, we bring our friends from the College of Social Work to help us in solving this problem. All the childrens' families were involved in the process of edu- cating their children. When a mother beats her son severely, we treat the situation by proper connections between the teacher and the mother. The children started to accept their teachers at schools... How can I improve the education through my vision and thought? The students at the middle schools cannot read or write. I began to sow in the children' minds that never do cheating even if you will fail in the exam. If you fail, I will teach you again. I teach you to learn not only to succeed. The students became aware of that. A child's father told us that his son might fail in the coming exams. I told him, let your son fails. Your son is now in the third year at the primary school and if he succeeded, he would transfer to the fourth year. In the fourth year, there are class- es for sciences and social studies and your son cannot read or write yet. Thus, it is not fair to let him get into the fourth year because he will never succeed. People began to accept our ideas. Thus, he left his son to fail and lost a year to save his whole future (A member of Giil Waʿiy Family)[31].

The interest of the students in providing educational activities to these disadvantaged or oppressed groups that do not receive high- quality educational services in schools, reflects an increase in their awareness, and the transformation of their voluntary activities into a more social cohesion. They attempted with their simple tools and small budgets to confront the reality in their societies to fill the gap in the role of the state towards these needy groups, in educational, social or cultural sides. Their educational message, which they want to deliver to the community, is primarily to build an integrated personality via comprehensive curricula not just a separate set of information without any link between them. They look at the problem of education in a comprehensive way and they are struggling with habits and misconceptions about education and the entire educational process that many institutions in Egyptian state have failed to achieve.

5.5.2 Volunteerism as Creativity and Innovation

The students have created various voluntary and charity activities that have a positive impact on the local community of Fayoum Governorate. The students endeavored to solve the energy problems in Egypt. They moved quicker than the government in facing the crisis. They implemented the biogas project in the poor areas of Fayoum Governorate. Moreover, this project also aimed to solve the problems of small farmers regarding fertilization in their land and the elimination of weeds affecting the productivity of crops. The students invented an appropriate solution which is the biogas project.

> Recently with the energy problems in Egypt, we asked farmers what are their problems with the gas cylinder? Because it costs now 50 or 60 Egyptian pounds in the black market. Therefore, we have realized that they have a problem in the waste and in the manure of cows which is the reason for the emergence of harmful yellow weeds. Consequently, they use a chemical spray for getting rid of these weeds (weed control) and buy inorganic fertilizers which cost 4000 Egyptian pounds every three months and this is a significant amount for them. We attempted to solve this problem and we thought about biofuels. Thus, we have established the unit of biogas under the ground so that the fermentation gets. We estimated an initial cost of 5,000 Egyptian pounds per unit, but this amount of money is higher than our financial resources. If we establish 30 biogas unites with a cost of 5000 Egyptian pounds, the amount would be 150 thousand pounds (The President of Enactus Fayoum).

---

[31] This female student is in the third year at the Department of Biology, College of Education.

*Figure 24. A student member of Enactus during the digging process for making the
biogas unit at Fayoum[32] .*

The project endeavored to resolve the energy problem in addition to providing
a healthy and suitable alternative for fertilization. This is a remarkable development in the quality of voluntary activities carried out by the students. It has exceeded providing individual timely services to provide services that solve the
problems of the local community and contribute to its development. The implementation of this type of projects needs a study and planning in advance and
the ability to convince the public to abandon traditional methods in favor of
using of modern methods. In fact, these obstacles could seriously threaten the
success of any project.

Because of the students' diligence and their belief in the importance of voluntary and charity work in serving the community, they reached to sixty-six
units in Fayoum. This is massive numbers for a group of young students who
are still receiving daily expenses from their parents. However, faith in voluntary
and charity work has made them a significant force to achieve what the governments and states can not.

---

[32] Pictures number (24, 25, 26, 27) was taken with a permission of the Enactus Fayoum.

Figure 25. A farmer seems happy for the new source of energy (biogas).

Currently, 66 units of biogas in Fayoum. The unit saves 2 to 3 gas cylinders per month if you have three cows. The two pipes that come out of the biogas unit, one for fertilizer is enough for two acres and the other pipe for gas. The fertilizer is better for the soil because the yellow weeds do not grow with that kind of fertilizer. The project solved the problem of gas cylinder and the problem of black market and also preserved the environment (A members of Enactus Fayoum)[33].

It is important to mention that the students of Enactus also devised a voluntary project based on the idea of entrepreneurship, which is the project of cleaning cars with steam instead of water. This is because Egyptian society is suffering from a water crisis due to the repercussions of the dam in Ethiopia. The students sought to invent a steam car wash machine to preserve water. This represents a high sense of responsibility for these students to confront the problems that beset the society.

The steam car wash machine project, which took the first rank in the Arab Republic of Egypt, is an important project. The car consumes about 100 to 150 liters per wash. A person will wash his car once or twice a week and this will waste much water. There are 7 million cars in Egypt. We calculated 7 Million cars with an estimated cost of 100 liters. Therefore, we waste 700 million liters per week for just washing cars. It is a disas-

---

[33] This student is in the second year at the Department of Plant, College of Science.

ter. Hence, the idea of the project rises. How can we decrease the consumption of water? The idea seemed to grow up in our minds, but we did not have the tools to implement it. We began to think about the idea of using a steam machine instead of washing cars by water. Washing car with steam machine consumes from 3 to 5 liters of water. We provided from 95 to 97% of the amount of water consumed in washing cars. It means saving every week more than 600 million liters of water (The President of Enactus Fayoum).

Moreover, the students are aware of the country critical situation and that water is the future crisis of Egypt. They endeavored to spread awareness about the culture of water conservation and to provide voluntary services to solve the problem of water in Egypt. They tried to change the structure of the prevailing culture in Egyptian society to solve its crises which are a reflection of this culture. The students attempted to introduce many improvements to the car wash machine to provide the service at an affordable price, as well as considering the environmental aspects and the dissemination of the culture of conservation of water. Creating a new culture for a large sector of Egyptian people towards the balanced consumption of water resources is a significant issue that needs public awareness.

> We started to bring these components, a motor to pull water and a boiler along with the safe buttons for the machine. It seems that we have problems such as the high pressure on using the machine which may make it explode. We got in contact with an experienced person in steam boiler machines. We made an initial model and it succeeded (A members of Enactus Fayoum)[34].

The voluntary activities have exceeded the traditional form to more sophisticated forms based on entrepreneurship, but at the same time, they have a humanistic and religious dimension. The students tried to challenge the limited conditions and possibilities in devising ways to carry out these activities. The idea of entrepreneurship is linked to voluntary and contribute to providing the necessary funding for the continuation of these projects and not stopping them after the completion of the activity. It also has an innovative and creative side.

5.5.3 Volunteerism: Crises, Plans, and Mechanisms

The student organizations take unique methods to activate establishing voluntary activities. Usually, many student groups take the scientific approach in selecting members who participate in voluntary and charity work. They also endeavored to attract the best student elements to achieve the goals of the student organization in providing services and voluntary activities both inside and outside the university with efficiency and excellence. Personal interviews for applicants to voluntary activities became familiar to student organizations at Fay-

---

[34] This student is in the second year at the Department of Plant, College of Science.

oum University after the revolution. The organizations such as Enactus and Snaʿ al-Hayah conduct interviews for students to select the superior elements.

> The other organizations, when a student asks to join them, they accept him at the same time. However, in Enactus, I have been interviewed for an hour just to know if I have been accepted or not. This attracted my attention. The interviewer asked where you see yourself after five years? What are your interests? What kind of activities did you participate? They wanted to know, how does this person will benefit the team? They are very selective (A member of Enactus Fayoum)[35].

> The interview has a specific set of questions, whether direct or indirect to know the experiences as well as the skills, whether it is useful in the field of marketing, or other fields and so on (The head of HR of Enactus Fayoum)[36].

Figure 26. A female member of Enactus interviewing a new candidate.

These criteria are new for the voluntary work of student organizations at Fayoum University. The student organizations are trying to attract the superior elements that can benefit volunteerism. In addition to the new members' interview, the student organization leaders try to invite students who have particular skills or abilities to help them carry out activities.

---

[35] A female student member of Enactus at the College of Arts.

[36] This female student is in the third year at the Department of English, College of Arts. She is the responsible for the Human Resources Department at Enactus Fayoum. Her tasks varied between selecting new members, follow up the working members and providing assessment for the working members. She is the one who is responsible for conducting interviews for the new members with the President of Enactus.

We focus on the eyes and tone of the student's voice to know if he is excited to join Enactus and work with us. Will this enThus,iasm change to work really or not? I tell him a situation and I asked if you are in my place, what will you do? The interview is not enough. This assessment also started in the camping (The head of HR of Enactus Fayoum).

There are students that I want them to join the team to be a designer, programmer or manager. I try to attract them to Enactus. As usual, I open the door for joining Enactus at the beginning of semester every year (The President of Enactus Fayoum).

The needs of the team or the projects determine the characteristics of students that should join the team. When undertaking projects related to the creation of the technological tools, there is a need for students from the College of Engineering who are proficient in this skill and this ultimately benefits the team. The interview is not the only way to accept new members. The candidates continue under observation through gatherings and workshops to reach a final assessment of the student's abilities and skills. The assessment process is ongoing with the new and old members as well. Moreover, it is made of their commitment and dedication in carrying out activities entrusted to them. Therefore, continuing training for the new members is useful in volunteering. It helps to avoid any deficiency or lack of skills among participants. Training on the skills is necessary to practice activities and voluntary work. Furthermore, it helps the new students to know the rules, the organizational structure, the objectives, and the general principles of the student family.

We started the first event and it was a party for the new students to know what their roles are? What do they need? And know a general idea about the activities. The primary idea was that Enactus is working on projects and that you are trying to apply these projects and make a difference in the local community (A members of Enactus Fayoum)[37].

We opened the recruitment (enrolment) and many students about 100 joined in this phase. We started to teach them what the meaning of project management, marketing, and funding is? We become to have a team for IT, for BR, for BM, and media. We began to develop our skills and we got the level to which we want to reach. We taught the new student the needed skills and the team began to move as harmonious unit (The President of Enactus Fayoum).

In Enactus, the new students are trained continuously on entrepreneurship, project management, and project marketing mechanisms to implement the tasks entrusted to them. Further, this training enriches students' experiences in receiving the latest methods of entrepreneurship and marketing, which contributes to the development of their skills and abilities in the future. The scientific method of work and training is in the interest of students regarding acquiring new skills and experiences that help in the development of voluntary work.

---

[37] She is a female student member of Enactus at the College of Arts.

It transmits the voluntary action from the concept of unplanned work to an organized work related to the skills and competencies of the operators.

Figure 27. A training session for Enactus students.

Workshops are also continuously organized at the level of Egyptian universities for most of the student organizations such as *Enactus, Resalah,* and *Snaᶜ al-Hayah.* These workshops aim to present projects and to exchange experiences among the participated students. This contributes significantly to overcome the obstacles and problems that stand in the face of volunteer work in universities. Moreover, the organizations are operated through a unique administrative structure with specific roles and responsibilities. In Enactus there is a precise identification of the roles for members.

> Enactus, unlike other organizations, it makes sure that the specialist is the only responsible for the task. You are doing a step and handed it over to the next responsible. Therefore, the project is completed correctly. I know that it is a circle and you are a part of it. The student enters Enactus as a particular person and gets out entirely a different person (A member of Enactus)[38].

> There is a president, three vice presidents and then a head of every team. We have in Enactus seven teams. There is a team for implementing projects and a team for the announcement (media) about Enactus and its projects at the university so that people can know who we are. In addition to, a team of Human Resource (HR) which is responsi-

---

[38]   A female student member of Enactus at the College of Arts.

ble for choosing and evaluating the new and old members, in an ongoing assessment of the members to benefit from them and how to empower them to bring out more than they have (the President of Enactus Fayoum).

In each student family, the advisor of the family is a professor and then the family rapporteur (the President) and then heads for social, cultural, sport, and scientific activities. There is also a treasurer who is responsible for the financial resources (The President of Giil Wa‛iy Family).

However, the difference between Enactus and the traditional structure of student families is that traditional family has a leading role in the family and a course of activities. However, Enactus is predominantly entrepreneurial and has a specific set of roles and responsibilities that contribute significantly to increasing effectiveness of the team and continuously improving the provided activities. The remarkable feature of voluntary work is the presence of periodic meetings among members, which is an essential mechanism for the consultation in the implementation and follow-up activities. There are weekly meetings and the team members meet or speak almost daily about the activities being carried out.

There are regular meetings for the members of the family to know how these activities are implementing (A member of the Giil Wa‛iy Family)[39].

Each team has a head and members and they are gathering for discussing what they have done. Moreover, all teams have a regular meeting with the President (The responsible for advertising and media in Enactus Fayoum)[40].

Although there is a clear structure, some student organizations as Enactus are not characterized by a monopoly of power. The spirit of the team overcomes the internal organizational divisions. Most of the decisions concerning the activities are discussed among all members and no individual or internal team is involved in controlling the decisions. The decision is a collective and not an individual decision.

I also learned how to respect each one in the team from the head of the team to the youngest member. There is no absolute power over the members in Enactus. Muhammad, as the President, takes the opinions of all the members below him. He usually makes discussions to take the final decision (The head of HR in Enactus Fayoum).

This thought based on specialization contributes profoundly to the success of voluntary and the implementation of activities with high efficiency. The democratic practices are eliminating any conflict among members of the same group. It also assists to the completion of activities as required because the idea of ac-

---

[39] This female student is in the third year at the Department of Biology, College of Education.

[40] This is a student at the third year of the Department of Civil Engineering, College of Engineering. He is responsible for the announcing of the Enactus' activities for the masses of students and the community. He is passionate about voluntary work.

countability is adopted in the group's work. Groups also follow the style of encouraging and supporting members. This method is prevalent among different student organizations. Encouraging through the emphasis on the objectives of the family or student organization helps to increase the belonging of the member to the group and, thus, do his best to achieve the aims of the group.

> I thought that I was not qualified to be a member of Enactus. I got encouragement from other members and heads of the teams (A member of Enactus Fayoum)[41].

> We are colleagues before anything and Muhammad has the advantage that he encourages people who are working with him. If a member's effort is limited, Muhammad encourages him and says excellent effort. Muhammad was characterized by giving power for members to work (A members of Enactus team)[42].

One of the prominent methods used by the student organizations in implementing voluntary activities is the process of studying project and making feasibility studies and determining of problems that may appear during work. Follow-up through and after the implementation is an essential mechanism of the fieldwork in voluntary activities. The continuing follow-up process leads to avoid any project failure but helps to improve it.

> I went to investigate the woman's problems, which we have realized that her husband is sick and staying at home. She also has children who need food. Therefore, she was forced to beg. Ok, this is the social and human side. We began to discuss it together and try to solve it together. As for her husband, we attempted to solve the problem of medication for him. We aimed to solve everything for the woman. We look at the economic aspect and search for the appropriate project for her circumstances. Did she work before? How many hours per day does she go out? How many hours can she work per day? What about her children's conditions in school? (The President of Enactus Fayoum).

> The man who drives the tricycle began to make many routes for transferring materials (in the recycling project). In fact, we were in need to put a flexible and sophisticated financial plan for the project in order not to lose (A member of Enactus Fayoum)[43].

It is important to mention that the student organizations have also adopted the idea of advertisement of their work. It is an essential mechanism in voluntary work. It helps student organizations to spread their ideas at the university and have a significant impact on obtaining financial support from sponsors outside the university. Advertising may be through banners or paper plates at the university or via Facebook. Most student families and student organizations have web pages on the social networking.

---

[41] This student is in the second year at the Department of Plant, College of Science.
[42] A female student member of Enactus at the College of Arts.
[43] This student is in the second year at the Department of Plant, College of Science

The idea was presented on balloons and we wrote phrases such as blood drop is equal to life and so on. The students who donate came to us (A member of the Giil Waʿiy Family)[44].

However, after the event *"Al-Dafah"* that was organized by Enactus, the students were silent because they saw our work on the real and on the Facebook (The responsible for the Announcement and Media in Enactus Fayoum).

As for the mechanisms of funding for voluntary and charity work, they are varied due to the limited budgets allocated to the student activities and the support directed by the university to the student organizations. Students try to find sources to finance their activities either by self-funding or by working to find sponsors who contribute to afford a part of the cost of these activities that exceed their financial capabilities.

At first, our team had no sponsor, but we collected five Egyptian pounds from our pocket money to bring identification cards for us to be known by students (A members of Giil Waʿiy Family)[45].

We are trying to reduce the cost of the components because the cost is high. The project is based on a self-funding and there is no help even from the local community or the businessmen (A member of Enactus Fayoum).

Moreover, voluntary contributions from members and attempts to reduce the costs are a way of coping with lack of funding. Thus, they work under challenging conditions and suffer hardship for the superior purpose; However, many student organizations are already looking for new mechanisms to fund these projects such as seeking to establish service and voluntary projects that provide some profit for spending on the other activities.

Exhibits provide some profit and the college never ask for that. The first exhibition was excellent. Through profit, we start to do other activities. The exhibition after hard work for a week or two weeks gains 500 Egyptian pounds. For example, we made a deal with the commercial libraries those sell office tools, books, and accessories to present their products in our exhibition and give us a certain percentage of profit (The President of Giil Waʿiy Family).

At the beginning of this project, I just collected paper and plastic. When it became a ton, I sold it. I called the sells manager at the factory that I have a ton of paper, a ton of plastic, and a ton of cans. Prices at sometimes vary. The money of what we sold, covers the cost of transportation, fuel, design, and everything. If any money remains, it helps us in a new project in Enactus (The President of Enactus Fayoum).

---

[44] This female student is in the third year at the Department of Biology, College of Education.

[45] This female student is in the second year at the Department of history, College of Education.

Figure 28. The exhibition of accessories at the College of Education.

In addition to the profit activities, the student organizations have tried to find sponsors to support them financially. The students searched for sponsors whose interests intersected with the establishment of voluntary activities. In addition, sponsors who wish to enter the campus and offer their services and goods to the public at the university. Therefore, the students offered the sponsors to provide publicity for their goods at the university in exchange for the sponsors' contribution to the establishment of service and volunteer activities.

> We tried to find a sponsor for the project. We thought about the governmental agencies because of our limited financial resources in Enactus and the farmers do not have money. We also searched for agencies that are interested in our project. We searched for agencies that have a problem with the gas cylinders. We found the official authorities are the ones who have the problem. We went to the Ministry of Environment and made a deal together because the Ministry of Environment supports every gas cylinder for citizens with a significant amount of money. We said to them: "we will go to every place in Fayoum to determine the places where the project will benefit and you support us. The Ministry of Environment covered 80% percent of the cost and the farmers cover 20% and the poor farmers who cannot afford to pay 20%, Enactus will pay it. The Ministry of Environment will deposit 4,200 pounds and the farmer will pay 800 pounds for the price of the concrete. The Ministry of the Environment began to bring the engineers, materials, and pipes to construct the biogas unit (The President of Enactus Fayoum).

We went to many sponsors and told them that we want you to support us. Of course, any commercial organization wants to enter the university because it is a wide space for audience and the sponsors began to say, what is the benefit to me? We said that we would make t-shirts with your name on it. The name of your organization will be written on the banner (A member of Giil Waʿiy Family)[46].

Moreover, students sometimes face the intransigence of sponsors. Students went to small companies responsible for selling goods and contracted with them to obtain a percentage of profit in return for giving the goods to students for ease of payment. For example, after the end of the exhibition, the price of goods is supplied to these companies. This is in addition to the attempts of small student organizations to collect donations from students and from people especially in times of Ramadan and other religious events.

> We made a deal with commercial companies to supply us with goods at low prices. We chose the goods that benefit the students. After selling the goods, we gave them the money because we did not have the actual amount of money for those goods (The President of Giil Waʿiy Family).

> We searched for young entrepreneurs to sponsor our project because there are no wealthy entrepreneurs agreed to help us. Therefore, we found young entrepreneurs and offered them to be a partner and get a profit (A members of Enactus)[47].

> In Ramadan, we collected donations from people in the streets to fund our projects. We contacted the doctors in the clinics and asked for support for charity (A member of Giil Waʿiy Family)[48].

Despite the students' attempts to activate the voluntary work, many obstacles are facing them. Firstly, there are lacks of funding, lacks support for student activities, and the problems of reconciling the study with volunteer work at Fayoum University.

It is important to indicate that the students believe that the university's intransigence in approving the establishment of student activities is one of the prominent problems facing student activity in general and charity and voluntary activities in particular. This is in addition to the intransigence of the sponsors and their exploitation of students to achieve their interests. One student said that sponsors humiliated us to provide some financial support for charitable activities.

> There are approvals from the university authorities must be taken to organize an exhibition or activity. This is not easy for all student organizations. You should first get the

---

[46] This female student is in the third year at the Department of Biology, College of Education.

[47] This student is in the second year at the Department of Plant, College of Science.

[48] This female student is in the second year at the Department of History, College of Education.

approval of the family's advisor and the college Vice- Dean for Student Affairs and finally the Dean (A members of Giil Waʿiy Family)[49].

> The approvals from the university administration for organizing the event took about one month or more. They kept the application without signing it because they were not enThus,iastic about the event. On the day of the event, we still not get the approval from the university. I was worried that the approvals are delayed, or the ceremony is canceled. We spoke to the university security and they told that they are not ready to protect the event. I told them that I could write a declaration that if something happened, I would be the responsible. It was a miracle that the approval arrived, but the university said no stranger would be allowed to enter the university (The President of Enactus Fayoum).

The university does not contribute significantly to supporting student activities. On the contrary, it increases the bureaucratic procedures and controls approvals for activities within the university. This is because the circumstances of the university and the political events affecting the exercise of activities. The university administration was also afraid of any strangers entering the campus and causing riots or violence. The university, at that time, was full of demonstrations and security chases every day for students in university dormitories or on campus.

However, this is not a justification for intransigence in issuing licenses and security approvals for training courses or hosting one of the trainers to give a lecture. This undoubtedly prevented the expansion of volunteerism and contributed significantly to decreasing the number of activities carried out by students within the university. Thus, most student organizations tend to provide voluntary activities away from the university.

> The political events have affected our activities because the security situation was very bad. A lot of our stuff has been burnet during the student demonstrations at the university (A member of Enactus)[50].

> We wanted to start the preparation for the event a week before, but the police entered the university. We delayed the preparation on Tuesday instead of Sunday. In this day, we are imprisoned in the university the whole day due to the student unrest. On Wednesday, a strike has begun at the Colleges of Engineering and College of Science (The President of Enactus Fayoum).

Moreover, the security opened its eyes to the students to monitor their movements and activities. It did not differentiate between political activities or charity and voluntary activities. During our gatherings or meetings, some hidden security personnel joins and hear and record what students say in their meetings and workshops. This, of course, affects student activity at the university. Students felt that they are watched all the time by the security forces. The political events also contributed to delaying the implementation of the activities and af-

---

[49] This female student is in the second year at the Department of History, College of Education.

[50] This student is in the second year at the Department of Plant, College of Science.

fected the desire of students to join student activity within the university. Student activities also face many rivalries between student organizations, which also work in voluntary and charity work. Competition among them in carrying out activities generates hidden and visible conflicts among students.

> In the college, student groups fight each other and releases rumors on each other. A student family gave us wrong information about the commercial institutions that provide goods for the exhibition. I paid 600 Egyptian pounds as loses. There is no help among student families. In case of cooperation between two student families, many problems happen because of the belonging to the family (The President of Giil Waʿiy Family).

The relations between student organizations that carry out charity work are full of tensions and lack of cooperation. It sometimes reaches to the degree of harm and causes problems that may lead to the collapse of voluntary work of these families. Some student organizations may also follow a sarcastic approach to what students do with the voluntary work. For example, these students are working for the university administration, or they co-operate with the security forces. Sometimes they are charged with sexual favors between male and female members of the team. This is in addition to the profanity words against those organizations.

> Some students, when we were working on the recycling project, said that you are working as a cleaner. Further, when we were preparing for a meeting and moving chairs to the place of the meeting, the students said to me that your job is to carry chairs (The responsible for Announcement and Media in Enactus Fayoum).

> As we are a closed community in Fayoum, there is a problem of rumors on the student organizations. Other students say that a boy and a girl have a sexual relationship in this organization (The President of Enactus Fayoum).

> The dialogue is closed. You are talking to people who do not understand what you say correctly. The culture of people was declining (The responsible for Announcement and Media in Enactus Fayoum).

Among the crises is the weakness of a culture of volunteering in the local community. The contribution is feeble and, therefore, has an unfavorable impact on work and volunteer activities. Many people are still looking at it as a waste of time, but in turn, volunteer work is developing the character of students and solving the crises of society. On this basis, voluntary and charity work as one of the student activities has given it a qualitative leap regarding programs, topics of activities, and target groups. Therefore, the revolution had a considerable impact on the development of voluntary work at Fayoum University. The students became more active in the society's issues and they solved many urgent problems that are facing their society. This is a remarkable change in student culture in post-revolution in Egypt.

5.6 Sixth Theme: linguistic Symbols, Gestures, and Expressions

Language is certainly a basic communication tool between human beings because it is a means of understanding and conveying ideas and feelings. Through language, man thinks, communicates, interacts, and shares with others in a way that achieves himself. Therefore, word is the source of deeds and actions. Language comes at the top point of the symbolic system of human, through which people can express their feelings, attitudes, ideas, and perceptions (Achard, 1993; Jadallah, 2011). It also helps to achieve cohesion among members of the same society or the same social group. Furthermore, "language is sensitive and responsive to all changes in a society; it is a true indicator of a society's intellectual, moral, and ideological trend" (Jadallah, 2011, p. 13).

Students have their own language that has been created and developed to reflect their cultural specificities and distinguish them from the adult community (Hummon, 1994). This language reflects the intellectual, social, political, and technological changes that have taken place in their society. The fast- paced lifestyle and the abundance of verbal and written communication have led to profound changes in the mind, culture, and language of young people. Therefore, they devised a unique vocabulary for themselves to reflect their personality and manifestations of their thinking. Moreover, the students at Fayoum University, like other students, use their own language in different situations. They spoke with a unique style and an expressive vocabulary. These slang words and phrases have a particular significance for students. This slang language is compatible with the speed of life in this era. The majority of this language is oral than written words. It has a vast amount of words, expressions, and symbols. It is a highly symbolic language with irony tone.

Through the experience of the researcher in the student community at Fayoum University, he noted the spread of many words, phrases, and non-verbal expressions among students, which represent a common language for them. The researcher was able to collect a combination of overt and covert vocabulary and phrases used by students of Fayoum University in their dialogues, conversations, and discussions inside campus. These words are easy, concise, symbolic, and relevant to what the students mean. Fayoum University students use a variety of vocabulary, including terms of the study, some terms of greetings, and others related to the students' interactions.

5.6.1 Terms of Study and Educational Process

Among students, there were several terms for courses, examinations, and lecturer's qualities of pride or hatred. Its humorous and comic nature sometimes characterizes it. These phrases are part of the etymological dictionary for students. Perhaps the vocabulary created by students helps them to get rid of the stress and tension that accompany the examination process. It express burlesque of courses that they hate and do not tend to. This is a type of defensive tricks used by students in dealing with examinations, courses, and non-friendly faculty members. For example, if a professor puts difficulties in front of students and there is no kind of flexibility or cooperation between students and a professor of a subject or a course, we find them call him by some personal attributes, for example:

> If a professor is silly and distasteful, we called him funny names due to his qualities. For example, if a professor has a long nose, we say *"Abu-Tawiylh"* upsets us in our lives. If a professor stays for a long time in a lecture, we say *"Al-Raghay"* which means the talkative man. If a professor talks a lot about his tournaments, achievements, and travels, we say *"Abu-Btuwlat"* which means the champion man but in an ironic tone. This professor is *"Baiyḍ"* means that this professor is so silly and hateful. This professor is like Tuesday *"Shabah Yuwm Al-talat"* because Tuesday is full of lectures. This professor is a *"Prince"* means that he is understanding and unique in his speech and gives an opportunity for discussion (Participant, D 8).

Through these words, it becomes manifestly apparent that students mock of the non-cooperative professors by sticking qualities that are not good to be ridiculed among the masses of students. In the case of sincere cooperation with students and providing an opportunity for them to discussion and presenting their points of view, the students call him words such as prince, which express appreciation of what this professor does. This is called slang identities as students characterize and categorize their professors and colleagues upon their social attributes (Hummon, 1994). These words illustrate tension between students and their professors. The authority relations between students and professors produce a kind of hatred manifested through the language of students.

When it comes to exams and evaluation, the words are extremely ironic. Examinations are especially necessary for students because it is the only tool to judge students' scientific and academic abilities. Therefore, many vocabularies described it such as:

> *"Ana shilt obah"* is said when a student failed in a single subject or a course (Participant, D 8).

> *"Khysht fi al-amtahan"* is said when the student failed in an exam as a whole.

> *"Ana mash maṣdaq nafsy ya lambi"* I cannot believe myself, Lambi is said when the student succeeded in an exam. This phrase represents joy, pleasure, and good news for those who succeed in an exam.

> *"Ana hirabt manyhum"* if a student is not expected to succeed in exams and suddenly, succeeded (Participant D8).

> *"Nakhla͑"* if a student wants not to attend a lecture (Participant D 3).

> *" Madaublar"* this phrase means that a student remains to repeat an exam for the same college year (Participant, B 5).

It is noted that these words are taken from some banners of the modern movies, which are said by actors and actresses in their cinematic works. It expresses their reality in a sarcastic and comic language that reflects a state of intellectual choas suffered by society and at its heart is the youth. Students use some of the words used by young children, such as the word *"Obah"* meaning something bad or not good according to children's language. They also use words from English such as *"Madaublar"* which is derived from "double" that means "two" and reflects that a student repeats the school year as a result of failure.

5.6.2 Greetings

It is noted that the greetings differed among students. It is characterized by being brief and straightforward phrases and indicates the existence of previous conversations between students on the Facebook or Chat. The most common expressions of greeting among students of Fayoum University are:

> *"Ya prince"*, *"Finak ya abny?"*, *"Fih ayh"* means what's up. *"Aṣahbi"* means Hi, my friend.*"Izayak ya abny?"* means Hi man*"ṣabah ṣabah"*, means good morning (Participant, D 3).

These words are just greetings among students to know each other's news. The words vary according to the degree of friendship between students and the degree of appropriateness of the word to the personality of listener. Words such as *"prince"*, *''asahbi''* indicate strong relations and sincere friendship among students. These phrases are usually answered in other terms to respond to greetings, including:

> *"Phol"* means fragrant Arabian jasmine *"Iashta. kullo tamam"* means everything is perfect. *"Kharah" means* very bad (Participant, D 8).

Moreover, these words express the mood of students and come in a symbolic form. If a student's mood is good and feels comfortable and optimistic, words such as *"phol"* will come to respond to the situation, which is similar to the person's mood with roses, beautiful bright flowers, and pure cream, which has nothing to disturb his mood. In the case of bad mood, the response is a *"kharah"* or *"zift"* an expression of depression and the existence of problems, where the label came from the asphalt, which is one of the petroleum derivatives, which is recognized by its dark brown colour and bad smell. It is also noted that greetings were quick and concise because students wanted to go to lectures quickly and due to the fast-paced lifestyle in their society.

In the case of departure comes to a group of words such as *"peace"* and is derived from the word peace and the word *"peace ya man,"* *"bayna telfonaat"* means we will talk in phones shortly. *"take care"* means take care of yourself. *"face baka"* means will contact via Facebook. The departure phrases indicate that there will be contact in another way other than direct contact is the use of telephone or Facebook. This is supported by the use of modern technology in continuous communication between university students from the real to the digital space. It is worth noting that many English words exist in the students' speech. This is an influence of the western culture over the student culture. The excessive use of the Internet and social media make that influence. In addition, watching American movies has a significant influence on the students' language.

5.6.3 Phrases of Praise and Disparagement

There is a set of words which students use in praising and appreciating other students. These words are varying, including:

> *"Al-wad dah dimaghoh hilwah"* means this student has intellectual potentials. *"Al-wad dah hariyt"* means this boy is studying hard. *"Al-bat di moza"* means this girl is beautiful. *"Al-wad dah moz"*. This boy is handsome. *"Al-bat di ṣaruwkh"* means this girl is a pretty. *"Al-bat di ṭalqah"* means this girl is a bullet as very beatuful (Participant, D 8).

These are slang epithets. They directly elicited to praise the intellectual, mental, and aesthetic aspects of the listener. For example, *"Al-wad dah dimaghoh hilwah"* means smart. This uses to praise the mental intelligence and ability to solve problems that he faces. Furthermore, the word *"hariyt"* is a common expression among students refers to a student committed to studying, who spends many hours in the study, attending lectures, and preparing assignment. The word " *hariyt"* came from plowing lands and showed in one of its aspects to make great effort and hardship in the collection of what the student aims at. Besides, *"Al-Bat Di ṭalqa"* is an expression of the supernatural beauty and a resembling of a girl's body as a bullet that hits the heart of everyone who looks at her because of her attractive beauty.

However, the terms of disparagement spread in the language of students at Fayoum University. Students use a variety of words that disparage the other and express the lack of acceptance of students to that behavior or that attribute. The most prominent words are:

> *"Al-wad dah khaniq"* means this boy is silly. *"Al-wad dah itm"* means this boy is foolish ridiculous. *"Al-wad dah ghatit"* means this boy is stupid. *"Al-wad dah huqna"* means this boy is like injection or make troubles to others. *"Al-wad dah manafsin"* means this boy is psychic. *"Al-wad dah khazuwq"* means this boy is scandalmonger. *"Al-wad dah parachute"* means this boy is a parachute (Participant, D 2).

Most of these words disparage the traits and behaviors that students dislike. This includes the qualities of the non-sense and interference in the affairs of others as well as hatred of others or to gossip and inform news among students and other bad qualities, which are hated by students.

There are many phrases that students use in everyday conversations to describe events they are going through. These phrases are vital in expressing what they have been told, or the described event. The students of Fayoum University use a wide range of vocabulary including:

"Alish" is a strange term and is saying continuously in the center of speech. It means contempt for the words or a person who speaks. If there are people, who speak on a particular issue or a problem and one speak about the subject and enter it in a form of films. The words that a person says may be true, but as long as the talk from this person, I do not like him or want to be underestimated by him, so everyone laughs at him. *"Teet"* like in this movie *"Teet"* is a stigma of any indeterminate spell. It cames when part of a film is interrupted or montaged by *"Teet"*. *"Aṣaḥbi"* Each student spoke to his colleague says *"Aṣaḥbi"* saying it with "A and S". This word is taken from a comedy page on Facebook, which is a common form of a man who deals with issues in the country with mockery and irony style. *"Fax" or "Fxan"* means that this matter is deactivated. It has done before, or it is needless.

"Rāshak maʿakum" means I will come with you on that subject or the path that you are going to. *"Hagah fashikhah"* means something massive. When an event or an issue is impressive and strong in convincing a student and that he did not imagine it. *"Okay shaghal"* It is an expression of a person's approval of an idea or a subject but not a complete approval or agreement. *"Ana makoom"* means a full approval of a case or a subject matter and is highly convinced of it.

Moreover, student ironically uses many political terms through his speech. They elicited these words and phrases from the events of the revolution. These words and phrases are *"Qalah mundasah"* which descripts of those who stir up discord between colleagues. Moreover, *"Taraf taliit"* this phrase was used intensively in the era of the January 25th Revolution of 2011. This phrase indicates lack of understanding of the intent of the speaker and ambiguity in his speech and actions. *"Flool"* means the remnants of fugitives from the field after the defeat in the war. The intention here is the members of the National Democratic Party, who fled the field of political life after the collapse of the regime. They became away from the masses without a single leadership.

"Anta gāy tʿmal anfalat amniy" the translation is, you intend to cause a security breach. This means to lower your voice and stop violence. This usually said in response to someone who uses his voice to impose his opinion or ask for demands. Another term is *"Muwtuw bighazikum"* used by students when one of them rejects the request of another. This phrase has used by a political leader of the Brotherhood group regarding refuse the demands of other political forces. *"Gamiid tahrir"* means I miss you so much. *"Tagy naʿmil iatlāf"* this used by students in flirting with girls. *"Al-shaʿb yurid raqam, telefuonik"* means I want your

phone number. It is a comic phrase for the revolution's slogan "people want to overthrow the regime."

It is important to mention that these words and phrases can turn the entire situation into hysterical laughter among colleagues or even add more irony to a particular situation. Normally, students were capable of adapting and using language through verbal projections and indirect signals. Students were able to invent this group of vocabulary for specific situations. These terms are widely used among Fayoum University students, especially when the speech is not typical to reality or that person has a different view and says it comically. Sometimes a person does not like this talk or agree to it. Thus, he says some words that are different from the scope of talk or issue rose.

5.6.5 Phrases of Insults

There is a set of words and phrases used by students as insults for others with bad behavior or morals or who cause harms and harassment to others. The expressions of insults are varying and including:

> *"Al-wad dah rikhīs"* means this student is not kind. *"Al-wad dah mash tamam"* means this student is not okay or bad. *"Wasikh"* means this student is dirty. *"Ibn al-wasīkhah"* or *"Ibn al-hablah"* means the son of an idiot. *"Al-wad dah ʿArṣ"* means this student is a cuckold. *"Teet"* means any insult (Participant, D 7)

> The word *"ʿArṣ"* kept circulation and people writing it so much at the university walls and on the streets and remained widely spread, *"ʿArṣ"* or cuckold.

These words indicate that a person has bad qualities and harms others. One of these bad traits is hatred, lying or gossiping about others. The use of these curses is widely observed among students, especially males and comes incidentally during the students' conversations and discussions. These students were affected by the wave of insults that was prevalent after the revolution among political forces. The insults were routine during the speeches of the politicians in talk shows programmes.

5.6.5 Gestures

Students of Fayoum University have a set of gestures that they use to denote certain phrases, events or characteristics without using the spoken language. The students usually make signs with their hands or eyes and these actions have a obviously clear indication for the university students. They understand and deliver the message in a obvious and expressive manner without strange person from the university know about the content of this message. One of the essential signs that play a linguistic role in the lives of students at Fayoum University is:

"Put the fingers of the thumb and the index finger under the chin" this means that this professor is silly and we do not want him(Participant, B 5)

"Put the hands above the eyes and raise them repeatedly" and this exam surprised them and unexpected. Thus, the students put their hands on their eyes and open them again as a breath from their pressure and anxiety.

"Putting the finger and thumb on the ears" means I will phone you (Participant, D 3)

5.6.6 Written Symbols

Generaly students use written language to facilitate communication between them via Facebook chat or through a cell phone. In their writings, the students of Fayoum University use social networking, chat programs, or mobile messages. The words are a mixture of English alphabet and Arabic numerals, and are spoken in Arabic. The style of writing in this way is called Franco-Arab.

It is important to mention that this method of writing gives full confidentiality to the words and messages sent by students to each other through modern means of communication. No one can identify it, only those who know how to write and what figures represent, which exist in sometimes at the beginning of the word, other times in the middle and at the end. Examples of words written in this way are:

"7abay" my darling. *"Ya 3am"* you, uncle. *"2hel7war"* what is the dialogue. *"la5as" means* summed up.

The number 7 expresses the letter "ح" number 3 for "ع" and number 2 for "خ". Thus, students use this technique in writing to create their own world and a language that distinguishes them from others and expresses their uniqueness. It also discriminates them from the language of adults who do not communicate rapidly and adequately from their point of view. This language helps them communicate their thoughts and feelings in a quick, concise, and encrypted way. Their innovation behind creating this type of writing is to create a world of their own away from the society of adults who have narrow horizons and rigid traditions, from their point of view.

In conclusion, the January 25th Revolution as a social and political event was a shock that brought Egyptians out of a long silence. The constant and rapid events which were experienced by students, both during and after the revolution, were new life situations for them accompanied by new vocabulary and terminology. Due to the continuity of these events, it turned into a reality of the students live their daily life. These events became an integral part of the students' life which pushed them to use that language fluently. They also even modified the vocabulary and use sentences in the projection or ridicule and mocking way. What is astonishing in the new political terminology that has imposed itself on the language of the students at the university is that its members use it in their daily discussions in various gatherings, as well as their conversations and their electronic comments. Those words that are political, inspired by the January 25th Revolution used to describe someone or a group of people, as well as being employed comically in many life situations.

Finally, the central and fundamental reason for the emergence of this language is the social and psychological development of students. Each generation has its own language and terminology that characterize it and shape its culture. The current generation of students is growing up now in a corrupt environment, in which consumerism culture that dominated the media institutions in the Arab World prevails in the face of fierce globalization that elevates the values of consumption and the market in the opposite of social values and cultural specificities. This is clearly represented in the spread of the foreign language expressions in the students' conversations at the university. Moreover, the society full of problems such as unemployment, corruption, and lack of political liberty. What are our expectations from this frustrated generation who cannot find a way to protest against this suppressive climate except to use a language that nobody else than them can comprehend?

Chapter VI: A New Theory for Change in Student Culture

This chapter summarizes the results of the study. The relationship between categories is discussed as well as a suggested theory. In addition, contributions of the new findings, implications for professional practices, recommendations for further research, and limitations and strengths of the study are addressed.

6.1 The Features of Change in Student Culture of Fayoum University

The major question of the study is how did Fayoum University student culture change after the January 25th Revolution of 2011? In order to comprehend the implications of and contributions of these changes, this chapter will be guided by the analysis of themes derived from the participant interviews. Using an inductive approach, this study analyzes the interview data from which five axial categories and one central category arises.

The five axial categories are (1) the daily activities of students at Fayoum University, (2) the students' perceptions of the educational system at the university, (3) the charity and voluntary activities, (4) the forms of social interaction, and (5) the linguistic symbols and expressions of the students. These five categories provide the scaffolding for the core category of the student elections and political activity. This chapter will begin with looking at the shifts in student culture in the post-revolution era and then looking at the axial categories and core category to understand these shifts. The current study has displayed set of results that answer the questions of the study. The most prominent findings of the study are the following:

- The students at Fayoum University practice a group of traditional non-productive hobbies, which do not help in the physical, psychological, and mental integration of the students.
- Fayoum University students exhibit a low value of time management. There are no clear rules for time management.
- Students' appetites for fast food meals in the restaurants or in the streets have increased. They refuse food served at the central restaurants of the university.
- The values of belonging and citizenship among all the student groups after the January 25th Revolution of 2011 have emerged. The degree of a sense of belonging of students to their country and their willingness to serve has also increased.
- The change of the pattern of relations between the students, university administration and professors from the authoritarian to the participatory democratic style, especially after the January 25th Revolution of 2011. On the

contrary, these relationships greatly declined after the events of the 30th of June 2013.

- The use of new electoral tools in the student elections campaigns such as electoral conferences, banners for candidates, and propaganda through the Facebook and Twitter.
- The prevalence of conservative ideas among students concerning hide the faces of female students or their photos on the electoral banners. These ideas spread among student organizations with the Islamic reference.
- The male students showed masculinity orientation with marginalizing the females' role in activities after the 30th of June 2013.
- The fierce competition between different student organizations such as the Muslim Brotherhood, the Salafis movement, Strong Egypt (Miṣr Al-Qawia), and the Independent students on the Student Union elections.
- Lack of cooperation between different student groups and increasing the degree of conflict among them, especially after the events of the 30th of June 2013. This is in addition to the intellectual closure as a result of prevailing the ideas of the organization followed by the students.
- Increasing social interaction of the students in the virtual society than in reality on the campus through the breadth of the use of the Facebook, YouTube, and Twitter in exchanging views among students.
- The students pursue violent behaviors in a counter of the harshness of the security forces where the students were forced to respond to repeated aggression.
- The flexibility of the students' language and their ability to express the ideas and meanings in their minds as well as the emergence of new vocabulary and terminology in the linguistic composition of the students.
- The Muslim Brotherhood student organization adopted strategies to secure demonstrations and protest vigils from the attacked of the security forces or from the student organizations hostile to them after the 30th of June 2013.
- There are different forms of solidarity between students at Fayoum University, including both explicit and hidden solidarity.
- The diversity of charity and volunteer activities directed to solve the problems of the local community at Fayoum Governorate.

6.2 The Suggested Theory

Theorizing has become an urgent necessity in the study of social issues in general and cultural studies in particular. It helps us to reach general conclusions that go beyond what is known or accepted. The theory is an intellectual attempt to explain a part of the social life of a society. What distinguishes sociological theory from general concepts is that it provides a framework for interpretation of a social phenomenon in a compatible and comprehensive way (Dressman, 2008; Harrington, 2005; Swedberg, 2012).

The grounded theory is aimed primarily at building an accurate theory that explains a phenomenon in its natural context (Charmaz, 2007). It also helps us, through concepts emerging from data, to understand the basic conditions that contributed to the formation of the phenomenon, dimensions, and factors affecting its future paths. The proposed theory attempts to explain shifts and changes in student culture of Fayoum University in post-revolution through the theoretical axis. These axes highlight the overlap and interplay of factors that led to the changes and the extent of their association or isolation from what the students live at the university. The current theory is mainly based on a set of premises that constitute it as following:

- Change in student culture is often gradual.
- Conflict is a normal process predominantly occurs after revolutions as a result of the political polarization in universities especially in the third world countries.
- Changing in political aspects of student culture is faster than social, value, and behavioral aspects.
- Students usually splintered into divergent groups having various political and social interests. The competition between different student organizations is increasing over elections of the Student Union and provision of activities to a vast range of students.
- Lack of cooperation between different student organizations is often a remarkable feature of student culture in post-revolution.
- Colleges and universities are characterized by an authority structure which is centralized and works against the students' interests.

6.2.1 The Axes of the Theory

The theory of accelerated change in student culture in the post-revolution era consists of four major axes that interpret how student culture changes in post-revolution. These axes have a complex network of interrelated relationships with each other. They express a process of cause and effect that lead to change in university student culture after a revolution. Although the process represents a circular relationship, it starts from one point and ends at a certain point.

The first axis: The students' perceptions of the educational system at a university, whether positive or negative, have a significant influence on the student political engagement. If the perceptions are positive the intensity of the student political activities and democratic practices at the university will increase. Moreover, the student activities, in this case, aim to building institutions that follow a democratic approach and they contribute effectively to the political process for rebuilding the state. If students' perceptions are negative about the educational system, in addition to their feelings of injustice and deprivation, they will be more involved in more political activities that aim to challenge the ruling regime. This assumption related to what Altbach (1989) declared that students in the third world countries have a more active role in changing policies in their countries.

They also try to confront university administration because any administration of a university is a tool of the regime in implementing his plans at the university. Administration of a university also represents a legitimate authority that students are confronting and trying to change it. In opposite, increasing political activities in a university will lead students criticizing the educational system and looking forward to new educational services that are compatible with their desires and interests.

The second axis: Social interaction among student groups are often increased after revolutions as a result of opening the public domain at university to various student factions and political trends for interacting and practicing activities on campus. Consequently, competition among student bodies increases the level of political activity after the revolution. Conflict relations between student groups may lead to violent practices at the university. Expansion of political activities at the university supports the increase of social interaction between various student groups with different ideologies. This highly contributes to increasing competition, conflict or attraction according to the type of political interest of each student group.

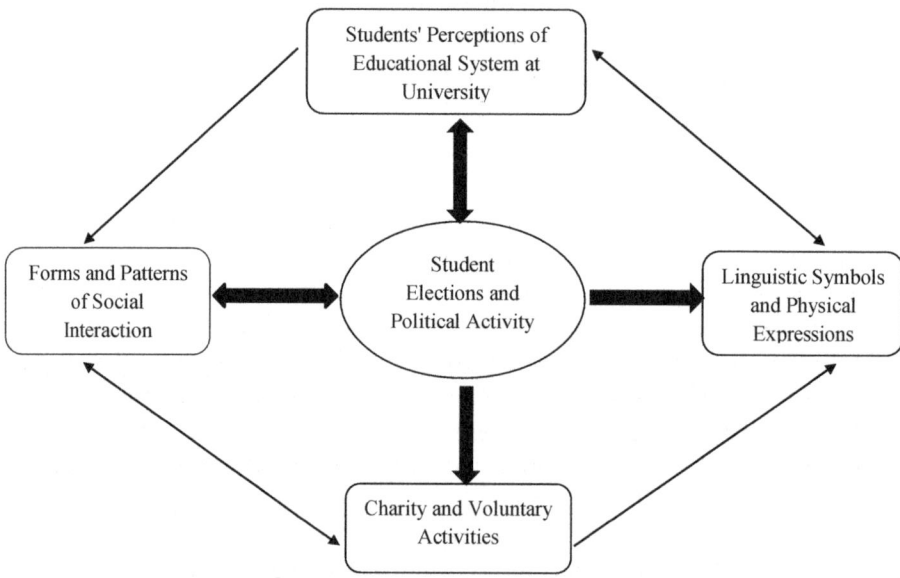

Figure 29. A model depicts a structure and structural relations among categories of student culture at Fayoum University in post-revolution.

Furthermore, providing voluntary and charity activities often lead to various social interaction relations among student groups, especially competition. This is because students try to dominate providing activities in and out campus. Relationships among student groups sometimes develop as a co-operation and solidarity.

The third axis: A correlation between the language of students and practicing political activity seems to exist. The increase in student political activity leads to an increase in vocabulary and linguistic expressions of students, which are dyed political and reflect overall events and attitudes experienced by students. University students invent written, verbal symbols, and expressions that characterize other student groups that compete with their group. Moreover, the increase in providing charity and voluntary activities of students leads to adopting many words and a vocabulary from outside university. These words take its

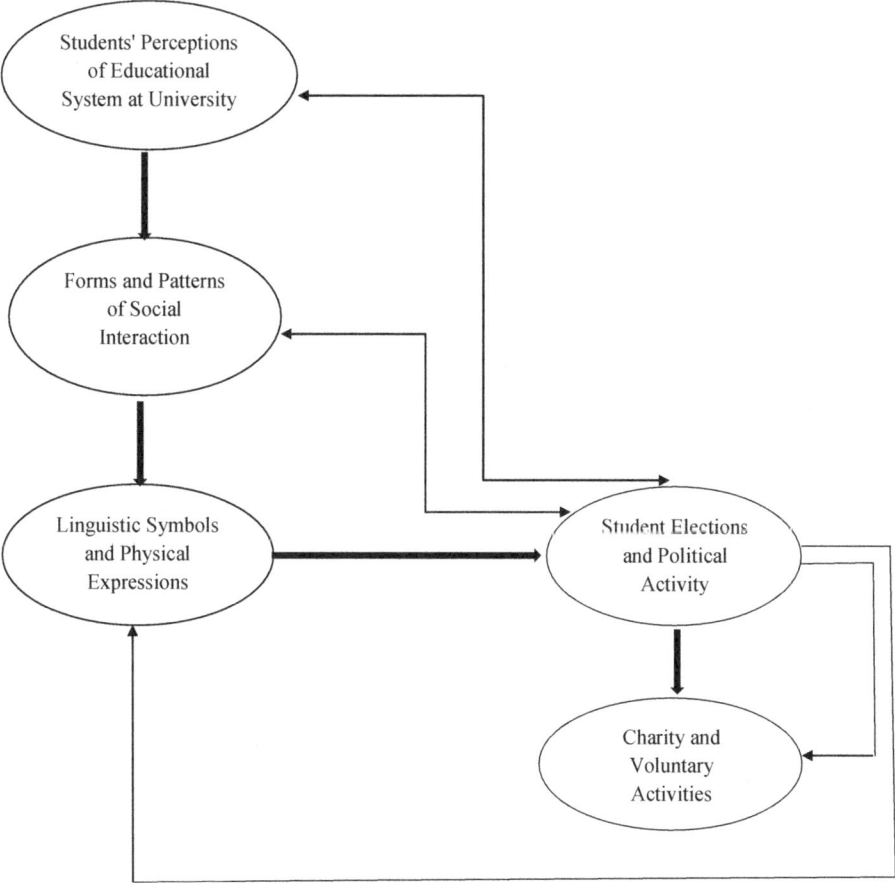

Figure 30. A process model of change in student culture at Fayoum University in post-revolution.

place in students' dictionary and they start to use them and give the words new meanings according to the situation.

The fourth axis: The charity and voluntary activity of students grow during changes in a post-revolution era, especially when an authoritarian regime restricts the political activities at the university. Alternatively, a conflict may occur between the state and one student group at the university which make the campus unsafe for practicing activities. Students may change their approach from political activities to charity and voluntary ones. This is because it is more secure than involving political activism in the uncertain political sphere. Practicing these activities help them to prove their identities and satisfy their desires as participants in the community's issues. It also portrays them as being on the side of society by trying to meet its needs and seeking to defend rights of the poor and the marginalized.

6.2.2 Testing and Validating the Suggested Theory

Evaluating the grounding theory is based on four main criteria to judge the applicability of the suggested theory. These four standards are fit, work, modifiability, and relevance (Glaser, 1992; Glaser & Strauss, 1967). I will use these four bases for evaluating the new theory which interprets the change in student culture in post-revolution at Fayoum University. This theory is preliminary and further investigations are needed to validate it for generalization to other universities around the globe.

First, students at Fayoum University after the January 25th Revolution have organized many protests for demanding education reform. They criticized all elements of the educational system at Fayoum University such as the curricula, professors, programmes, infrastructure, university textbook, university administration, and academic preparation for the labour market. Students were not satisfied and wanted to change the old educational system or to improve it. Students were aware of the low-quality education at the university and they wanted to turn it into a high-quality institution.

Given the fact that there was a wide area of freedom at that time, most students engaged in various political activities. Students organized many political gatherings, workshops, and meetings to discuss the ongoing issues in Egypt. This led to a variety of social interaction relationships among students. Therefore, solidarity and cooperation relationships were prominent among student groups (The Brotherhood students, the Salafists, Strong Egypt, and the Independent students) during and after the revolution. Consequently, competition increased among students due to the Student Union elections.

After the coup in Egypt, demonstrations and excessive political activism were reported. This increased social interaction especially conflict among student groups that had different political orientations. This was reported by clashes between the Independent students and the Muslim Brotherhood students in different times and places at Fayoum University. With the oppressive behaviors of the security forces towards student demonstrations, students' violent actions were directed against the police and the civic security at university.

It is noted that students' vocabulary increased, and it derived from political expressions. Students used many political words in their conversations such as *"ṭalqah, Qalaḥ Mundasaḥ""Taraf Taliit,"* and *"Anta Gāy T'mal Anfalat Amniy".* The state almost suspended political work at all universities including Fayoum University. The security forces broke into the university to end the student demonstrations. Therefore, a significant portion of students went to provide voluntary and charity activities outside Fayoum University. This was not safe for them because hundreds of students were jailed and others were also injured or dismissed from the university. Therefore, the expansion of charity and voluntary activities increased competition among student groups that provided these activities in and out of Fayoum University.

Second, the theory is generated from the data of the interviews, focus groups, and participant observations. The interviewees were students at Fayoum University. I discussed results with some students of the study's sample, so that the suggested theory may be considered as a suitable contribution to studies of student culture after revolutions and societal transformations. Thus, the fit criterion is achieved.

The categories of the suggested theory are linked by a set of mutual relations which present a cause and effect for the change in student culture. It is a circle of change that starts with the first category which is the student's perceptions of the educational system, and ends at being involved in more voluntary activities. This illustrates the process in which change has occurred in student culture at Fayoum University. Therefore, the second criterion is successfully accomplished.

The suggested theory can offer interpretations for similar phenomena. It can be used for studying change in student culture in post-revolutions in other societies. It may provide useful contributions to knowledge. In this case, the third criterion is also fulfilled. The new theory is under development; therefore, it is ready to accommodate new concepts or even categories according to the new data. Thus, the last criterion is checked.

6.3 Implications for Student Affairs Professionals and Policy Makers

The findings of this study have many implications for practice and policy. First, the Student Affairs Circles should work to facilitate setting up student regulation that frames student activities within the university. It is incumbent upon those responsible for university education in Egypt to let students develop a regulation that expresses their hopes and aspirations that guarantees the margin of freedom they want. These is in addition to expressing their opinions and participate in the decision-making of the university that relate to their education.

Second, the Student Affair Circles at Egyptian universities must promote a dialogue between student factions and work to create a more inclusive campus environment. The Brotherhood students, the Salafis, the Lefts, and the Independent students should have continued dialogue among themselves. Practitioners should emphasis on the notions of accepting others, living peacefully, and respecting differences. It should also construct centers for social justice on campus and enhance cross-campus collaboration (Broido & Reason, 2005). This is essential now during conflict among student groups at Egyptian Universities.

Third, the Student Affairs professionals ought to provide meaningful discussions with students about what it means to be an active member of a society in a post-revolution. The role of a student affairs adviser is to create calmness during the storm and provide an opportunity to assist students to have a role in leadership. This could be accomplished through regular political awareness workshops (Bickford & Reynolds, 2002). This is, in addition, to develop leading programs in political education. Such programs work on the formation of the correct political awareness of rights and duties of the individual; therefore, do not leave room for destructive ideas and extremists, which seek to sabotage the minds of young people and demolition.

Fourth, practitioners can also have alumni serve as a supervisor or external participator over the student lifecycle to provide rich and positive experiences to students. This will provide guidance towards the essence of student life and activities. Fifth, university policies and procedures should be regularly reviewed to explore how they contribute to the upgrowth of student activism and violence. This is a vital issue in the successive events experienced by Egypt now.

Last, Student Affair Circles, in co-operation with the policy-makers, can provide a booklet for student code of conduct for demonstration and political work. The need to develop an explicit policy for the campus in which the desired behaviours are determined and consistent with the customs and traditions of the university is a vital demand. This is in addition to the policies that ensure student safety and the allocation of places to demonstrate and express their views. All of these policies are to respect the rights of students and maintain their safety within the university. This will also contribute to a secure campus environment for students, faculty, and staff. These recommendations will encourage the university administrators to adopt policies that will be compatible with the changes in student culture at Fayoum University.

6.4 Recommendations for Further Research

This study raises some important questions for the research community. First, this study used a small sample of the Muslim Brotherhood students and the Independent students, who studied at Fayoum University. Future research that discusses a larger sample of the Muslim Brotherhood students in various regions in Egypt would be beneficial to understand, on a broader scale, if other Brotherhood students experience similar shifts as that many of the participants in this study experienced. Furthermore, a study of sample situated in various regions of Egypt would help to understand if other Brotherhood students are undergoing a similar process with regards to deprivation, discernment, and abuse by the university administration and security forces along with the fact that this process is leading to shifting in their political activities or cultural identity.

Additionally, other regions and universities may provide different contributions to the shifts in student culture that could not be accounted for in this study. I believe it would also be interesting to compare the changes in student culture after a revolution in urban areas versus rural or suburban areas. In many urban areas in Egypt such as Cairo, Alexandria, and the like, the Muslim Brotherhood students would likely have much more access to the broader community, political forces, and opponents. It would be worth researching to clarify in an independent study.

Another useful extension to this research would be to consider the impacts of low-quality education and expected unemployment pressures in increasing the amount and type of the student political activities in Egyptian universities. This will also help in completing a theory about student culture after societal changes.

Lastly, I believe the quantitative research could yield valuable data. Coupling a longitudinal study for the Muslim Brotherhood students participating in the study could help understand what programs and support structures work to help them better to reintegrate in the community. Moreover, many independent studies needed to verify the relationships presented in this study. For example, a study that explores the relationship between the patterns of social interaction and forms of political activities as well as between the increase of charity activities and decline political work at university etc.

6.5 Strengths and Limitations of the Study

It is a fact that any qualitative study has some strengths and limitations. Although the qualitative method is suitable for this study because the small number of the participants, the problem of generalizing results still exists. Moreover, the results of the current study may provide a theoretical perspective to explore the changes in student culture in universities in post-revolution. Therefore, this is considered a highly significant contribution to the student culture literature.

Although there was an accuracy of conducting interviews and participant observations in this study, some participants refused to be interviewed which could be a disadvantage to the study. The uprising question in this situation is: what do these people think and view the student culture after the revolution? It might be that these students have valuable experience and different assumptions regarding the student community in a post-revolution. They may have valuable information and experienced severe situations which may be vital to the study.

Despite the implementation of an exploratory investigation via a focus group, it may restrict the researcher's view to ask students more deep questions about controversial issues that might exist at Fayoum University after the revolution. This might avoid essential data to be included in the study. Furthermore, choosing two groups of students from different political and social backgrounds as a sample for the study is also considered as an advantage.

Although my attempts to be objective while dealing with the phenomenon of student culture at Fayoum University, the process of analyzing and presenting data might be influenced by my academic background as a doctoral student affiliated to Fayoum University. I also have a liberal and open view that considers the students' activism a legitimate right. This may also influence the way in which I present the study results.

Appendix

Appendix A

ALA-LC Romanization Symbols for Arabic Letters

Letter	Name	ALA-LC
ا	alif	ā
ب	bā’	b
ت	tā’	t
ث	thā’	th
ج	jīm	j
ح	ḥā’	ḥ
خ	khā’	kh
د	dāl	d
ذ	dhāl	dh
ر	rā’	r
ز	zayn/zāy	z
س	sīn	s
ش	shīn	sh
ص	ṣād	ṣ
ض	ḍād	ḍ
ط	ṭā’	ṭ
ظ	ẓā’	ẓ
ع	‘ayn	ʿ
غ	ghayn	gh
ف	fā’	f
ق	qāf	q
ك	kāf	k
ل	lām	l
م	mīm	m
ن	nūn	n
ه	hā’	h
و	wāw	w; ū
ي	yā’	y; ī
ء	hamzah	’
ة	tā’ marbūṭah	h; t
ى	alif maqṣūrah	ā
َ	fatḥah	a

	kasrah	i
ِ	kasrah	i
ُ	ḍammah	u
َا	fatḥah alif	ā
ِى	kasrah yāʾ	ī
ُو	ḍammah wāw	ū
َى	fatḥah yāʾ	ay
َو	fatḥah wāw	aw
ً	fatḥatān	an
ٍ	kasratān	in
ٌ	ḍammatān	un

Source: Library of Congress, USA: https://www.loc.gov/catdir/cpso/roman.html

Appendix B

(1) The Statistics of the Sample (the Muslim Brotherhood Students).

Name	Age	Gender	Faculty	Father's Education	Mother's Education	Address
B1	21	Female	Education	Pedagogy Diploma	High school	Fayoum
B2	22	Male	Dar al-Uloom	High school	Uneducated	Beni suif
B3	22	Male	Medicine	B.S. of Commerce	B.S. of Commerce	Cairo
B4	21	Male	Dar al-Uloom	High school	Non-Educated	Fayoum
B5	20	Male	Engineering	High school	High school	Fayoum
B6	21	Male	Agriculture	Uneducated	Uneducated	Fayoum
B7	20	Male	Education	High school	High school	Fayoum
B8	21	Female	Education	Uneducated	Uneducated	Fayoum
B9	21	female	Education	High school	High school	Fayoum
B10	21	Male	Dar al-Uloom	Uneducated	Uneducated	Gharbia

(2) The Statistics of the Sample (the Independent Students)

Name	Age	Gender	Faculty	Father's Education	Mother's Education	Address
D1	20	Male	Engineering	B.S. of Education	B.S. of Education	Fayoum
D2	21	Male	Education	Uneducated	Uneducated	Fayoum
D3	20	Male	Education	Uneducated	Uneducated	Fayoum
D4	21	Male	Social Work	High school	High school	Fayoum
D5	21	Male	Dar al-Uloom	High school	High school	Fayoum
D6	20	Male	Engineering	Uneducated	Uneducated	Fayoum
D7	20	Male	Arts	B.S. of Education	High school	Fayoum
D8	22	Female	Arts	B.S. of Education	B.S. of Education	Fayoum
D9	21	Male	Education	Uneducated	Uneducated	Fayoum
D10	20	male	Agriculture	B.S. of commerce	B.S. of law	Minia

Appendix C

The Statistics of Fayoum University 2014/2015

Colleges	Students			Faculty Members	Administrative Employee	Graduate Students
	Male Students	Female Students	Total			
College of Archaeology	297	313	610	91		
College of Arts	820	3061	3881	168		
College of Education	507	2731	3238	132		
College of Computing and Information	249	173	422	57		
College of Agriculture	97	164	261	307		
College of Science	2096	812	2908	238		
College of Specific Education	188	1004	1192	97		
College of Social work	1214	1913	3127	101		
College of Dar al-Uloom	1100	2333	3433	112		
College of Early Childhood Education	0	895	895	44		
College of Tourism and Hotels	302	187	489	79		
College of Medicine	326	509	835	388		
College of Dentistry	28	50	78	30		
College of Nursing	147	361	508	89		
College of Engineering	942	286	1228	228		
College of Pharmacy	110	58	168	5		
Institute of Nursing	197	146	343	-		
Total	8620	14996	23616	2166	3851	5384

Appendix D

The Interview Guide

Background Questions

1. What is your name?
2. How old are you?
3. Where were you born?
4. What is your major?
5. What is the highest level of education of your father?
6. What is the highest level of education of your mother?
7. What is your father occupation?
8. What is your mother occupation?

Main Tour Question

How do you see the student's community at Fayoum University following the January 25th Revolution of 2011 in Egypt?

Daily Life Activities

1. How do you spend your day at the University?
2. How do you choose your clothes when you go to college? On which basis?
3. What is the most prominent hobby that you practice continuously?
4. How do you spend your leisure time?
5. What are the youthful words and vocabulary that you use in your talks? What does it mean?
6. What are the most prominent students' celebrations at Fayoum University?
7. Do university students use Twitter and Facebook more than anything else?

Social Interactions

1. How do you see the students' relationships after the January Revaluation?
2. In your opinion, to what extent the student community at Fayoum University is coherent or there is a split among students after the revolution?
3. What are the main demands of the students and how they have changed their ways to claim their rights?

Relationship with University Administration

1. What is the type of relationship between students and the Authority (Dean and Vice Deans- university President) in your college?
2. Do you think the nature of the relationship between students and Dean and Vice Deans in your college changed after the revolution? If so, how?

3. From your point of view, has the administration tried to realize students' hopes and aspirations in both academic and social life on campus after the revolution?
4. Did the college administration contact you to participate in the decisions that concern you?
5. What is your impression about the relationship between the students and the faculty members after the revolution in your college?

Political participation

1. What are the kinds of the political practices exercise by students at Fayoum University?
2. What campus activities have the students participated in?
3. Are you a member of a political party?
4. Do you promote the ideas of your party at the university? Do you think this is useful?
5. From your point of view, what is the amount of political freedom guaranteed at Fayoum University?
6. Are there still forms of suppression of freedoms being practiced within the university?
7. How do you think: should allow the political work in the university or prevented it?
8. From your point of view, does the atmosphere at Fayoum University encourages democracy and political practice?

Student Elections

1. How do you see the student elections at Fayoum University?
2. Have you participated in student elections at Fayoum University to choose your college's Student Union and the university Student Union?
3. What criterion did you choose students in the elections?
4. Tell me about your impression of the students' election at Fayoum University?
5. How did the students cover the cost of banners and election conferences?
6. How do you see the new students' regulations?
7. Why universities refused the students regulation after 2013?

Student Demonstrations

1. Tell me about the student demonstrations at Fayoum University?
2. What is the goal of the student demonstrations and riots?
3. Tell me about the process of organizing the demonstrations at Fayoum University?

4. In your opinion, is the process of securing demonstrations and marches necessary within the university?

The Policy of Education at the University

1. What is your opinion about the ability of the current educational system at Fayoum University to create conscious and educated generations?
2. Do you think that the educational system at university able to qualify you for the labour market?
3. What is your opinion about the university professor and lecturers performance in post-revolution at Fayoum University?

Appendix E

The Approval Letters for Conducting the Field Study at Fayoum University

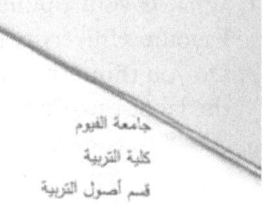

جامعة الفيوم
كلية التربية
قسم أصول التربية

السيد الأستاذ الدكتور / محمد فاروق عبد السميع

عميد الكلية

تحية طيبة وبعد ،،،،،،

برجاء من سيادتكم التكرم بالموافقة علي إعطائي خطاباً موجهاً إلى السيد مدير إدارة الأمن الجامعي
بجامعة الفيوم تفيد بأني مسجل لدرجة الدكتوراه بقسم أصول التربية في موضوع " أثر ثورة ٢٥ يناير ٢٠١١
في تغيير ثقافة المجتمع الطلابي . دراسة حالة لجامعة الفيوم " وذلك باستخدام المنهج الاثنوجرافي وهو
منهج يستلزم معايشة الظاهرة محل البحث ، وإنني بصدد جمع مادة علمية عن الحراك الطلابي داخل
الجامعة ليتسنى لي لنا فهم وتفسير هذا الحراك وإمكانية ترشيده ودرء خطورته علي المجتمع ، مما يتطلب
تواجد الباحث في بعض المواقف التي يجري فيها حوارا مع بعض الطلاب داخل حرم الجامعة.

وتفضلوا بقبول فائق التحية والتقدير ،،،،،،،،،

مقدمة لسيادتكم
ناصر شعبان علي طلبة
مدرس مساعد بقسم أصول التربية

264

السيد الاستاذ / مدير ادارة الامن الجامعي

تحية طيبة وبعد،،،،،

نحيط سيادتكم علما بأن الباحث/ ناصر شعبان علي طلبة مسجل لدرجة دكتور الفلسفة فـي التربيـة

بقسم : اصول التربية تخصصص اصول التربية بموافقة مجلس الكلية علي التسجيل بتاريخ: ٢٠١٣/٦/١٢

وموافقة نائب رئيس الجامعة بتاريخ: ٢٠١٣/٨/٢١.

وعنوان رسالته:

أثر ثورة ٢٥ يناير في تغيير ثقافة طلاب الجامعة " دراسة حالة لجامعة الفيوم"

برجاء تيسير مهمة الباحث في تطبيق أدوات الدراسة المتعلقة بموضوع رسالته.

- مكان التطبيق : جامعة الفيوم

- عينة التطبيق: عينة عشوائية من طلاب الجامعة

- منهج التطبيق :

المنهج الاثنوجرافي وهو منهج يستلزم معايشة الظاهرة محل البحث والتي نرصد طبيعـة الحـراك الطلابي داخل الجامعة ليتسنى فهم وتفسير هذا الحراك وامكانية ترشيده ودرء خطورته علي المجتمـع ممـا يتطلب تواجد الباحث في بعض المواقف التي يجري فيها حوارا مع بعض الطلاب داخل حرم الجامعة.

- القائمون بالتطبيق : الباحث

- الأدوات التي سيتم تطبيقها:

١ـ المقابلات المتعمقة.

٢ـ الملاحظة بالمشاركة.

- زمن التطبيق: العام الدراسي ٢٠١٤/٢٠١٥

وتفضلوا سيادتكم بقبول فائق الاحترام

المختص   رئيس القسم   مدير إدارة الدراسات العليا

٢٠١٤/١٢/٨

وكيل الكلية لشئون الدراسات العليا والبحوث

وقائم بعمل عميد الكلية

(أ.د/ محمد فاروق عبد السميع)

بسم الله الرحمن الرحيم

جامعة الفيوم

كلية التربية

السيد الاستاذ الدكتور/ خالد حمــزة

رئيس الجامعــة

تحية طيبة وبعد،،،

اتشرف بأحاطة سيادتكم علما بشأن الطلب المقدم من الباحث/ ناصر شعبان على طلبه المدرس المساعد بقسم اصول التربية بالكلية ومسجل رسالة الدكتوراه بعنوان: "ثقافة طلاب الجامعة في ضوء بعض التغيرات المجتمعية المعاصرة (دراسة حالة لجامعة الفيوم) والذى يلتمس فيه موافقة سيادتكم على حصوله على البيانات والمعلومات التالية:

- بيان بأعداد الطلاب المقيدين بكليات الجامعة المختلفة للعام الجامعى ٢٠١٥/٢٠١٤.
- بيان بأعداد أعضاء هيئة التدريس بكليات الجامعة المختلفة.
- إحصاء بأعداد طلاب الدراسات العليا بالجامعة.
- إحصاء بأعداد العاملين بالجهاز الإدارى بالجامعة.
- إحصاء بأعداد الطلاب والطالبات بكل كلية من كليات الجامعة.
- إحصاء بنسبة الطلاب البنين إلى البنات فى الجامعة.

حيث أن هذه البيانات سوف تفيده فى الدراسة الميدانية لرسالة الدكتوراه الخاصة بسيادته، وذلك بعد موافقة المشرف الرئيسى.

والأمر معروض على سيادتكم للتفضل بالموافقة،،،

وتفضلوا بقبول فائق الشكر والتقدير

عميد الكلية

ا.د/ آمال ربيع كامـــل

جرجا - الفيوم مرمز بريدى (٦٣٥١٤) تليفون (٠٨٤/٦٣٣٤٩٩٢) فاكس (٠٨٤/٦٣٤٠٥٣٨) - عمومى (٠٨٤/٦٣٤٢٦٧٣)

Al Fayoum. Cod. 63514, Tel (084-6334992), Fax: (084) 6340538 – (084) 6342673

APPENDIX F

The Concepts Matrix

1 The concept of participation

Indicators
- Participation in the Presidential elections.
- Participation in the Parliament elections.
- Participation in the political debates.
- Participation in preparing the student regulation.
- Participation in the Student Union elections.
- Participation in the student activities at Fayoum University.

2 The concept of food disorder

Indicators
- Eating fast food.
- Differences in timing of meals.
- Eating foods in unclean restaurants "in the streets".
- Eating more carbohydrates.

3 The concept of social justice

Indicators
- The Coordination Office and the absence of social justice.
- Differences in dealing with student groups.
- Giving certain jobs to the sons of a particular social class.
- Exclusion certain student groups from political work at the university.

4 The concept of freedom

Indicators
- Arrest and detain students.
- Break up demonstrations and strikes by force.
- Calling the security forces to end student demonstrations.
- Preventing the practice of political activities at the university.
- The administration repressed the student's voices.

5 The concept of democracy

Indicators
- The Coup.
- Preventing student protests by force.
- The elections of the university administrations.
- Canceling the Students Union elections.

- Running student elections.
- The law of political isolation.
- The toppling of the elected President.
- Presidental elections fraud.

6 The concept of violence

Indicators
- Clashes between students and the security forces.
- Shooting gas and smoke bombs.
- Clashes between students and the civil security.
- Destroying the university's infrastructure.
- Throwing stones at the security forces.
- The numbers of injuries and victims.
- Burning university's infrastructure.

7 The concept of charity work

Indicators
- Medical convoys for the poor villages.
- Community development projects.
- Books and clothes exhibitions.
- Blood donation campaigns for hospitals.
- Literacy education for adults.
- Construction of small projects for the poor.

8 The concept of a university textbook

Indicators
- The policy of printing and allocating textbook at the university.
- The card or "al-Sheet" for the book.
- More than four textbooks for one subject or a single course.
- The university textbook and the student's marks.
- The high prices of the university textbook.

9 The concept of rebellion

Indicators
- Organizing demonstrations.
- Making strikes in front of the Dean's office.
- Organizing marches.
- Violation the law of demonstrations.

10 The concept of solidarity

Indicators
- Sympathy in happy and sad situations.
- Solidarity in cases of death or the need for money.
- Participating in paying bail for the arrested students.
- Solidarity with the detained students through graffiti.
- Helping students who fail in exams.
- demanding the university administration to release the arrested students.

11 The concept of causal language

Indicators
- Phrases for good qualities.
- Phrases for bad qualities.
- Insults.
- written symbols.
- Greetings phrases.
- Body language.

12 The concept of time

Indicators
- Sleep and wake up times.
- The lecture time is the basis.
- Sleep schedules vary.
- Random timings.

13 The concept of power

Indicators
- The power relationship between students and the university administration.
- The power relationship between the anti-regime groups (The Muslim Brotherhood) and the regime support groups.
- The authoritarian relation between male and female in the religious groups.
- Power relations between students and professors.

BIBLIOGRAPHY

ʿAbbas, R. (1995). *Tārykh jāmʿt al-Qāhirh* [The history of Cairo University]. Cairo, Egypt: Al-Hy'h Al-ʿāmh lill Kitāb [Egyptian General Authority for Book], [Arabic].

ʿAbdallah, A. (1985). *The student movement and national politics in Egypt 1923-1973*. London, UK: Al-Saqi Books.

ʿAbdallah, N. (2013). Egypt's revolutionary youth: From street politics to party politics. SWP comments11, the project "Elite change and new social mobilization in the Arab world".German Institute for International and Security Affairs, Germany.

ʿAbdel-Fatah, S. (2013). *Al-mārhalhal-intkālyah, krāāh fī al-mashhāād al-māsry* [Transition period, insights in the Egyptian situation]. Cairo, Egypt: Dar Al-Bashīīr, [Arabic].

ʿAbdel-Hamed, M. (1994). Al-ṭabaqah al-wasṭaī fī miṣr [The middle class in Egypt]. In Ahmed Abdallah(ed.), *Humoum miṣr wa azmat al-ʿaquwal al-shabāb* [The concerns of Egypt and the crisis of young minds] (pp. 11-28). Cairo, Egypt: Marakaz Al-Giil Lill Darasāt Al-Ijtmaizah Wa Darasāt Al-shabāb [The Generation Center for Social and Youth Studies], [Arabic].

ʿAbdel-Satar, sh. (2016). *īshāmāt al-ānshṭah al-ṭolābīh fī tanmiat maharāt al-hīyaāt liṭolāb āl- jāmʿt: Drāsāt min manẓūr al-khidmah al-ījtmāih* [The contributions of the student activities for the development of life skills for university students: study form perspective of general practice in social work]. Master dissertation, Assuit University, Assuit, Egypt, [Arabic].

ʿAbdel-ʿaal, N. (2015). *Fāʿlyat mūāqʿ al-tawṣl al-ijtmāy fī tanmiat bʿad āl-kīyam al-ijtmāih ladī ṭolāb al-jāmʿt* [The effectiveness of the social media sites in developing social values for university students]. Master dissertation, Mansoura University, Mansoura, Egypt, [Arabic].

ʿAbdel-Rahman, M. (2015). *Egypt's long revolution: Protest movements and uprisings*. New York, USA: Routledge.

ʿAbdel-Muwguwd, S. (2014). *Al-athar al-ijtmāih wa-al-mjttmāih tāmoul al-shabāb āl-jāmʿt maʿ mūāqʿ al-tawṣl al-ijtmāy āl-ialīktrawinyh* [Social and societal impacts for university youth interaction with Social Media: A Comparative ecological study in Upper, lower Egypt and Cairo]. Doctoral dissertation, Ain Shams University, Cairo, Egypt, [Arabic].

ʿAbdel-Wahed, M. (2005). *Taquwim al-ānshṭah al-ṭolābīh be jāmʿt Assuit* [An evaluative study of the student activities in Assuit University]. Doctoral dissertation, Assuit University, Assuit, Egypt, [Arabic].

ʿAbdou, D., and Zaazou, Z. (2013). The Egyptian revolution and post soscoeconmic impact. *Topics in Middle Eastern and African Economies*,15(1), 92-115.

Abu-Al-Ftuwh, A. (2010). *Shāhid alá tārykh al-harkah āl- īslāmiah fī miṣr 1970-1984.*[Witiness for the history of the Islamic Movement in Egypt]. Cairo, Egypt: Dar Al-Shuruwk, [Arabic].

Abu-Alʿla, A. (1984). *Al-tārbih āl-syāsiah* lill *shābāb* [Political education for youth]. Cairo, Egypt: Dar Nahadit Miṣr, [Arabic].

Abu-Khres, H. (2015). *Thaūrt 25 yaniir watāthirh alá manẓūmāt al-kīyam al-ijtmāih lill shābāb āl-jāmʿt ma*ʿ[The January 25th Revaluation and its impact on social value system for University youth]. Master dissertation, Fayoum University, Fayoum, Egypt, [Arabic].

Abu-Omer, H. (2015). *Duwr al-bārāmij al-hawāryāh āl-syāsiah fī al-faḍāʾyiāt al-miṣrīyah fī tāshkiyl maʾārif al-shābāb al-jāmʿt ma*ʿ *wa-itiyjahāthm nahwa al-kaḍāiyah al-syāsiah al-muʿāṣrah* [The role of political talk show programs in Egyptian channels in the formation of the young Egyptian university knowledge and attitudes towards contemporary political issues in Egypt during the period from June 2011 to June 2013. Field study]. Master dissertation, Mansoura University, Mansoura, Egypt, [Arabic].

Abu-Nuwr, A. (2013). *ṭolāb ṭib biytiray al-Wadiy al-Jadiyd yughlyqwn al-kullīyat īʿtaraḍa ʿalá naqaṣ al-khadamāt* [Veterinary students at the New Valley University closing the college doors in protest at the lack of services]. El youm7 newspaper, March 31/2013 Retrieved at: http://www1.youm7.com/News.asp?NewsID=1000735&SecID=296, [Arabic].

Abu-Sikiin, H. (2013). *Al-wataniyah wa- al-mūwātnah fī miṣr al-thaūrah* [Nationalism and Citizenship in Egypt Revolution]. *Magālat al-Diymuqrāṭiah* [Journal of Democracy] (52), 161-151, [Arabic].

Achard, P. (1993). *La sociologie du langage.* Paris, France: Presses Universitaires de France.

Adieb, N. (2009). *Al-thakāfa al-syāsiah lill shābāb* fī al-jāmʿt ma*ʿ al-Miṣrīyah* [Political culture of the university youth in the Egyptian society, study of the main tributaries of the formation of the political culture]. Cairo, Egypt: al-Hyʾh āl-ʿāmh lill Kitāb[The General Authority for Book], [Arabic].

Adieb, S. (1990). *Marhālat al-taʾlīm al-ʿali fī miṣr al-qadiymah* [Higher education in ancient Egypt]. Master dissertation, Zagazeg University, Zagazeg, Egypt, [Arabic].

Ahmed, A. (1993). *Drāsāt fī ʿalm al-ījattmʿa al-tarbiwaī* [Studies in Educational Sociology]. Alexandria, Egypt: Dar Al-Maʿāraf Al-jāmʿiyah, [Arabic].

Ahmed, A. (1987). *ẓāhirat al-īghtirāb bayna ṭolāb al- jāmʿt* [The phenomenon of alienation among university students]. Doctoral dissertation, Ain Shames University, Cairo, Egypt, [Arabic].

Akhbar Altaalim (2013). Amn kullīyat al-ṣaidalah fī jāmʿt al-Qāhirh yamnaʿ al-ṣahafiin man taghaṭizat al-Muẓahrat al-ṭolābiah [The security of College of Pharmacology at Cairo University prevents journalists from covering student demonstrations]. Akhbar Altaalim Newspaper, April 21/2013 Retrieved at: http://www.akhbaraltaalim.com/index.php/news/onenews/6970, [Arabic].

ʿAli, A. (2012). *State and revolution in Egypt: The paradox of change and politics.* Brandeis University Crown Center for Middle East Studies.

ʿAli, A. (2011). Thaūrt 25 yanir: *Al-shābāb yaṣnʿ al-mustahiil* [January revolution, people makes impossible. Cairo, Egypt: Al-Hiy'ah Al-ʿāmah leh Quṣuwr Al-Thaqāfah [The General Authority for Cultural Palaces], [Arabic].

ʿAli, M. (2009). *Mumārasat al-ānshitah al- ṭolābiya al-ghiyir taqlidiah fī tanmiat simāt al-mūwātin al- ṣālih ladī ṭolāb āl- jāmʿt* [The role of practicing the untraditional student activities in developing citizenship among university students]. Doctoral dissertation, Cairo University, Giza, Egypt, [Arabic].

ʿAli, S. (1996). *Al-taʿlīm fī al-haḍārah al-miṣrīyah al-qadiymah* [Education at the Egyptian ancient civilization]. Cairo, Egypt:ʿĀlam Al-Kutub, [Arabic].

ʿAli, S. (2007). *Nahwa īstarātiyjiah litaṭūiyr al-taʿlīm al-ʿāli fī miṣr* [Towards a strategy for developing the higher education in Egypt]. Cairo, Egypt: Al-Ahram Al-Āqtaṣādiy, [Arabic].

ʿAli, S. (2008). *Jāmʿaāt taḥatt al-hiṣār* [Universities under siege]. Cairo:ʿAllam Al-Kitāb, [Arabic].

ʿAmar, H. (1964). *Banāʿ al-bashar* [Build humans]. Cairo, Egypt: Dar Al-Maʿāraf, [Arabic].

ʿAmar, H. (1996). *Al- jāmʿt bayna al-rasālah wa- al-muʾūssah* [University between mission and institution]. Cairo, Egypt: Al-Dar al-ʿArabiyah lill Kitāb, [Arabic].

ʿAllam, R. (2012). Al-thaūrt al-moḍādah [Counter Revolution]. In Mahmoud Abd Al-fadeel(ed.), *Al-thaūrt al-Miṣrīyah, al-dawāfaʿ, al-atajāhat wa al-tahadiyāt* [Egyptian revolution motivations, trends and challenges] (pp. 375-416). Doha, Qatar: Al-Mararkaz Al-ʿAarabiy Lill Abahath Wa Darāsāt Al-syāsisāt [Arab Center for Research and Policy Studies], [Arbic].

Al-ʿAdly, F. (1981). *Anthropologia al-tarbiyah* [Educational Anthropology]. Cairo, Egypt: Dar Al-Kitāb Al-Gāmʿiy, [Arabic].

Al-Asdudiy, N. (2012). Dūwr mūwāqʿ al-tawṣl al-ijtmāy fī idrdarāk al-*shābāb* al-jāmʿt maʿ hurriyāt al-rāʾī wa- al-mushārikah *āl-syāsiah* fī thaūrt 25 yanir [The role of the social media in the students' perception of freedom of speech and political participation in the January 25th Revolution]. Master dissertation, Mansoura University, Mansoura, Egypt, [Arabic].

Al-ʿAzabawy, Y. (2014). Duwr al-shābāb wa-al-harākāt al-ījattmʿiah al-jadidah fī thaūrt 25 yanir [The Role of the youth and the new protest movements in the January 25th Revolution]. Al- bwaba News, January 5/2014 Retrieved at: http://www.albawabhnews.com/62037, [Arabic].

Al-Bana, D. (2011). Al-ʿamāl al-taṭauʿiy ladī ṭolāb āl- jāmʿt, al-wakiʿ wa-al-māmu'l: Drasa maydania bi jāmʿt Al-Azhr [Voluntary work for university students, hopes and realty.: Field study in al-Azhar University]. *Magāliyat Kullīyat al-Tarbiyah bel al-Azhr*, [Journal of College of Education at Al-Azhar University], 145,130-152, [Arabic].

Al-Barbary, A. (2013). Tahadiyāt al-marhalah: Mawaqāt al-īntaqāl al-dimuqraty fi miṣr baʿd thaūrt 30 yawnyah. [The progressive challenges of the democratic transition in Egypt after the 30th of June Revolution]. *Magāliyat Al-Syāsiah Al-Dawaliyah* [Journal of International policy], Novemeber, 12/2013. Retrieved at: http://www.siyassa.org.eg/NewsContent/, [Arabic].

Al-Bashary, T. (2014). Thaūrt 25 yaniir *wa-al-ṣraʿ hawla al-sultah* [The January 25th Revolution and conflict on the Authority]. Cairo, Egypt: Dar Al-Bashīīr, [Arabic].

Albrecht, H. (2005). How can opposition support authoritarianism? Lessons from Egypt. *Democratization*, 12(3), 378-397.

Alexander, A., and Aouragh, M. (2014). Egypt's unfinish revolution: The role of the media. *International Journal of Communication*, (8), 890-915.

Alexander, R. (1982). Participant observation, ethnography and their use in educational evaluation: A review of selected works. *Studies in Art Education*, 24(1), 63-69.

Al-Gamiry, A. (2012). *Miṣr tastʿiyd rouh: Thaūrt 25 yaniir wa iʿādat biynā' al-dawlah* [Egypt restores its soul: The January 25th Revolution and reconstruct the state]. Cairo, Egypt: Dar Nahadit Miṣr, [Arabic].

Al-Ghubashy, M. (2011). The praxis of the Egyptian revolution. Middle East Report, 258, 2-13. Published by: Middle East Research and Information Project, Inc. (MERIP).

Al-Hadiddy, D., and Rifʿat, I. (2013). Ātahād ṭolāb jāmʿt Al-Azhar yuṭalibuwn befaṣl mas'uwliy al-mudon al-jāmʿiyh baʿd tasamum 228 ṭālabān basabab suwa' al-ṭaʿām [Students' union of Al-Azhar University are demanding to dismissal students' hostel officials after the poisoning of 228 students because poor conditions of food]. El youm7 Newspaper, April 1/2013 Retrieved at: http://www1.youm7.com/News.asp?NewsID=1002218&SecID=12, [Arabic].

Al-Hadiniy, A. (1999). *Al-muhamshiyn wa-al-syāsah* fi *miṣr* [The marginalized people and politics in Egypt]. Cairo, Egypt: Marakaz Al-Ahrām Lill Darasāt Al-Syāsiah Wal Al-Istarātijiyah [Al-Ahram Center for Political and Strategic Studies], [Arabic].

Al-Jimyʿiy, A. (1982). *Al–jāmi'h al-Miṣrīyah wal al-mujtama' 1908-1940* [The Egyptian University and society 1908-1940]. Cairo, Egypt: Marakaz Al-Ahrām Lill Darasāt Al-Syāsiah Wal Al-Istarātijiyah [Al-Ahram Center for Politics and Strategies Studies], [Arabic].

Al-Kuwari, A., and Madi, A. (2009). *Limādhā intaqal al-ākharun ilá al-dimuqrātih wa-tākhrah al-ʿrab? Drāsah muqārnah le-al-dūwall al-ʿrabih maʿ al-dūwall al-ākhrah* [Why the others transmuted to democracy and the Arab not: A comparting analysis]. Beirut, Lebanon: Marakaz Darāsāt Al-Wahida al-ʿArabiyah, [Arabic].

Al-Mahdy, A. (2015). Drāsah taquymiyah lill al-ānshitah al-ṭolābiya bkullīyat al-ṭab al-bashary bejāmʿt Banha [Evaluation of the students' activities at the faculty of medicine –Banha University]. Master dissertation, Banha University, Banha, Egypt, [Arabic].

Al-Nagar, A. (2009). *Al-inhiyār al-iqtaṣādiy fi ʿṣar Mubarak* [The economic collapse in Mubaruk's ear]. Cairo, Egypt: Marakaz Al-Maharusah, [Arabic].

Al-Rafaʿy, A. (1989). *ʿṣar Mohamed Ali* [The age of Mohamed Ali].The 5th edition, Cairo, Egypt: Dar Al-Maʿāraf, [Arabic].

Al-Sabaʿy, I. (2016). *īstarātiyjiah muwqtarah le-tamuwiil al-ānshitah al- ṭolābiya be-al- jāmi'at al-Miṣrīyah fi duwʿ al-ātajāhāt al-muaʿsrah* [Asugessted strategy for funding the students' activities at the Egyptian universities in the light of contemporary trends]. Doctoral dissertation, Assuit University, Assuit, Egypt, [Arabic].

Al-Sayīd, S. (2015). *Muʿḍalat al- īstiʿab: Al-harakat al-shababiah fi Miṣr Khra'ṭ al-faʿlien wa ʿawamil al-taghier* [The dilemma of accommodates. Youth movements in Egypt, actors' maps and stumbling factors]. Cairo, Egypt: Al-Mararkaz Al-Aqlimy Lill Darasāt Al-Istarātijiyah [The Regional Center for Stratigic studies], [Arabic].

Al-Sayīd, M. (2002). *Al-āqtāṣād al-miṣriy wa-al-tahadiāt al-āuwdāʿ al-rāhinah :al-āsbāb wa- al-hilawl* [The Egyptian economy and the challenges of the current situations: Causes and solutions]. Cairo, Egypt: Dar Al-Shuruwk, [Arabic].

Al-Sharkawy, B. (2012). Al-majliys al-iʿalī lill kuwāt al-muwsalhah hākmin syāsian [The Supreme Council of the Armed Forces as a governor]. In Mahmoud Abd Al-fadeel(ed.), *Al-thaūrt al-Miṣrīyah, al-dawāfaʿ, al-atajāhat wa al-tahadiyāt* [Egyptian revolution motivations, trends and challenges] (pp.522-495). Doha, Qatar: Al-Mararkaz Al-ʿAarabiy Lill Abahath Wa Darāsāt *Al-syāsisāt* [Arab Center for Research and Policy Studies], [Arabic].

Al-Talidy, B. (2012). *Al-islāmiiuwn wa-al-rabiʿ al-ʿrabiy: Al-ṣaʿwd, al-tahadiyāt, tadābiyr al-hukim*[Islamists and the Arab spring: Ascension, challenges and governors tactics]. Beirut, Lebanon: Marakaz Namā' Lill Abahath Wa Al-Darāsāt [Namaa Center for Research and Studies], [Arabic].

Altbach, Ph. (1989). Perspectives of student political activism. *Comparative Education*, 25(1), 97-110.

Altbach, Ph., and Cohen, R. (1990). American student activism: The post-Sixties transformation. *The Journal of Higher Education*, 61(1), 32-49.

Altbach, Ph. (1991). Student politics and culture. *Higher Education*, 22(2), 117-118.

Amin, G. (2011). *Thaūrt miṣr* [The revolution of Egypt]. Cairo, Egypt: Dar ʿiyn, [Arabic].

Amin, G. (2011). Mādhā *hadath lill al-thaūrah al-Miṣrīyah* [What happened to the Egyptian revolution]. Cairo, Egypt: Dar Al-Shuruwk, [Arabic].

Aouragh, M. (2012). Framing the internet in the Arab revolutions: Myth meets modernity. *Cinema Journal, 52*(1), 148-156.

Arendt, H. (1970). *On violence*. New York, USA: Harcourt Brace Jovanovich, Inc.

Arendt, H. (1963). *On revolution*. New York, USA: Viking Press.

Arnold, C., and Kuh, G. (1992). Brotherhood and the bottle: A cultural analysis of the role of Alcohol in fraternities. Bloomington, IN: Center for the Study of the College Fraternity.

Astin, W. (1998). The changing American college student: Thirty-year trends, 1966-1996 (Electronic version). *The Review of Higher Education, 21*(2), 115-135.

ʿAttallah, F. (2012). *Dūr jāmʿt januwb al-wadiy fi al-tanmiat āl-syāsiah lill ṭolāb: Drāsah mydāniah bjāmʿt januwb al-wadiy* [The role of South Valley University in development of the students' political participation. Field study]. Master dissertation, South Valley University, Qina, Egypt, [Arabic].

ʿAzaam, H. (2013). With photos students for Egypt organize the conference "we will develop our university" in Fayoum. Al-Dostor Newspaper, March 10/2013, retrieved at: http://www.dostor.org/159712

Baldwin, J. (1988). Habit, emotion and self-conscious action. *Sociological Perspectives, 31* (1), 35-57.

Barany, Z. (2012). Comparing the Arab revolts: The role of the military. *Journal of Democracy, 22*(4), 28-39.

Barhoum, M. (1983). Attitudes of university students toward women's work: The case of Jordan. *International Journal of Middle East Studies, 15*(3), 369-376.

Beinin, J. (2011). Workers and Egypt's January 25 revolution. International Labour and Working-Class History, 80, 189-196.

Beissinger, M., Jamal, A., and Mazur, K. (2015). Explaining divergent revolutionary coalitions: Regime strategies and the structuring of participation in the Tunisian and Egyptian revolutions. *Comparative Politics, 48*(1), 1-21.

Bennett, T., Grossberg, L., and Morris, M. (2005). *New keywords: A revised vocabulary of culture and society*. Oxford, UK: Black Publishing ltd.

Berry, R. (1954). *Realms of value: A critique of human civilization*. Harvard University Press.

Biber, Sh., and Leavy, P. (2006). *The practice of qualitative research*. 2nd Edition. California, USA: Thousand oaks, Sage Publications, Inc.

Bickford, M., and Reynolds, N. (2002). Activism and service-learning: Reframing volunteerism as acts of dissent. *Pedagogy, 2*(2), 229-252.

Biraimah, K. (1994). Class, gender, and societal inequalities: A study of Nigerian and Thai undergraduate students. *Higher Education*, 27(1), 41-58.

Bishop, J., Lacour, M., Nutt, N., Yamada, V., and Lee, J. (2004). Reviewing a decade of change in the student culture. *Journal of College Student Psychotherapy*, 18, 3-30.

Bishop, J., Bishop, M., Gelbwasser, L., Green, Sh., Zuckerman, A., Schwartz, A., and Labaree, D (2003). Nerds and freaks: A theory of student culture and norms. *Brookings Papers on Education Policy*, 6, 141-213.

Birkholz, S. (2013). Confronting gerontocracy: The youthful character of the Egyptian revolution. Working Papers, No 9, for Middle Eastern and North African Politics. Freie Universität Berlin.

Bogdan, R., and Biklen, S. (2006). *Qualitative research for education: An introduction to theories and methods* (5th edition). Boston, USA: Education Group.

Boktor, A. (1963). *The development and expansion of education in the United Arab Republic*. Cairo, Egypt: The American University in Cairo Press.

Bradley, J. (2012). *After the Arab Spring: How Islamists hijacked the Middle East revolts*. New York, USA: Palgrave Macmillan.

Bradley, J. (2008). *Inside Egypt: The land of the Pharaohs on the brink of a revolution*. New York, USA: Palgrave Macmillan.

Brake, M. (2003). *Comparative youth culture: The sociology of youth cultures and youth subcultures in America, Britain and Canada*. New York, USA: Routledge.

Bray, Z. (2008). Ethnographic approaches. In Donatella della Porta and Michael Keating(ed.), *Approaches and Methodologies in the Social Sciences. A pluralist perspective* (pp 296-316). Cambridge University Press.

Breckler, S., and Wiggins, E. (1989). On defining attitude and attitude theory: once more with feeling. In A. R Pratkanis, S. J. Brecker, and A.G. Greenwald, (Eds.). *Attitudes structure and function* (pp. 407-427). Hillsdale, NJ: Erlbaum

Brimeyer, T., Miller, J., and Perrucci, L. (2006). Social class sentiments in formation: influence of class socialization, college socialization, and class aspirations. *The Sociological Quarterly*, 47(3), 471-495.

Broido, E. M., and Reason, R. D. (2005). The development of social justice attitudes and actions: An overview of current understandings. *New Directions for Student Services* (110), 17-28.

Brown, R. (1968). An investigation of the relationship between the intellectual and the academic aspects of college life. *The Journal of Educational Research*, 61(10), 439-441.

Bu-Nuꜥman, S. (2012). *Falsafāt al-thaūrt al-ꜥrabiyah* [The philosophy of the Arab Revolutions]. Beirut, Lebanon: Marakaz Namā' Lill Abahath Wa Al-Darāsāt [Namaa Center for Studies and Research], [Arabic].

Bush, R. (2007). Politics, power and poverty: Twenty years of agricultural reform and market liberalisation in Egypt. *Third World Quarterly*, 28(8), 1599-1615

Byrd, W. (2014). Cross-racial interactions during college: A longitudinal study of four forms of interracial interactions among elite white college students. *Societies*, 4, 265–295

Cnaan, R., Smith, K., Holmes, K., Haski Levenhal, D., Handy, F., and Brudney, J. (2010). Motivations and benefits of student volunteering: Comparing regular, occasional and non-volunteers in five countries. *Canadian Journal of Non-Profit and Social Economy Research*, 1(1), 65-81.

Caplan, S. (2003). Preference for online social interaction: A theory of problematic internet use and psychosocial well-being. *Communication Research*, 30(6), 625-648

Cermakova, Z., and Holda, D. (1992). Changing values among Czech students: Before and after November 1989. *European Journal of Education*, 27(3), 303-314.

César, M., and Kumpulainen, K. (2009). *Social Interactions in Multicultural Settings*. Netherlands: Sense Publishers.

Chalcraft, J. (2012). Horizontalism in the Egyptian revolutionary process. *Middle East Report*, 262, 6-11.

Chang, J., Denson, N., Saenz, V., and Misa, K. (2006). The educational benefits of sustaining cross-race interaction among undergraduates. *Journal of Higher Education*, 77, 430–455.

Change, J. (2005). Faculty-student interaction at the Community College: A focus on students of color. *Research in Higher Education*, 46(7), 769-802

Chung, K., Liu, C., and Chen, E. (2001). University students' attitudes towards mental patients and psychiatric treatment. *International journal of social psychiatry*, 47(2), 63-72.

Chaney, A. (2013). Revolt on the Nile: Economic shocks, religion, and political power. *Econometrica*, 81(5), 2033–2053.

Charmaz, K. (2007*). Constructing grounded theory. A practical guide through practical analysis*. London, UK: Sage Publications.

Clarke, K. (2014). Unexpected brokers of mobilization: Contingency and networks in the 2011 Egyptian uprising. *Comparative Politics*, 46(4), 379-397.

Cole, D (2010). The effects of student-faculty interactions on minority students' college grades: Differences between aggregated and disaggregated data. *The Journal of the Professoriate, an affiliate of the Center for African American Research and Policy.*

Cole, J. (1982). *Anthropology for the Eighties: Introductory readings*. New York: Free Press, 1982.

Collins dictionary (2016). July 10/2016, Retrieved at: http://www.collinsdiction ary.com/dictionary/english/habit.

Cook, B. (2001). Islam and Egyptian higher education: Students attitudes. *Comparative Education Review*, 45(3), 379-411.

Cotton, R. and Wilson, B. (2006). Student-faculty interactions: Dynamics and determinants. *Higher Education*, 51, 487–519.

Cox, O. (1974). The problem of societal transition. *American Journal of Sociology*, 79(5), 1120-1133

Croswell, J. (2007). *Qualitative inquiry and research design: Choosing among five traditions*. (2nd Edition). California, USA: Thousand Oaks, CA: Sage Publications, Inc.

Crotty, M. (1998). *The foundation of social research: Meaning and perspective in the research process*. London, UK: Sage Publication, Inc.

Della Porta, D. (1995). *Social movements, political violence, and the state A comparative analysis of Italy and Germany*. Cambridge University Press.

Denzin, N., and Lincoln, Y. (1998). *The landscape of qualitative research: Theories and issues*. California, USA: Thousand Oaks, Sage Publication, Inc.

Denzin, N., and Lincoln, Y. (1994). "Introduction: Entering the field of qualitative research." In N.K Denzin and Y.S Lincoln (eds.) *Handbook of Qualitative Research*, (pp. 1-18). California, USA: Thousand Oaks, Sage Publication, Inc

Dey, I. (1993). *Qualitative data analysis, a user-friendly guide for social scientists*. London, UK: Routledge.

DeWalt, K., and DeWalt, B. (2011). *Participant observation: A guide for fieldworkers*. London, UK: AltaMira Press, a Division of Rowman & Littlefield Publishers, Inc.

Douglass, P. (1966). Campus subculture and academic achievement. *Improving College and University teaching*, 14(1), 43-45.

Dressman, M. (2008). *Using social theory in educational research*. New York, USA: Routledge.

Eagleton, T. (2000). *The idea of culture*. Malden, USA: Blackwell publishing.

Eargle, Z. (1963). Social class and student success. *The High School Journal*,46(5), 162-169

Egyptian Cabinet: Information and Decision Support Center, (2006). Future issues: the Egyptian youth culture. Vol 2. pp 2-31. Quarterly series, Center for Future Studies.

Eisner, W. (1991). *The enlightened eye: Qualitative inquiry and the enhancement of educational practice*. New York, USA: Macmillan Publishing Company.

Eisenhart, M. (1988). The ethnographic research tradition and mathematics education research. *Journal for Research in Mathematics Education*, 19(2), 99-114.

Elizabeth A., and Marie, S. (1991). College students' attitudes, beliefs and behaviours about AIDS: Implications for Family Life Educators: *Family Relations*, 40 (3), 258-263.

Engle, T. (2002). CIRP press release: CIRP freshman survey. Retrieve, July 9, 2002, from the University of California, Los Angeles, the Graduate, School of Education & Information Studies, the Higher Education Research Institute.

Englesberg, P. M. (1992). University student culture in China, 1978-1990: Formal and informal organization. Doctoral Dissertations, University of Massachusetts Amherst.

Emme, E. (1943). Changes in student attitudes. *The Phi Delta Kappan*, 25(5), 109-111.

Farag, M. (2013). Al-muqadamāt āl-syāsiah lill thaūrt al-Miṣrīyah [The political foregrounds of the Egyptian Revolution]. In Abd-Alkader Yassen(ed.), *25 yanāiir mabāheth wa shihādāt* [The January 25th investigation and witnesses] (pp.77-98). Beirut, Lebanon: Al-Mararkaz Al-ᶜAarabiy Lill Abahath Wa Darāsāt Al-Syāsisāt [The Arab Center for Research and Policy Studies], [Arabic].

Farghaly, R. (2012). *Āṭafāl al-shawarᶜ, al-jans wa -al-ᶜduwan* [The street children, sex and aggression]. Cairo, Egypt: Al-Dar Al-Miṣrīyahal Al-Lubanāinia.

Farhaat, H. (2015). *Tᶜraḍ āl-shabāb āl-jāmᶜt leh qaḍāiya al-fasād al-idāriy bmūāqᶜ al- ākhbāriah waᶜlāqtah bmuwstwī al-ṭamuwh* [The exposition of university students to administrative corruption issues at news programs and its relation of their ambitions]. Master Thesis, Monifiya University, Monifiya, Egypt, [Arabic].

Fayoum University (2015). Fayoum University website. Retrieved at 15/2/2015 time 9, 00 pm: http://www.fayoum.edu.eg/FUAboutcollegepage2.aspx

Fayoum University (2014). *Dalīl al-Darasāt al-ᶜaliah* [Post graduate booklet]. Fayoum, Egypt: Al-Karmah, [Arabic].

Fayoum University (2014). *Dalīl al- jāmᶜt fi ᶜid al-ᶜalīm* [University's yearly book at the festival of science]. Fayoum, Egypt: Al-Karmah, [Arabic].

Ferjani, N. (2011). *Yawmyaat thaūrt al-fuol* [The diary of the Jasmine Revolution]. Cairo, Egypt: Al-Hy'h Al-ᶜāmh lill Kitāb [The Egyptian General Book Authority], [Arabic].

Fetterman, D. (2010). *Ethnography step by step*. 3rd edition. California, USA: Thousand Oaks, Sage publication, Inc.

Flick, U. (2007). *Designing qualitative research*. London, UK: Sage publications, Ltd.

Flick, U. (2009). *An introduction to qualitative research*. 4th Edition. London, UK: Sage publications, Ltd

Foran, J. (2009). Theorizing the Cuban revolution. *Latin American Perspectives*, 36(2), 16-30.

Foran, J. (1993). Theories of revolution revisited: Toward a fourth generation. *Sociological Theory*, 11(1), 1-20.

Furnhum, A., and McManus, C. (2004). Students attitudes to university education. *Higher Education Review*, 36(2), 29-38.

Geertz, C. (1973). *The interpretation of cultures: Selected essays*. New York, USA: Basic Books.

Given, L. (2008). *The sage encyclopaedia of qualitative research methods*. California, USA Thousand Oaks, CA: Sage Publications, Inc.

Glaser, B. (1992). *Emerging vs. forcing: Basics of grounded theory analysis*. USA, Mill Valley: Sociology Press.

Glaser, B., and Strauss, A. (1967). *The discovery of grounded theory*. USA, Chicago: Aldine.

Golafshani, N. (2003). Understanding reliability and validity in qualitative research. *The Qualitative Report*, 8(4), 597-606.

Goldberg, E. (1992). Peasants in revolt- Egypt 1919. *International Journal of Middle East Studies*, 24(2), 261-280.

Goldstone, A. (2001). Toward a fourth generation of revolutionary theory. *Annual Review of Political Science*, 4, 139-187.

Ghoniem, A. (2014). The roots of economic challenges facing Egypt in the aftermath of the January 25th Revolution. *Jean Monnet Occasional Paper* No. 9. Institute for European Studies (Malta).

Ghonimah, KH. (2008). Barnāmig muqtarah lill al-kīyam al-ījtmāih lizyādat mushārkat al- shābāb fi al-ʿamal al-taṭawyī [A suggested program in social work to increase the students in voluntary work]. Doctoral dissertation, Cairo University, Giza, Egypt, [Arabic].

Gray, M. (1998). Economic reform, privatization and tourism in Egypt. *Middle Eastern Studies*, 34 (2), 91-112.

Gray, L., and Saracino, M. (1991). College students' attitudes, beliefs and behaviors about AIDS: Implications for family life. *Family Relations*, 4(3), 258-263.

Graham, H., and Gurr, T. (1970). Violence in America: Historical and comparative perspectives. *American Sociological Review*,35(1), 118-120.

Guba, E., and Lincoln, Y. (1985). *Naturalistic inquiry*. California, USA: Newbury Park, Sage Publications, Inc.

Gumʿah, S. (1984). *Al-shabāb wa al-mushārikah āl-syāsiah* [Youth and political particpation]. Cairo, Egypt: Dar Al-Thaqāfiah, [Arabic].

Gurr, T. (2016). *Why men rebel*. Forties anniversary edition. New York, USA: Rutledge.

Habashy, M. (2012). Manẓūmāt al-kīyam lad ṭolāb al- jāmʿt fi miṣr fi duw' baʿḍ al-mutagāyrāt wa duwr al- jāmʿt fi al-tʿāmul maʿhā [The core value for the university students in Egypt in the light of some contemporary issues and the role of university in dealing with]. *Magāliyat Kullīyat al-Tarbiyah* [The *Journal of College of Education*], Suez Canal University, (22),1-84, [Arabic].

Haferkamp, H., and Smelser, N. (1992). *Social change and modernity*. University of California Press.

Hamada, A. (2012). 25 Yaniir 2011 Al-qa'id Al-faʿil wa Al-midan [25 January, the leader, the activist and the field). In Abd-Alkader Yassen(ed.), *25 yanāiir mabāheth wa shihādāt* [The January 25th investigation and witnesses] (pp. 79-100). Beirut, Lebanon: Al-Mararkaz Al-ʿAarabiy Lill Abahath Wa Darāsāt Al-Syāsisāt [The Arab Center for Research and Policy Studies], [Arabic].

Hamersley, M., and Atkinson, P. (2007). *Ethnography: Principle and practice.* 3rd edition, London, UK: Taylor and Francis laniary.

Hammad, A. (2013). *Al-thaūrt al-tā'aha ṣarāʿ al-khawadhah wa al-liyhiah wa al-miydān* [The lost revolution: the conflict of helmet, Beard and field, 3rd Edition. Cairo, Egypt: Marakaz Al-Maharusah Lill Nashir [Al-Maharusah Center for Publishing], [Arabic].

Hamza, M. (2011).ʿish [Braed]. In Mamdouh Hamza (ed.), *Rasā'il al-thaūrt* [Messages of the revolution1] (pp. 10-35). Cairo, Egypt: Al-Marakaz Al-Qawmmay Al-Miṣrī [The Egyptian National Council], [Arabic].

Harb, M. (2001). Al-waʿī al-syasi lad ṭolāb al- jāmʿt: Al-wāqʿ wa al-mustaqbal [Political awareness among university students: reality and future]. Master dissertation, University of Alexandria, Alexandria, Egypt [Arabic].

Harman, K. (2002). Merging divergent campus cultures into coherent educational communities: Challenges for higher education leaders. *Higher Education*, 44(1), 91-114.

Harrington, A. (2005). *Modern social theory: An introduction.* Oxford University Press.

Hays, Sh. (1994). Structure and agency and the sticky problem of culture. *Sociological Theory*, 12(1), 57-72.

Heaton, J. (2004). *Reworking qualitative data.* London, UK: Sage Publication, Inc.

Heikal, M. (2013). *Miṣr ilá āyana mābaʿd Mubarak wa zamānh* [Egypt to where; After Moubark]. Cairo, Egypt: Dar Al-Shuruwk, [Arabic].

Helmy, M. (1981). *Al-qaim al-Muʿaṣrah byen ṭolāb āl- jāmʿt wa ʿalaqitha bel tanmiah: Drāsah mydāniah leh ṭolāb āl- jāmʿt Helwan* [Contemporary values among university students and its relationship to development: A field study for students of Helwan University]. Doctoral dissertation, Helwan University, Helwan, Egypt, [Arabic].

Hirschkind, C. (2012). Interview with Alaa Abd Al-Fattah, Tahrir Square, 12 pm, July 19th. *Anthropological Quarterly*, 85(3), 917-925.

Horowitz, H. (1986). The 1960s and the transformation of campus cultures. *History of Education Quarterly*, 26(1), 1-38.

Human Rights Watch's Report, (2014). All according to plan, the Rab'ah massacre and mass killings of protesters in Egypt. USA, Scott Nelson/Redux. https://www.hrw.org/sites/default/files/related_material/egypt0814_brochure_web.pdf

Hummon, D. (1994). College slang revisited: Language, culture and undergraduate life. *The Journal of Higher Education*, 65(1), 75-98.

Hurs, B., Wallac, R., and Nixo, S. (2013). The impact of social interaction on student learning. *Reading Horizons*, 52(4), 375-398.

Husneen, M. (1981). *Al-banā' al-ṭabaqiy fī miṣr 1952-1970*.[Construction class in Egypt 1952-1970]. Cairo, Egypt: Dar Al-Thaqāfiya Lill Tabaa wal Nasher, [Arabic].

Hussien, S. (2007). *Al-ʿuwlamah al-thaqāfiyah wa tātherha ʿalá al-thaqāfah al-tarawyhiah lill shābāb fī al-jāmʿt maʿ* [The cultural globalization and effect on recreational culture for university students]. Master dissertation, Banha University, Banha, Egypt, [Arabic].

Hussien, B. (2015). Thaūrt 25 yaniir al-miṣrīyah: Al-syāsiah al-amirykiyah tigāh ṣaʿwad wa ṣaqwat houkm al-akhwān al-muslimiyn [The Egyptian January 25th Revolution: American policy toward the rise and fall of the Muslim Brotherhood]. Master dissertation, Birzeit University, Birzeit, Palestine, [Arabic].

Hussein, M. (1972). The revolt of the Egyptian students. *MERIP Reports*, (11), 10-14. Stable URL: http://www.jstor.org/stable/23567678

Hutcheson, S., and Chapman, D. (1979). Patterns of Student Interaction in Clark-Trow Subgroups. *Research in Higher Education*,11(3), 233-247.

Idris, M. (2011). Muqadamāt āl-thaūrt [The introductions of the revolution]. In Amr Hashm Rabiaa(Ed.), *25 yaniir qra'at āuwalia wa ruwiah mustāqbliah* [January 25 revolution preliminary reading and future vision] (pp.7-22). Cairo, Egypt: Marakaz Al-Ahrām Lill Darasāt Al-Syāsiah Wal Al-Istarātijiyah [Al-Ahram Center for Political and Strategic Studies], [Arabic].

Inglis, D., and Hughson, J. (2003). *Confronting culture, sociological vistas*. London, UK: Polity press in association with Blackwell publishing ltd.

Jadallah, M. (2011). *Lughat al-shabāb wa lughat al-thaūrt* [The language of youth and the language of revolution]. Alexandria, Egypt: Dar Al-Maʿāraf Al-jāmʿiyah, [Arabic].

Jerome, T. (2001). Changes in locus of control beliefs in polish university students before and after democratization. *The journal of social psychology, 132(2), 217-222.*

Johansson, T. (2007). *The transformation of sexuality gender and identity in contemporary youth culture*. Hampshire: Gower House.

Kashif, E. (2001). Namaṭ al-qaim *byen* ṭolāb āl- jāmʿt wa ʿalaqitha beṭurqhum fi Muwagahat azmat al-huwiah [Value pattern among university students and its relationship to their methods in facing identity crisis]. *Al-Magālah Al-Miṣrīyah Lill Darasāt Al-Nafsiah* [The *Egyptian Journal of Psychological Studies]* (3), 465-528, [Arabic].

Katz, D., and Kahn, R. (1978). *The social psychology of organization*, (2th.). New York, USA: john Wiley.

Kayla, S. (2013). *Waḍ⁺ al-thaūrt al-ˤrabiyah wa al-miṣrīyah* [The case of the Arab revolutions and its destiny]. Damascus, Syria: Dar Al-Kawthir Lill Nashir [Al-Kawthir for Publishing], [Arabic].

Kefaya Movement (2014). The movement of Kefaya Facebook page, January 10, 2014 retrieved at: https://ar-ar.facebook.com/Kefaya.Movement/

Kenneth, G. (1999). Campus culture and the experiences of Chicano students in predominantly white colleges and universities. paper presented at the annual meetings of the association for the study of higher education (24th, San Antonio, TX, November18-21,1999).

Khatib, L. (2013). Political participation and democratic transition in the Arab World. *Journal of International Law, 34(2), 314-340.*

Kimbrough, W. (2003). *Black Greek 101: The culture, customs and challenges of Black fraternities and sororities.* 2end Edition: Rosemont Publishing & Printing Crop.

Kleinberg, O. (1979). *Students, values and politics: A cross cultural comparison.* New York, USA: free press.

Kneller, G. (1968). *Educational anthropology: An introduction.* New York, USA: John Willey and Son.

Kolar, N. (2012). Civil disobedience and university politics in post-revolution Egypt, Higher Education Blog, Retrieved at: http://www.hanoverresearch.com/2012/04/civil-disobedience-and-university-politics-in-post-revolution-egypt/.

Konings, P. (2002). University students' revolt, ethnic militia and violence during political liberalization in Cameroon. *African Studies Review, 45(2), 179-204.*

Krober, A., and Kluckhohn.C. (1952). A critical review of concept and definitions. *Papers of the peabagy Museum of American. Archaeology and Ethnology, 47(1), 1-18.*

Kuh, D., and Whitt, E. (1988). The Invisible tapestry: Culture in American colleges and universities. *ASHE-ERIC Higher Education Report* No. 1. Washington, D.C. Association for the Study of Higher Education.

Kuh, G., and Shouping, H. (2001). The effects of student-faculty, interaction in the 1990. *The Review of Higher Education, 24(3), 309-332.*

Kuh, G. (1995). Cultivating high-stakes student culture research. *Research in Higher Education, 36(5), 563-576.*

Kullina Khaled Saeid (2013). Kolinā Khaled Saeid Facebook page. August 16, 2013. Retrieved at: https://ar-ar.facebook.com/KolenaKhaledSaeid.

Kuper, A. (1999). *Culture: The anthropologists' account.* Harvard University Press,

Lacy, W. (1978). Interpersonal relationships as mediators of structural effects: College student socialization in a traditional and an experimental university environment. *Sociology of Education, 51(3), 201-211.*

Lafore, L. (1964). One campus, two cultures. *Science, New Series*, 145(3634), 790-795.

Lal, Z. (2007). *Al-'uwnf fi 'alam mutaghyr* [Violence in a changing time]. Riyad, KSA: Ramdk, [Arabic].

Lane, D. (1973). The impact of revolution: The case of selection of students for higher education in Soviet Russia, 1917-1928. *Sociology* 1973 7: 241 is available at: http://soc.sagepub.com/content/7/2/241

Lawler, A. (2010). Collapse? What collapse? Societal change revisited. *Science, New Series*, 330(6006), 907-909.

Laylah, A. (2012). Limāzā qāmat al-thaūrt? Bahith fi āhawāl al-duwalah wa al-mujtmaʿ [Why the revolution has occurred? A survey of the state and society]. In Mahmoud Abd Al-fadeel(ed.), *Al-thaūrt al-Miṣrīyah, al-dawāfaʿ, al-atajāhat wa al-tahadiyāt* [Egyptian revolution motivations, trends and challenges] (pp. 23- 50). Doha, Qatar: Al-Mararkaz Al-ʿAarabiy Lill Abahath Wa Darāsāt Al-syāsisāt [Arab Center for Research and Policy Studies], [Arabic].

Laylah, A. (2007). *Halt al- ṭabaqah al-mutawasṭah; Madkhal raṣd āwaḍā' al-mujt-maʿ al-ʿarabiy* [The Status of the Arab middle cases, an approach to monitor the situation of the Arab society]. Alexandria, Egypt: Makatabt Al-Āskandriyah [the Library of Alexandria], [Arabic].

LeCompte, M., and Goetz, J. (1982). Problems of reliability and validity in ethnographic research. *Review of Educational Research, 52(1)*, 31-60.

Lesch, M. (2011). Egypt's spring: Causes of revolution. *Middle East policy council*, XVIII, (3), Pp35-48.

Levine, A., and Cureton, J. (1998): Student politics: The new localism. *Reviews of Higher Education,(21)*, 137-150.

Levine, A., and Keith, W. (1979). Student activism in the 1970s: Transformation not decline. *Higher Education*, 8(6), 627-640.

Levy, D. (1981). Student politics in contemporary Latin America. *Canadian Journal of Political Science / Revue canadienne de science politique*, 14(2), 353-376.

Liping, S. (2008). Societal transition: New issues in the field of the sociology of development. *Modern China*, 34 (1), 88-113.

Lipset, S. (1964). The political behaviour of university students in developing nations. *Social and Economic Studies*, 14(1), 35-75.

Lipset, S. (1972). *Rebellion in the university: A history of student's activism in America*. New York, USA: basic books.

Madi, A. (2015). *Al-'uwnf wa al-tahawiylat al-dymuqratiyah fi miṣr baʿd al-thaūrt* [Violence and democratic transition in Egypt after revolution]. Cairo, Egypt: Dar Al-Bashīīr, [Arabic].

Mahmoud, M. (1986). *Al-Azhahr jāmʿ wa jāmʿt* [Al-Azhar mosque and university]. Cairo, Egypt: Al-Hy'h Al-ʿāmh lill Maṭabʿ [The General Authority for Printers], [Arabic].

Mahmoud, Y. (2008). Āzmat al-jāmʿāt al-ʿarabiah [The crisis of the Arab universities]. Cairo, Egypt: Al-Dar Al-Miṣrīyah Al-Lubnaniah, [Arabic].

Mahmoud, Y. (1991). Muwshklaat liṭolāb āl- jāmʿt fī misr wa torkhm fī moghhtaha [The problems of university students in Egypt and their methods to facing it]. Magāliyat Darasāt Tarbuwyah [Journal of Educational Studies], (49 -50), 200-245, [Arabic].

Mahmoud, Y. (1991). Taghāyrāt al-kīyam liṭolāb āl- jāmʿt khilal 30 sanah [Change the values of university student's during thirty years]. Magāliyat Darasāt Tarbuwyah [Journal of Educational Studies] (51), 17-195, [Arabic].

Mariam Webster (2016). July 10/2016, Retrieved at: http://www.merriam-webster.com/dictionary/custom.

Mariam Webster (2016). July 28/2016, Retrieved at: http://www.merriam-webster.com/dictionary/attitude.

Mars, P. (1975). The Nature of Political Violence. Social and Economic Studies. 24(2), 221 238.

Marvasti, A. (2004). Qualitative research in sociology. London, UK: Sage Publication Ltd.

Marzouk, A. (2011). Takuwin al- ʿaqal al-miṣrīy wa īshkaliyat najah thaūrt 25th yaniir: Ru'yah tarbauwyah [The formation of the Egyptian mind and the challenges of success for the 25th January Revolution: An educational vision]. Mu'wtamar thaūrt 25th yaniir wa mustaqabal al-taʿlim fī Miṣr [The January 25th Revolution Conference and the Future of Education in Egypt], Cairo University, Institute of Educational Studies and Research 13-14 July 2011.

Mashayekhi, M. (2001). The revival of the student movement in post-revolutionary Iran. International Journal of Politics, Culture and Society, 15(2), 283-313.

Mason, J. (2002). Qualitative researching. 2nd Edition, London, UK: SAGE Publications Ltd.

Marshal, SH., and Stacher, J. (2012). Egypt's generals and transnational capital. Middle East Report, (262), 12-18.

Martini, J., and Taylor, J. (2011). Commanding democracy in Egypt: The military's attempt to manage the future. Foreign Affairs, 90(5), 127-137.

Mauch, J. (1994). Universities in transition in the Czech Republic: The case of the University of South Bohemia, Paper presented at the Annual Meeting of the Association for the Study of Higher Education (19th, Tucson, AZ, November 10-13.

Maxwell, J. (1996). Qualitative research design. California, USA: Newbury Park, CA: Sage.

McCabe, T., White, K., and Obst, P. (2007). The importance of volunteer functions to university students. Australian Journal on Volunteering, 12(2),50-58.

McQuail, D, (1987). Mass communication theory: An introduction. 2nd Edition, California, USA: Thousand Oaks, Sage publication Inc.

Meringolo, A. (2015). The struggle over the Egyptian public sphere. Instituto Affari Internazionali.

Miner, J. (1971). Changes in student attitudes toward bureaucratic role prescriptions during the 1960 s. *Administrative Science Quarterly*, 16(3), 351-364.

Michiya Shimbori, T., Ban, K. Kono., H, Yamazaki, Y., and Kano, M., Murakami (1980). Japanese student activism in 1970 s. *Higher Education*, 9(2), 139-154.

Milem, J. (1998). Attitude change in college students: Examining the effect of college peer groups and faculty normative groups. *The Journal of Higher Education*, 69 (2), 117-140

Miṣr El Kheir (2015). Miṣr el-kheir web site, March 20, 2015. Retrieved at: http://misrelkheir.org/, [Arabic].

Mitchell, N (2010). The participant researcher relationship in educational research. Doctoral dissertation, university of Nottingham, Nottingham, United Kingdom.

Mittermaier, A. (2014). Bread, freedom, social justice: The Egyptian uprising and a Sufi Khidmah. *Cultural Anthropology*, 29(1), 54–79.

Moffatt, M. (1991). College life: Undergraduate culture and higher education. *Journal of Higher Education*, 62(1), 44-61.

Morgan, E (2004). *Collective political violence: An introduction to the theories and cases of violent conflicts*. New York, USA: Rutledge.

Morin, M., Glickman, J., and Brooks-gun, J. (2015). *Parenting and the home environment*. In Ann Farrell, Sharon Kagan and E.kay.M. Tisdall *"The SAGE Handbook of Early Childhood Research"*, PP 15- 35. London, UK: SAGE Publications Ltd.

Mughiyth, K. (2009). University and politics: Glorious past, rich experiences, miserable Reality. *Journal of Comparative Poetics*, 29, 64-88.

Mughiyth, K. (2014). *Hitafat al-thaūrt al-miṣrīyah wa nuṣuwṣha al-kamilah* [Chants of the Egyptian revolution and its full texts]. Cairo Egypt: Al-Majlis Al-'Alī Lill Thaqāfiya [The Supreme Council of Culture], [Arabic]

Mughiyth, F. (2004). Al-mushārikah āl-syāsiah liṭolāb āl- jāmʿt, al-waqaʿ wa al-mustakabal [The political participation for the university students, reality and future. Doctoral dissertation, University of Tanta, Tanta, Egypt, [Arabic].

Muhammad, A. (2012). Duwr al-ānshṭah al-thaqāfiya fi tahiyqyq al-āmin al-fakiry ladī ṭolāb jāmʿt Al-Suwes: Drāsah mydāniah [The role of student activities in achieving the ideological security for the students of university of Canal Suez, filed study]. Master dissertation, university of Canal Suez, Al-Ismaʿiliyya, Egypt, [Arabic].

Mustafa, N. (2011). *Al-thaūrt al-Miṣrīyah namudhaj haḍārī* [Egyptian revolution as a civilized example]. Cairo, Egypt: Dar Al-Bashīir, [Arabic].

Mutlu, K. (1996). Examining religious beliefs among university students in Ankara. *The British Journal of Sociology*, 47(2), 353-359

Najjar, F. (1976). State and university in Egypt during the period of socialist transformation, 1961-1967. *The Review of Politics*, 38(1), 57-87.

Naṣif, H. (2012). Why the Egyptian Army did not shoot? *Middle East Report*, (265),18-21.

Naṣr, H. (2005). *Al-thaqāfiya al-syāsiah liṭolāb kullīyat al-tarbiyah waʿlāqtah bel al-mumārasah al-syāsiah* [The political culture of faculty of education students and its relationship with political participation]. Master dissertation, Mansoura University, Mansoura, Egypt, [Arabic].

Nelson Laird, t., Bridges, B., Holmes, M., Morelon, C., and Williams, j. (2004). African American and Hispanic student engagement at minority serving and predominantly white institutions. Paper presented at the Annual Meeting of the Association for the Study of Higher Education, November 4 – 7, 2004 Kansas City, MO.

Nichols, W. (1993). Partying and the mysteries of student culture. *The Antioch Review*, 51(4), 537-550.

Nieburg, H. (1969). *Political violence. the behavioural process.* New York, USA: St Martin's Press.

Nkomo, M. (1984). *Student culture and activism in black South African universities: The roots of resistance.* London, UK: Westport, Conn: Greenwood Press.

Northedge, L. (2011). Egypt: First steps. *The World Today*, 67(3), 4-7.

Nusīr, M. (2013). *Duwr al-internet fī tashkel al-kīyam al-ijtmāih ladī al-shabāb āl-jāmʿt: :Drāsah mydāniah alá ʿaynah man liṭolāb jāmʿt al-Monufia* [The role of the internet in formation the social values for university students : Filed study on the students of Monufia University]. Master dissertation, Menoufia University, Menoufia, Egypt, [Arabic].

Oxford Dictionary. (2016). Definition of value. June13/2016 retrieved at http://www.oxforddictionaries.com/definition/english/value

Oxford Dictionary (2013). March 10/2013, Retrieved at: http://oxforddictionaries.com/us/definition/american_english/belief

Oxford Dictionary (2016). July 18/2016, Retrieved at: http://oxforddictionaries.com/us/definition/american_english/norm

Oxford Dictionary (2016). July 18/2016, Retrieved at: http://oxforddictionaries.com/us/definition/american_english/expectation

Patton, M. Q. (2002). *Qualitative evaluation and research methods* (3rd edition.). California, USA: Thousand Oaks: Sage Publications, Inc.

Petras, J. (1965). A student comments on the significance of the 'Berkeley revolution': Politics of democracy: *The Free Speech Movement*. The Phi Delta Kappan, 46(7), 343-346. Retrieved from http://www.jstor.org/stable/20343367

Petrie, F. (1923). *Social life in ancient Egypt*. England, Kessinger Publishing, LLC (September 10, 2010).

Qandil, A. (2003). *Al-mushārikah al-syāsiah lill-shābāb al-jām't* [The political participation for university youth]. Master dissertation, Mounifia University, Mounifia, Egypt, [Arabic].

Qashquwsh, M. (2013). Hidud al-duwr al-syāsiy lill jiyush [The limits of the political role of the armies]. *Magāliyat Al-Dimuqratiah* [The Journal of Democracy], 52, 50-58, [Arabic].

Qayati, M. (2013). Faj'ayatah al-thaūrt al-miṣrīyah [The suddenness of the Egyptian revolution] In Abd-Alkader Yassen (ed.), *25 yanāiir mabāheth wa shihādāt* [The 25th January investigation and witnesses] (pp141-170). Beirut, Lebanon: Al-Mararkaz Al-ʿAarabiy Lill Abahath Wa Darāsāt Al-Syāsisāt [The Arab Center for Research and Policy Studies], [Arabic].

Rabiaʿ,W. (2013). ṭolāb *kullīyat al-handasah be* Jāmʿt *Al-Qāhirh aʿlanuwh ʿan iḍarab shamil fī al- kullīyat* [Engineering college students at Cairo University declare a comprehensive strike within the college. El youm7 newspaper, April 14/2013 Retrieved at: http://www.youm7.com/News.asp?NewsID=1018 211.

Radwan, A. (2016). *Duwr al-faḍā'iyāt al-ʿrabiyah fī nashir al-thaqāfiya al-qānuniyah ladī al-shabāb āl-jāmʿt fī miṣr* [The role of the Arab satellite channels in spreading the lawful culture for the university youth in Egypt]. Master dissertation, Mansoura University, Mansoura, Egypt, [Arabic].

Ramadan, A. (2012). *Al-ṣarāʿ al-ijtamāʿiy wa al-syāsī* fī ʿaṣr *Mubarak* [Social and political conflict in the era of Mubarak], 2nd Edition. Cairo, Egypt: Al-Hy'h Al-Miṣrīyah Al-ʿāmh lill Kitāb [The Egyptian General Book Authority], [Arabic].

Ramadan, A. (1998). *Taṭawur al- harakah al-kawmiyah* [The evolution of the national movement]. Cairo, Egypt: Al-Hy'h Al-Miṣrīyah Al-ʿāmh Lill Kitāb [The Egyptian General Book Authority], [Arabic].

Rashwan, D. (2011). Mawaghat al-thaūrtal al-muḍāḍah wa isatkamāl al-thaūrtal: Kiyf? [Counter Revolution and complete the revolution: How?] . In Amr Hashm Rabiaa(Ed.) *25 yaniir qra'at āuwalia wa ruwiah mustaqbliah* [January 25th Revolution preliminary reading and future vision] (pp417-426), 3nd Edition. Cairo, Egypt: Marakaz Al-Ahrām Lill Darasāt Al-Syāsiah Wal Al-Istarāti-jiyah [Al-Ahram Center for Political and Strategic Studies], [Arabic].

Reid, D. (1990). *Cairo University and the making of modern Egypt.* Cambridge university press.

Reyes, D. (2015). Inhabiting Latin politics: How college shape students' political styles. *Sociology of Education*, 88(4), 302-319.

Roccu, R. (2013). *The political economy of the Egyptian revolution: Mubark, econmic reforms and failed hegemony.* UK: Palgrave Macmillan.

Robson, P., and Sell, L. (1998). Perceptions of college life, emotional well-being and patterns of drug and Alcohol use among Oxford undergraduates. *Oxford Review of Education*, 24, (2), 235-243

Russell, B. (2006). *Research methods in anthropology, qualitative and quantitative approaches*. 4th Edition, UK: Altamira Press,

Saied, S. (2007). *Al-dimukratiah* [Democracy]. Cairo, Egypt: Dar Nahadit Miṣr, [Arabic].

Sakran, M. (2001). *Waẓā'f āl- jām't al-miṣrīyah fi duw' al-ātajahāt al-mu'aṣrah* [Functions of the Egyptian university in light of traditional and contemporary trends]. Cairo, Egypt: Dar Al-Thaqāfiya Lill Nashir Wa Al-Tawzi', [Arabic].

Sakran, M. (2001). *Al-ṭolāb wa al-āstaz āl-jāmī* [Student and the university professor]. Cairo, Egypt: Dar Al-Thaqāfiya, [Arabic].

Sakran, M. (1989). Mawakif ṭolāb āl- jām't fī miṣr man bad al-kadaiyah al-mu'aṣrah[The position of the university students in Egypt from some contemporary issues]. *Magāliyat Darasāt Tarbuwyah* [Journal of Educational Studies], 4(16), 80-120, [Arabic].

Sakurai, K. (2004). University entrance examination and the making of an Islamic society in Iran: A study of the post-revolutionary approach to "Konkur". *Iranian Studies*,37(3),385-406.

Saldaña, R. (2009). The coding manual for qualitative researcher. London, UK: Sage Publication.

Sayīd, A. (2008). Al-'laqah bayna mumārasat al-ānshaṭah al-riyādivah wa al-mas'wliah al-ijtmāih ladī ṭolāb jām't Assuit [The relationship between practicing the sport activities and social responsibility for students of Assuit University]. Master dissertation, Assuit university, Assuit, Egypt [Arabic].

Shaaban, A. (2013). Men al-nutfah ala al- thaūrt [From the beginning to the revolution] In Abd-Alkader Yassen, *25 yanāiir mabāheth wa shihādāt* [The January 25th investigation and witnesses] (pp. 21-38). Beirut, Lebanon: Al-Mararkaz Al-'Aarabiy Lill Abahath Wa Darāsāt Al-Syāsisāt [The Arab Center for Research and Policy Studies], [Arabic].

Schutt, R. (2006). *Investigating the social work: the process and practice of research*. 5th edition. California, USA: Thousand Oaks. Sage publications, Inc.

Shaheen, R. (2011). Al-tahadyāt allty tuwājyhaha miṣr ba'd al- thaūrt [The challenges that confront Egypt after the revolution]. *Ahram Digital Magazine*, June 27/2011. Retrieved at: http://digital.ahram.org.eg/articles.aspx?Serial=55 3105&eid=361

Shan, X., and Guo, Z. (2011). Angry youth of the new century and the patriotism of young People: *Chinese Education and Society*, 44(2–3), 95–103.

Shann, M. (1992). The Reform of higher education in Egypt. *Higher Education*, 24(2), 225-246

Shehata, D. (2011).The fall of the Pharaoh: How Hosni Mubarak's reign came to an end. *Foreign Affairs*, 90(3), 26-32.

Shimey, Sh. (2016). *Al-mujtamāt al-iftrādih wa duwrhā fī tanmīat al-mahāarat al-ĭjtmāih lill tolāb* [Virtual communities and their roles in the development of social skills for students]. Master dissertation, Fayoum University, Fayoum, Egypt, [Arabic].

Sheppard, P. (1989). The relationship between student activism and change in the university: with particular reference to McGill University in the 1960S. Master dissertation, McGill University, Montreal, Québec, Canada.

Shillito, M., and Marle, D. (1992). *Value its measurement, design and management*. New Yok, USA: John Wiley& sons Inc.

Sīliym, M. (2014). *Duwr al- jāmᶜt fī tanmiyat al-shakhsiyah al-qauwmiah al-Miṣrīyah fī duw' al-mutagāyrāt al-muᶜāṣrah* [The role of the university in the development of the Egyptian national character in the light of contemporary challenges]. Doctoral dissertation, Ain Shames University, Cairo, Egypt, [Arabic].

ṣiyam, Sh. (2009). *Thaqāfiat al-ihatyjāj man al-ṣamt ilá- al-ᶜyṣīān* [The culture of protest from silence to disobedience]. Cairo, Egypt: Miṣr Al-ᶜArabiyah Lill Nashir Wa Tawziᶜ [Arabic Egypt for Publishing], [Arabic].

Shīrīff, S. (2006). *Al- thaqāfiat al-syāsiah ltolāb al-Azhar wa ᶜlaqataha maᶜ baᶜḍ al-mutaghyirāt* [Political culture for al-Azhar University students and its relationship with some variables. Field study] . *Magāliyat Kullīyat al-Tarbiyah* [the Journal of *College of* Education] *131, (2), 19-49.* [Arabic]

Smircich, L. (1983). Concepts of culture and organizational analysis. *Administrative science Quarterly*, 28, 339-358.

Shokr, A. (2011). The price of stability: Egypt's democratic uprising. *Economic and Political Weekly*, 46(7), 10-12.

Shokr, A. (2011). Harakāt al-ihatyjāj man al-istᶜadād al-mādawī ilá qalab al-thaūrt [Protest movements from the last preparation to the heart of the revolution]. In Amr Hashm Rabiaa(Ed.), *25 yaniir qra'at āuwalia wa ruwīah mustāqbliah* [January 25th Revolution preliminary reading and future vision] (pp. 27-61), 3nd Edition. Cairo, Egypt: Marakaz Al-Ahrām Lill Darasat Al-Syāsiah Wal Al-Istarātijiyah [Al-Ahram Center for Political and Strategic Studies], [Arabic].

Shuwman, M. (2012). *Al-jawānib al-thaqāfiya fī al-thaūrt al-miṣrīyah* [The cultural dimensions of the Egyptian revolution]. In Kamal Abed-Alatef and Waled Abd- Al-hay (ed.), *Al-īnfagar al-ᶜArabī al-kabiir, fī al-ābaᶜd al-thaqāfiya wal al-syāsiah* [The great Arab explosion, the cultural and political dimensions.] (pp119-146). Doha, Qatar: Al-Mararkaz Al-ᶜAarabiy Lill Abahath Wa Darāsāt Al-syāsisāt [The Arab Center for Research and Policy Studies], [Arabic].

Silver, H. (2003). Does a university have a culture? *Studies in Higher Education*, 28(2),157-169.

Simplicio, J. (2012). The university culture. *Education*, 133(2), 336-339.

Statera, G. (1979). Students politics in Italy from utopia to terrorism. *Higher Education*, 8(6), 657-667.

Stevens, G. (1969). Egypt since the Revolution by P. J. Vatikiotis. *Middle East Journal*, 23(2), 236-237. http://www.jstor.org/stable/4324442.

Stone, A. (1974). The Korean student revolution: A political analysis. *Occasional papers on Korea*, (2), 132-143. Retrieved from http://www.jstor.org/stable/414 90394

Strauss, A., & Corbin, J. (1990). *Basics of qualitative research: Grounded theory procedures and techniques.* California, USA: Newbury Park, Sage Publications, Inc.

Strauss, A. & Corbin, J. (1998). *Basics of qualitative research techniques and procedures for developing grounded theory.* 2nd edition. California, USA: Thousand Oaks. Sage publications, Inc.

Suchlicki, J. (1969). *University students and revolution in Cuba, 1920-1968*: Coral Gables, Fla., University of Miami Press.

Suliman, H. (2013). *Miṣr al-taghayrāt al-syāsiah wa -al-tahdiāt al-dimoqrātiah bᶜd thaŭrt 2011*[Egypt: Political changes and challenges of democratization post 2011 revolution], Master dissertation, Birzeit University, Birzeit, Palestine, [Arabic].

Swedberg, R. (2012). Theorizing in sociology and social science: turning to the context of discovery. *Theory and Society*, 41(1), 1-40.

Tadros, M. (2011). Sectarianism and its discontents in post-Mubarak Egypt. *Middle East Research and Information Project, Inc. (MERIP), Middle East Report*, No. 259, North Africa: The Political Economy of Revolt, pp. 26-31.

Tanter, R., and Midlarsky, M. (1967). A theory of revolution. *The Journal of Conflict Resolution*, 11(3), 264-280.

Tantawi, M. (1992). *Al-ᶜauwāmil al-mo'ūthrah fī thaqāfat ṭolāb āl- jāmᶜt: Drāsah mydāniah* [The factors that influence the university student's culture. A filed study on Zagaziek University].Doctoral dissertation, Zagazek University, Zagazek, Egypt, [Arabic].

Tawil-Souri, H. (2011). Egypt's uprising and the shifting spatialities of politics. *Cinema Journal*, 52(1), 160-166.

Teti, A. (2011). Political parties and movements in post-revolutionary Egypt. *Istituto per gli studi di politica internazionale*, 42, October2011.

Teti, A. & Gervasio, G. (2012). After Mubarak, before transition: The challenges for Egypt's democratic opposition. *Journal for and about social movements*, 4(1), 102-112.

The Egyptian Ministry of Higher Education (2017). Higher education in numbers between 2014 -2017. March 11, 2018, Retrieved at: http://portal.mohesr.gov.eg/ar-eg/Pages/Higher-education-in-numbers.aspx

The Movement of 9th March (2013). *Majmuat al- ʿaml man ājgl istaqlāl al- jāmʿt* [The 9th March movement: A group working for the university independence]. Facebook page. 9 March Facebook page, October,18,2013 Retrieved at: https://arar.facebook.com/%D8%AD%D8%B1%D9%83%D8%A9-9-%D9%85%D8%A7%D8%B1%D8%B3%D9%85%D8%AC %D9%85%D9%88%D8%B9%D8%A9%D8%A7%D9%84%D8%B9%D9%85 %D9%84%D9%85%D9%86%D8%A3%D8%AC %D9%84%D8%A7%D8%B3%D8%AA %D9%82%D9%84%D8%A7%D9%84%D8%A7%D9%84%D8%AC %D8%A7%D9%85%D8%B9%D8%A-188384427861990/. , [Arabic].

Tignor, R. (1967). The revolution in egypt's economic system: From private enterprise to socialism, 1952-1965. *The American Historical Review*, 72(4), 1455-1456.

Tilly, C. (2003) *The Politics of Collective Violence*. Cambridge University Press.

Touraine, A. (1994). *Qu'est-ce que la démocratie*. Paris, France: Librairie Arthème Fayard.

Tucker, J. (1978). While Sadat shuffles: Economic decay, political ferment in Egypt. *MERIP Reports*, 65, 3-9+26

Stable URL: http://www.jstor.org/stable/3010875

Van Maanen, J., and Barley,S. (1984). Occupational communities: Culture and control in organizations. *Research in Organizational Behavior*, 6, 287-365.

Wahba, KH. (2011). The Egyptian revolution 2011: The fall of the virtual wall -the revolution systems thinking archetype. The29th International System Dynamics Conference, Washington, DC, USA, July 24-28, 2011.

Wallace, W. (1966). *Student culture: Social structure and continuity in a Liberal Arts College*. Chicago, USA: Aldine Publishing Company.

Warnath, C. (1961). What college students think. A review. *The Family Life Coordinator*, 10(4), 85-86.

Webster Dictionary (2016). Retrieved at: http://www.merriamwebster. com/ dictionary/Violence.

Wells, A., Hirshberg, D., Lipton, M., and Oakes, J. (1995). Bounding the case within its context: A constructivist approach to studying detracting reform. *Educational researcher*, 24(5), 18-24.

Williams, R. (1989). *Culture is ordinary 'in resources of hope*. London, UK: Arnold McGuigan.

William, L. (1978). Interpersonal relationships as mediators of structural effects: College student socialization in a traditional and an experimental university. *American Sociological Association*, 51(3), 201-211.

Willis, J. (2007). *Foundations of qualitative research*. California, USA: Thousand Oaks, Sage Publications, Inc.

Wilson, B. (1969). Youth culture, the universities and student unrest source: *Critical Survey*, 4(1), 70-77.

Winegar, J. (2012). The privilege of revolution: Gender, class, space and affect in Egypt. *American Ethnologist*, 39(1), 67-70.

Yassien, A. (2013). Tarākumāt al-shuruwt al-iqtaṣādiah wa- al-ijatmāiah lill al-thaūrt [The accumulation of the economic and social reasons for the revolution]. In Abd-Elkader Yassen(ed.), *25 yanāiir mabāheth wa shihādāt* [25 January investigation and witnesses] (pp.39- 76). Beirut, Lebanon: Al-Mararkaz Al-ʿAarabiy Lill Abahath Wa Darāsāt Al-Syāsisāt [The Arab Center for Research and Policy Studies], [Arabic].

Yin, R. (2003). *Case study research design and methods*. 3rd edition, California, USA: Thousand Oaks, Sage Publications, Inc.

Zahran, G. (2012). Al-itigāhāt al-manātyqiyah wa-ʿlaqtha balmarkaz āthnā' Thaūrt 25 yaniir fi miṣr [Spatial trends and their relationship to the center during the January 25 revolution in Egypt] . In Mahmoud Abd Al-Fadeel(ed.) *Al-thaūrt al-Miṣrīyah, al-dawāfaʿ, al-atajāhat wa al-tahadiyāt* [Egyptian revolution motivations, trends and challenges] (pp.156- 133). Doha: Doha, Qatar: Al-Mararkaz Al-ʿAarabiy Lill Abahath Wa Darāsāt Al-syāsisāt [Arab Center for Research and Policy Studies], [Arabic].

Zimmermann, E. (2011). *Political Violence, crises and revaluation. Theories and research*. 2nd edition, New York, USA: Rutledge.

ABSTRACT

Since the January25th Revolution of 2011 in Egypt, there has been much attention given to the changes and transitions at Egyptian universities. The revolution was accompanied by high expectations and hopes for social and political development of Egypt. Therefore, the question emanated as to what extent these hopes have been realized in student culture, which social tensions shaped them and how they are behaved? This study conspicuously contributes to the description of changes in student culture within the context of an Egyptian university (Fayoum University) in post-revolution.

The purpose of this study is to help cover the shortage in the literature on the change in student culture at colleges and universities after revolutions as well as positioning it within the literature of broader student culture and student activism in higher education. The study aims to present a theory that helps to create an understanding of how student culture has changed and to provide a comprehensive picture for this change in order to assist policy makers in Egyptian higher education to consider these changes in their future policies.

Moreover, the central question raised by the study was: how Fayoum University student culture has changed with the January 25th Revolution of 2011? There are also sub-questions that require further investigation. What is the concept of university student culture? And what are the most important elements and dimensions of student culture? What is the January 25th Revolution of 2011? And what are its goals and trends? What is the essence of student culture after the January 25th Revolution of 2011, at Fayoum University? And what are the specific changes that have occurred in student culture after the January 25th Revolution of 2011?

As for the methodology, I developed a multi-perspective approach to reconstruct tensions that characterized student culture in view of the different sociopolitical positions of students with regard to the revolution. Therefore, I used the qualitative method as an overarching approach for this study. My aim was to articulate a critical dimension of the political and institutional dynamics that examined students' aspirations, thoughts, and practices. More specifically, I implemented the grounded theory-case study methodology to conduct a semi-structured interview of the target population at Fayoum University.

Additionally, the sample of the study was chosen purposefully from the students who are the Muslim Brotherhood supporters as well as the students who are considered politically independent. Data was received through twenty individual interviews with the study's sample and was triangulated through focus groups, participant observation, and archival documents and photography.

The study results were significant to a greater understanding of the emergence of new values among students at Fayoum University, such as the activation of values of citizenship, belonging, co-operation, and positive initiative after the revolution. Furthermore, there is a change in the form of relations between the students and the university administration from an authoritarian model to a more democratic model and, after June 2013, back to a more authoritarian style. There is active political involvement and there are a variety of political activities that profoundly reflect a real change in the students' mentality such as organizing fair Student Union elections and setting a new student regulation. Moreover, there has been a diversity of charity and volunteer activities directed to solve the problems of the local community at Fayoum Governorate. Also, there are various forms of solidarity between Fayoum University students, both explicit and hidden.

However, there is a low degree of cooperation between different student factions, which increases the degree of conflict between them, especially after the events of the 30th June 2013. The fierce competition among different student organizations such as the students of the Muslim Brotherhood, the Salafis movement, Strong Egypt, and independent students on the student elections and providing activities to students. This is in addition to an intellectual closure as a result of prevailing the ideas of the organizations followed by students. Besides, conservative ideas are prevalent among students concerning showing female students' of photos as well as the spread of a masculine orientation towards marginalizing the role of female students in activities after 30 June 2013. There were also a wide range of violent behaviours of the Brotherhood students in response to the brutal actions of the security forces. Finally, the study suggests a theory to interpret the changes in student culture in Egyptian universities in post-revolution.